WORKBOOK B

HIGH SCHOOL
HANDBOOK
2

HOLT, RINEHART AND **WINSTON**
Harcourt Brace & Company

Austin • New York • Orlando • Chicago • Atlanta • San Francisco • Boston • Dallas • Toronto • London

Printed in the United States of America

ISBN 0-03-098489-0

6 7 8 9 10   082   05 04 03 02 01

NOTE TO THE STUDENT: Excerpted literary works used in *Holt High School Handbook 2: Workbook B*

The following excerpt was used to illustrate sentence style:
from *Moby-Dick*, by Herman Melville, 108

The following excerpts were used to illustrate points of mechanics:
from "Mutability," by Percy Bysshe Shelley, 119
from "Friendship," from *Essays: First Series, 1841,*
  by Ralph Waldo Emerson, 147
from *Huckleberry Finn*, by Mark Twain, 155
from "Sonnet 14" in *Sonnets from the Portuguese,*
  by Elizabeth Barrett Browning, 153

The following excerpt was used to illustrate the research process:
from *The Readers' Guide to Periodical Literature, 1991,* 200

Table of Contents

WRITER'S QUICK REFERENCE

GRAMMAR AND USAGE

CHAPTER 1 PARTS OF SPEECH

CHAPTER 2 AGREEMENT

PHRASES, CLAUSES, SENTENCES

CHAPTER 6 **PHRASES**

CHAPTER 7 CLAUSES

CHAPTER 8 SENTENCE STRUCTURE

CHAPTER 9 SENTENCE STYLE

CHAPTER 10 SENTENCE COMBINING

MECHANICS

CHAPTER 11   CAPITALIZATION

CHAPTER 12   PUNCTUATION

CHAPTER 13   PUNCTUATION

CHAPTER 14 SPELLING AND VOCABULARY

COMPOSITION

CHAPTER 15 THE WRITING PROCESS

CHAPTER 16 PARAGRAPH AND COMPOSITION STRUCTURE

CHAPTER 17 THE RESEARCH PAPER

RESOURCES

Name _____ Date _____ Class _____

WORKSHEET 1

Common Usage Problems A

The following guidelines will help you avoid errors in usage.

adapt, adopt   *Adapt* means "to change or adjust something in order to make it fit." *Adopt* means "to take something and make it one's own."

all right   *All right* means "satisfactory," "unhurt; safe," "correct," or, in reply to a question or to preface a remark, "yes." *Alright* is a nonstandard spelling of *all right*.

all the farther, all the faster   These expressions are used informally in some parts of the United States. In formal situations, use *as far as* or *as fast as*.

altar, alter   *Altar* is a noun meaning "a table or stand at which religious rites are performed." *Alter* is a verb meaning "to change."

alumni, alumnae   *Alumni* (əlumʹ nī) is the plural of *alumnus* (a male graduate). *Alumnae* (ə lumʹ nē) is the plural of *alumna* (a female graduate). As a group, the graduates of a coeducational school are usually called *alumni*.

and etc.   The abbreviation *etc.* stands for the Latin words *et cetera*, meaning "and others" or "and so forth." Consequently, *and* should not be used before *etc.*

and which, and who   The expressions *and which* and *and who* should be used only when a *which* or a *who* clause precedes them in the sentence.

Exercise A   From the choices in parentheses, select the correct word or words for each of the following sentences.

1. First-aid kits should contain bandages, first-aid cream, scissors, a quarter for a telephone call, a pencil, (and etc., etc.)

2. Do you think that human beings can (alter, altar) the course of destiny?

3. My mother and Mrs. Chang, both (alumni, alumnae) of Pratt Institute, went there to see an exhibition of paintings.

4. The first paved street in Tokyo was Ginza, (and which, which) you should visit.

Exercise B: Revising   Each of the following sentences contains an error in usage. On the line provided, write the corrected sentence.

1. Certain Japanese folk dances were adopted from early religious rites.

_____

2. Deven looked everywhere for our waiter and who had disappeared.

_____

3. Four hundred miles is all the farther this car will go on one tank of gas.

_____

4. Whatever you decide will be alright with me; I'm very adaptable.

_____

Name _____ Date _____ Class _____

 **WORKSHEET 2** *Common Usage Problems B*

The following guidelines will help you avoid errors in usage.

bad, badly *Bad* is an adjective. *Badly* is an adverb. In standard English, the adjective form should follow only a sensory verb, such as *feel, see, hear, taste,* or *smell,* or other linking verbs.

being as, being that Avoid using either of these expressions for *since* or *because.*

born, borne *Born* means "given life." *Borne* means "carried; endured."

brake, break As a verb, *brake* means "to slow down or stop." As a noun, it means "a device for slowing down or stopping." As a verb, *break* means "to cause to come apart; to shatter." As a noun, it means "a fracture" or "a short period of rest."

bring, take *Bring* means "to come carrying something." *Take* means "to go carrying something."

bust, busted Avoid using these words as verbs. Use a form of *break* or *burst,* depending on the meaning.

clothes, cloths *Clothes* means "wearing apparel." *Cloths* means "pieces of fabric."

Exercise From the choices in parentheses, select the correct word or words for each of the following sentences.

1. I felt so (badly, bad) to hear the sad news.

2. (Being that, Because) Eric is shy, he doesn't say much.

3. Please (bring, take) your guitar when you come to my party.

4. He hit the (break, brake) so hard that he almost broke his foot.

5. How did my new cassette player get (broken, busted)?

6. Seminole jackets are made from long, narrow strips of different-colored (cloths, clothes) carefully sewn together.

7. To our joy, my first nephew was (born, borne) early last night.

8. (Being as, Because) Bernard Malamud is my favorite writer, I was excited to find one of his novels at the yard sale.

9. Did Carla (bring, take) her camera when she visited her home in Panama?

10. A grandmother several times over, the woman had (born, borne) all that fate had dealt her.

Name _____ Date _____ Class _____

WORKSHEET 3 *Common Usage Problems C*

The following guidelines will help you avoid errors in usage.

coarse, course   *Coarse* is an adjective meaning "rough or crude." *Course* is a noun meaning "a path of action," "one part of a meal," or "a series of studies." *Course* is also used after *of* to mean "naturally" or "certainly."

credible, creditable, credulous   *Credible* means "believable." *Creditable* means "praiseworthy." *Credulous* means "too ready to believe."

data   *Data* is the plural form of the word *datum*. In informal English, *data* is frequently used with singular pronouns and verbs. In formal usage, however, *data* takes plural pronouns and verbs. *Data* means "information."

des´ert, desert´, dessert´   *Des´ert* is a noun meaning "a dry region." *Desert´* is a verb meaning "to leave or abandon." *Dessert´* is a noun meaning "the final course of a meal."

emigrate, immigrate   *Emigrate* means "to leave a country or a region to settle elsewhere." *Immigrate* means "to come into a country or a region to settle there."

famous, infamous, noted, notorious   *Famous* means "widely known." *Infamous* means "having a bad reputation." *Noted* means "distinguished for a particular quality or achievement." *Notorious* means "widely but unfavorably known."

formally, formerly   *Formally* means "in a proper or dignified manner, according to strict rules." *Formerly* means "previously; in the past."

Exercise: Proofreading   Most of the following sentences contain errors in usage. If a sentence contains an error, cross out the error and, when necessary, write the correct word on the line provided. If a sentence is correct, write *C*.

1. To have worked a hundred hours with homeless children is a credulous achievement.   _____

2. One of my father's favorite sayings is "What's next—dessert or desert the table?"   _____

3. Court is formerly opened with a bailiff's cry of "Oyez, Oyez!"   _____

4. Have you tried out the new public golf coarse?   _____

5. Isa's family emigrated from Japan when she was nine years old.   _____

6. Personally, I don't think that a cartoon character makes the most credulous spokesperson for an airline.   _____

7. Sure, they fell for the joke; you know how credible they are.   _____

8. Alan Shepard, Jr., is notorious as the first American in space.   _____

9. The Chinese ballet dancer immigrated from his homeland to find creative freedom.   _____

10. To prepare her report, Judy used current data that were published by the Department of the Treasury.   _____

QUICK REFERENCE

Name _____ Date _____ Class _____

 **WORKSHEET 4** ***Common Usage Problems D***

The following guidelines will help you avoid errors in usage.

good, well   *Good* is an adjective. *Well* may be used as an adjective or as an adverb. Avoid using *good* to modify an action verb. Instead, use *well* as an adverb meaning "capably" or "satisfactorily."

hisself, theirselves   In formal situations, do not use these words for *himself* and *themselves.*

its, it's   *Its* is the possessive form of *it. It's* is the contraction of *it is* or *it has.*

kind(s), sort(s), type(s)   With the singular form of each of these nouns, use *this* or *that.* With the plural form of each, use *these* or *those.*

miner, minor   *Miner* is a noun meaning "a worker in a mine." As a noun, *minor* means "a person under legal age." As an adjective, it means "less important."

moral, morale   As an adjective, *moral* means "good; virtuous." As a noun, it means "a lesson of conduct." *Morale* is a noun meaning "spirit; mental condition."

myself, ourselves   In formal situations, avoid using pronouns ending in *–self* or *–selves* to replace personal pronouns as subjects or objects.

Exercise: Proofreading   Each of the following sentences contains at least one error in usage. Cross out the error or errors and write the correct word or words on the line provided.

1. Doyle and myself worked together on this project. _____

2. Always consult your technical documentation for explanations for these kind of problems. _____

3. The children helped theirselves to more vegetable curry. _____

4. Aside from a few miner mechanical problems, the engine still runs good. _____

5. "A weekend of rest and recreation will raise the troops' moral," the captain said. _____

6. Its too hard to do the whole job all by myself. _____

7. Check it out; Ron's got hisself a new skateboard. _____

8. These old speakers sound as well as my new pair does. _____

9. Sorry, kids, miners are not allowed in this establishment. _____

10. Should we help this bird that has fallen out of it's nest? _____

Name _____ Date _____ Class _____

Common Usage Problems E

The following guidelines will help you avoid errors in usage.

nauseated, nauseous *Nauseated* means "sick." *Nauseous* means "disgusting" or "sickening."

off, off of Do not use *off* or *off of* for *from.*

passed, past *Passed,* the past tense of the verb *pass,* means "went beyond." As a noun, *past* means "time gone by." As an adjective, it means "of a former time." As a preposition, it means "beyond."

peace, piece *Peace* means "calmness; the absence of war or strife." *Piece* means "a part of something."

persecute, prosecute *Persecute* means "to attack or annoy someone constantly." *Prosecute* means "to bring legal action against someone for unlawful behavior."

personal, personnel *Personal* is an adjective meaning "individual; private." *Personnel* is a noun meaning "a group of people employed in the same work or service."

phenomena *Phenomena* is the plural form of the word *phenomenon,* which means "an event that can be perceived and explained." Do not use *phenomena* as a singular noun.

Exercise A From the choices in parentheses, select the correct word or words for each of the following sentences.

1. The aurora borealis is a spectacular (phenomenon, phenomena) of nature.

2. Take these forms to the director of (personal, personnel) for approval.

3. For his contribution in bringing an end to the first Arab-Israeli war, Dr. Ralph J. Bunche was awarded the Nobel Prize for (piece, peace) in 1950.

4. The district attorney has announced plans to (persecute, prosecute) the case.

Exercise B: Revising Each of the following sentences contains an error in usage. On the line provided, write the corrected sentence.

1. As the team past the stands, a cheer went up.

_____

2. When she woke up this morning, she had a headache and felt nauseous.

_____

3. This is the most interesting phenomena that I have ever encountered.

_____

4. Why don't you borrow some change off of Rhoda?

_____

Name _____ Date _____ Class _____

 **WORKSHEET 6** *Common Usage Problems F*

The following guidelines will help you avoid errors in usage.

plain, plane   As an adjective, *plain* means "not fancy" or "clear." As a noun, it means "an area of flat land." *Plane* is a noun meaning "a flat, geometric surface" or "a carpenter's tool" or "an airplane."

real, really   *Real* is an adjective. *Really* is an adverb meaning "actually" or "truly." Although *real* is commonly used as an adverb meaning "very" in everyday situations, avoid its use in writing.

same, said, such   These words are sometimes used as pronouns in business or legal writing. Avoid using them in this way in general writing.

slow, slowly   *Slow* is an adjective. *Slowly* is an adverb. Although *slow* is also labeled as an adverb in many dictionaries, this usage applies only to informal situations and colloquial expressions, such as *drive slow* and *go slow*.

some, somewhat   In formal situations, avoid using *some* to mean "to some extent." Use *somewhat*.

than, then   *Than* is a conjunction used in comparisons. *Then* is an adverb meaning "at that time" or "next."

their, there, they're   *Their* is a possessive form of *they*. As an adverb, *there* means "at that place." As an expletive, it is used to begin a sentence. *They're* is the contraction of *they are*.

Exercise: Proofreading   Most of the following sentences contain errors in usage. If a sentence contains an error or errors, cross out the error and, when necessary, write the correct word or words on the line provided. If a sentence is correct, write C.

1. Make sure that everyone walks real slow around the pool; it's too dangerous to run.   _____

2. Possession of the wheelbarrow goes to Lucius Nicks; same shall have all rights regarding such.   _____

3. Don't worry; this test is real easy.   _____

4. Let me know if their coming or not; then I can make some plans.   _____

5. This play you wrote is much longer then an hour.   _____

6. Hurry! We're really late and it's going to take us an hour to get their.   _____

7. As we crossed the plain, hundreds of birds rose before us.   _____

8. My watch must be slow; I can't believe it's really ten o'clock.   _____

9. This year, my brother Luke is finally taller then Papa.   _____

10. As we approached the crossing, the train slowed some and blew its whistle.   _____

Name _____ Date _____ Class _____

 **WORKSHEET 7** *Common Usage Problems G*

The following guidelines will help you avoid errors in usage.

them   Do not use *them* as an adjective. Use *those*.

to, too, two   *To* is used as a preposition or as the sign of the infinitive form of a verb. *Too* is an adverb meaning "also" or "overly." As an adjective, *two* means "totaling one plus one." As a noun, it means "the number between one and three."

type, type of   Avoid using the noun *type* as an adjective. Add *of* after *type*.

waist, waste   *Waist* is a noun meaning "the midsection of the body." As a noun, *waste* means "unused material." As a verb, it means "to squander."

where, when   Do not use *where* or *when* for *that*.

who's, whose   *Who's* is the contraction of *who is* or *who has*. *Whose* is the possessive form of *who*.

your, you're   *Your* is a possessive form of *you*. *You're* is the contraction of *you are*.

Exercise A: Revising   Each of the following sentences contains error(s) in usage. On the line provided, write the corrected sentence.

1. Have you read the too great modern poems "The Hollow Men" and *The Waste Land*?

   _____

2. Poet T. S. Eliot, who's belief was that modern life was characterized by some type loss, wrote both of these poems early in his career.

   _____

3. He saw where people of his day needed a bedrock of belief too regain their vitality.

   _____

4. Without faith, he believed, to many lives were being waisted in confusion.

   _____

5. Read these poems, and decide whether they speak to you're experience.

   _____

Exercise B   From the choices in parentheses, select the correct word or words for each of the following sentences.

1. The commuters noticed (that, where) the subway was running late.

2. Take (your, you're) time answering the question.

3. Yes, this copier can make color copies (to, too, two).

4. (Who's, Whose) washing the dishes tonight?

5. Get (them, those) dogs out of the bathtub right now!

QUICK REFERENCE

Name _____ Date _____ Class _____

The Double Negative

A **double negative** is a construction in which two negative words are used where one is enough. Although they were acceptable up to and during Shakespeare's time, double negatives are now considered nonstandard.

Double negatives often contain the following words: *barely, hardly, neither, never, no, none, nothing,* or *scarcely*. Many double negatives contain *n't*, the contraction of *not*, and another negative word.

NONSTANDARD: The baby wouldn't eat none of her breakfast.

STANDARD: The baby **would** eat **none** of her breakfast.

STANDARD: The baby **wouldn't** eat **any** of her breakfast.

NONSTANDARD: You shouldn't take no rides from strangers.

STANDARD: You **shouldn't** take rides from strangers.

STANDARD: You **shouldn't** take **any** rides from strangers.

STANDARD: You **should** take **no** rides from strangers.

The words *but* and *only* are considered negative words when they are used as adverbs meaning "no more than." In such cases, the use of another negative word with *but* or *only* is considered informal.

INFORMAL: There weren't but two seats left.

FORMAL: There were but two seats left.

FORMAL: There were only two seats left.

Exercise: Revising   On the line provided, revise each of the following sentences to eliminate the double negative. Although the following sentences can be corrected in more than one way, you need to give only one revision.

EXAMPLE: 1. I don't have none left.

I don't have any left.   or   *I have none left.*

1. I was so sleepy that I couldn't hardly keep my eyes open.

_____

2. If she hadn't only called sooner, we would have helped.

_____

3. The manager said there wasn't no reason for making us wait so long.

_____

4. Bennie will never get nowhere until he starts believing in himself.

_____

5. Neither of them wants nothing to do with it.

_____

Name _____ Date _____ Class _____

Review

Exercise A: Proofreading   Each of the following sentences contains one or more errors in usage. If a sentence contains an error or errors, cross them out, and write the correct word or words on the line provided.

1. Its up to Sandy and myself to find a band for the dance.   _____

2. The police couldn't find no evidence of a brake-in.   _____

3. They all held they're breath as they past the border patrol.   _____

4. After his run, George panted, "Sure, I'm alright."   _____

5. When the plain begins it's descent, start looking for the airport.   _____

Exercise B: Proofreading   Most of the following sentences contain errors in usage. If a sentence contains an error, cross out the error and, when necessary, write the correct word above the line. Circle the number of any sentence that is correct.

[1] Last July, I accompanied the Reverend Kemp and his wife Angela on a sightseeing trip too Alaska. [2] While on the plane, we saw a double rainbow—a marvelous phenomena that we felt was a lucky sign. [3] At the hotel, we unpacked our cloths and began to plan what we would do the next day; but the possibilities were huge, and we didn't know where to start. [4] Finally, we decided that we wouldn't neither stay in our rooms nor eat lunch at the hotel; instead, we would go for a drive. [5] As we headed for the car, I saw on a poster where the World Eskimo-Indian Olympics were being held that very day. [6] "Doesn't this sound like fun?" I asked.

[7] The Kemps agreed, and as soon as we arrived at the fairgrounds, we introduced ourselves two a Mrs. McBride. [8] She was a friendly woman who was happy to tell us about the games and which were about to begin. [9] I was surprised some at the many different events that had been scheduled. [10] Said games included tests of skill, such as the Alaskan high kick, and tests of strength, such as drop-the-bomb.

[11] In the Alaskan high kick, a person whose sitting on the ground tries to kick a ball suspended in midair. [12] An event requiring exceptional balance, the Alaskan high kick is an example of the type skills that were traditionally needed by native Alaskans. [13] The drop-the-bomb competition begins when three men lift another man off the ground. [14] The man who is held by his wrists and ankles must remain perfectly horizontal while them three other men carry him. [15] The contestant who is carried the longest way without letting hisself sag wins the event.

[16] As Mrs. McBride finished describing the games, she smiled and said to ourselves, "This is the thirty-first year we've held the Eskimo-Indian Olympics." [17] Than she proudly pointed out Cecelia Chanerak, who was sailing through the air during the blanket toss. [18] In this event, a group of people stretch out a hide blanket and throw a man or a woman all the farther they can; the winner must jump the highest and keep the best balance. [19] I must confess that I got a bit nauseous watching people fly up so far in the air, but I managed to snap a picture anyway. [20] We had a real good time that day, and when I got back home, I eagerly described the Eskimo-Indian Olympics to my family and friends.

Exercise C: Revising   Most of the following sentences contain errors in usage. On the line provided, revise each sentence containing an error. If a sentence is correct, write C.

EXAMPLE: 1. Oh no, I've busted my watch!
Oh no, I've broken my watch!

1. The children built the treehouse theirselves, without any help from they're parents.

   _____

2. All living creatures must adopt to their environments.

   _____

3. "I'm sure that python hasn't any intention of pursuing us," said Ms. Feldman.

   _____

4. Before dawn, the minors had brought there equipment to the mines.

   _____

5. For desert, he served his infamous carrot cake.

   _____

6. "I'm sorry," I gasped, "but there isn't nothing I can do two help you."

   _____

7. Being that gasoline is a source of pollution, we need another type fuel.

   _____

8. My mother hadn't hardly sat down when she caught a fly ball.

   _____

9. The morale of the story is "You can't altar the facts."

   _____

10. Hill's Bakery, formally Bill's Baked Bread, will reopen next Monday.

    _____

Chapter 1: Parts of Speech

WORKSHEET 1 *Types of Nouns A*

A **noun** is a word used to name a person, a place, a thing, or an idea. A **common noun** is a general name for a person or persons, a place, or a thing. A **proper noun** names a particular person, place, or thing. Common nouns are not capitalized; proper nouns are.

COMMON NOUN: scientist   PROPER NOUN: Albert Einstein

A **concrete noun** names an object that can be perceived by the senses. An **abstract noun** names a quality, a characteristic, or an idea.

CONCRETE NOUNS: moon, daisy   ABSTRACT NOUNS: hope, idealism

Exercise A   In the following sentences, underline the common nouns once and the proper nouns twice. On the lines provided, write correctly any proper nouns that are not capitalized. Do not include dates, such as *1975*.

EXAMPLE: 1. <u>Sacajuwea Hunter</u> and <u>Charla ramsey</u> are wheelchair
<u>racers</u> with incredible <u>spirit</u> and <u>courage</u>. *Ramsey*

1. Sacajuwea and Charla have a very special friendship that
developed because of their mutual interest in athletics.   _____

2. Saca, who is a long-distance racer, lost both of her legs when she
was a young child; charla, who is a sprinter, was born with a
disease that damaged her spinal column.   _____

3. In 1984, both girls went to the International Games in new york. _____

4. Crowds admire the girls' determination and commitment.   _____

Exercise B   In the following sentences, classify each underlined noun as concrete or abstract. On the line provided, write *C* if the noun is concrete or *A* if the noun is abstract.

EXAMPLE: ___*C*___ 1. We planted <u>petunias</u> in the garden.

_____ 1. In Japan many homes have a place of <u>honor</u> in which the family displays a
favorite scroll or a vase of flowers.

_____ 2. Amalia Mesa-Bains and Michael Ríos are among the many Hispanic artists
who launched their <u>careers</u> in the Mission District of San Francisco.

_____ 3. In one afternoon the <u>crew</u> repaired eleven helicopters.

_____ 4. We purchased tomatoes, lettuce, and corn grown by local <u>farmers</u>.

_____ 5. Congress debated the <u>merits</u> of the bill late into the night.

GRAMMAR/USAGE

Chapter 1: Parts of Speech

Types of Nouns B

A **collective noun** names a group.

team (of horses)   platoon (of soldiers)   batch (of muffins)

A **compound noun** consists of two or more words used together as a single noun. Some compound nouns are written as one word, some as separate words, and others as hyphenated words.

highway   high school   son-in-law

Exercise A In each of the following sentences, decide if the italicized words are collective nouns or compound nouns. On the lines provided, write *collective* or *compound*.

EXAMPLE: 1. The dance *troupe* is much better this year. *collective*

1. Will the *attorney general* be present?   _____

2. In Scotland, each *clan* is known by a distinctive plaid tartan.   _____

3. I get along very well with my *mother-in-law*.   _____

4. A *colony* of ants had taken up residence in the doghouse.   _____

5. The *airport* was almost deserted at that time of day.   _____

6. Why does *New York* get all the best plays?   _____

7. We arrived just as the *orchestra* was tuning up.   _____

8. Dad, there's a film on about the *Battle of Britain*.   _____

9. Please, put all trash in the *wastebasket*.   _____

10. According to statistics, the vast *majority* of Americans agree on
    that point.   _____

Exercise B In each of the following sentences, underline the collective nouns once and the compound nouns twice.

EXAMPLE: 1. The commander of the <u>troop</u> called <u>headquarters</u> for
             orders.

1. The four-year-old practiced walking on tiptoe across the living room.

2. Do sea horses live in the Gulf of Mexico?

3. The coalition comprises mainly those who wish to ban the burning of garbage.

4. A number of blackbirds are making their nests in our home.

5. Is a group of wolves called a pride or a pack?

Name _____ Date _____ Class _____

Types of Pronouns A

A **pronoun** is a word used in place of a noun, more than one noun, or another pronoun. The word that a pronoun stands for is called the **antecedent** of the pronoun.

We contacted the mayor, and **she** agreed to help. [*We* and *she* are pronouns. *Mayor* is the antecedent of the pronoun *she*.]

A **personal pronoun** refers to the one speaking (first person), the one spoken to (second person), or the one spoken about (third person). A **reflexive pronoun** refers to the subject of a sentence and directs the action of the verb back to the subject. An **intensive pronoun** emphasizes a noun or another pronoun. A **demonstrative pronoun** points out a person, a place, a thing, or an idea.

PERSONAL PRONOUNS: **I** had never met **him**.

REFLEXIVE PRONOUN: Did Tony hurt **himself**?

INTENSIVE PRONOUN: Twain **himself** couldn't have done better.

DEMONSTRATIVE PRONOUN: Where did Ellen hear **that**?

Exercise   Underline the pronouns in the following sentences. Label each pronoun as *personal*, *reflexive*, *intensive*, or *demonstrative*.

EXAMPLE: 1. <u>It</u> is a surprise to see <u>you</u>. *personal; personal*

1. In 1973, we launched a space laboratory called *Skylab I*. _____

2. Scientists were surprised when it suddenly returned to earth in 1979. _____

3. They had planned to send it into a higher orbit where it would stay until 1983. _____

4. The possibility of *Skylab*'s scattering debris upon reentry greatly concerned them. _____

5. That is true because scientists themselves couldn't guarantee people complete safety. _____

6. According to some people, we had not been responsible enough in the exploration of space. _____

7. You would be surprised how many people voiced concern about this. _____

8. I myself wouldn't have wanted to be around the landing area. _____

9. Can you tell me what eventually happened to *Skylab I*? _____

10. It fell from orbit in 1979 and scattered itself over the Indian Ocean and Australia. _____

GRAMMAR/USAGE

Chapter 1: Parts of Speech

WORKSHEET 4 | *Types of Pronouns B*

An **interrogative pronoun** introduces a question. A **relative pronoun** introduces a subordinate clause. An **indefinite pronoun** refers to a person, place, or thing that is not specifically named.

INTERROGATIVE PRONOUN: **What** is your name?

RELATIVE PRONOUN: The movie, **which** was great, lasted two hours.

INDEFINITE PRONOUN: **Some** of the oranges are ripe.

Exercise A   In each of the following sentences, underline the type of pronoun indicated in parentheses. There may be more than one of that type of pronoun in the sentence.

EXAMPLE: 1. <u>Who</u> is doing a report on Mexican artists? (interrogative)

1. A book about Mexican artists titled *Out of the Volcano: Portraits of Contemporary Mexican Artists* focuses on many of Mexico's most gifted artists. (indefinite)

2. All of the photographs that appear in the book, whose authors are Margaret Sayers Peden and Carole Patterson, are part of a museum exhibit. (relative)

3. What does somebody who is a tapestry artist create? (interrogative)

4. Marta Palau creates woven hangings, woolen sculptures, and such. (indefinite)

Exercise B   Underline the pronouns in the following sentences. Label each pronoun as *interrogative, relative,* or *indefinite.*

EXAMPLE: 1. <u>Several</u> came to the opening. *indefinite*

1. Whose sculptures appear in the two photographs over here?   _____

2. Both are the work of the Mexican sculptor Angela Gurría.   _____

3. Which of the students knows anything about Gurría's work that can be shared with the class?   _____

4. One of Gurría's designs, *Monument to Workers on the Deep Drainage System,* was constructed with the help of many.   _____

5. Something that requires more than two thousand workers to build has to be amazing.   _____

6. What is the name of the photographer who was born in 1902 in Mexico City?   _____

7. Manuel Alvarez Bravo is someone whose photographs are revered.   _____

8. Few in the world of photography are as admired as Bravo.   _____

9. Another of the Mexican artists that interests people is the photographer, painter, and sculptor Francisco Toledo.   _____

10. Toledo, whom some have compared to Picasso, is multitalented.   _____

Chapter 1: Parts of Speech

Adjectives

An **adjective** is a word used to modify a noun or a pronoun. Adjectives modify nouns or pronouns by telling *what kind, which one,* or *how many (how much)*. The most frequently used adjectives, *a, an,* and *the,* are called articles.

A **small blue** boat pulled up to the dock. [The adjectives *small* and *blue* modify *boat* and tell what kind; *a* and *the* are articles.]

Some words may be used either as adjectives or as pronouns. Remember that an adjective *modifies* a noun and that a pronoun *takes the place of* a noun.

ADJECTIVE: **That** jacket is mine.

PRONOUN: **That** is my jacket.

Sometimes nouns are used as adjectives.

NOUNS: post office   hospital

ADJECTIVES: **post office** policy   **hospital** room

NOTE: Don't confuse a noun used as an adjective with a compound noun. If a noun and its modifier are listed together in the dictionary, the word group is a compound noun.

COMPOUND NOUNS: city hall   Middle Ages

Exercise A   Underline each adjective in the following sentences. Do not include articles.

1. William Least Heat-Moon's first book, *Blue Highways: A Journey into America,* chronicled his journey across the United States in 1978.

2. That interesting book attracted many readers and even made the bestseller lists.

3. In *PrairyErth,* Heat-Moon narrows his focus to a single Kansas county.

4. The book's unusual title comes from the shorthand term scientists use for the unique soils of the nation's central states.

5. In Heat-Moon's skillful hands, Chase County becomes a microcosm of the nation.

Exercise B   Underline each adjective in the following sentences (do not include articles). Then draw an arrow to the word or words that the adjective modifies.

EXAMPLE: 1. The churning waters rose over the weakened dam.

1. The spirited laughter of the happy children was heard across the street.

2. The commemorative celebration of the seventy-fifth anniversary of that store was held at a large downtown hotel.

3. Many outstretched hands reached for the cool water.

4. The two winter storms dumped much snow on the remote mountain village.

5. A neighborhood spokesperson said heavy traffic was deadly and dangerous to students of a nearby school.

GRAMMAR/USAGE

Chapter 1: Parts of Speech

Action Verbs and Linking Verbs

WORKSHEET 6

A **verb** is a word used to express an action or a state of being. An **action verb** expresses physical or mental activity.

PHYSICAL ACTIVITY: laugh, run, write, skate, argue, build

MENTAL ACTIVITY: consider, fear, wish, remember, realize, suspect

A **transitive verb** is an action verb that takes an object—a word or words that tell who or what receives the action. An **intransitive verb** is an action verb that does not take an object. A verb can be transitive in one sentence and intransitive in another.

TRANSITIVE VERB: The musician **played** my favorite song.

INTRANSITIVE VERB: The musician **played** for an hour.

A **linking verb** connects the subject with a word that identifies or describes it. The most commonly used linking verbs are forms of the verb *be* and other verbs such as *appear, become, feel, grow, look, remain, seem, smell, sound, stay, taste*, and *turn*. Some linking verbs may be used as action verbs.

LINKING VERB: The light **grew** dim.

ACTION VERB: My mother **grew** these roses in her garden.

Exercise A On the line provided before each sentence, write *AV* if the italicized word is an action verb or *LV* if it is a linking verb.

EXAMPLE: ___AV___ 1. When you are called, *state* your name.

_____ 1. You may *ask* questions when it *is* your turn.

_____ 2. Simon *looks* very confident, but he is actually extremely nervous.

_____ 3. Mother *felt* my forehead to see if I had a fever.

_____ 4. He is a clown and always *performs* for the children.

Exercise B Underline the verbs in the following sentences. On the lines provided, write each verb followed by *TV (transitive verb)*, *IV (intransitive verb)*, or *LV (linking verb)*.

EXAMPLE: 1. It seems as though the Statue of Liberty has always been in New York Harbor. *seems, LV; has been, LV*

1. The Statue of Liberty, which is a major American landmark, is probably the best-known structure in the world. _____

2. It possesses a twofold appeal: It symbolizes human liberty, and it unfailingly awes with its colossal size. _____

3. In newspaper editorials, Joseph Pulitzer persuaded the American people that they needed the statue. _____

4. The people agreed, and in 1886, the nation celebrated the dedication of the Statue of Liberty. _____

Name _____ Date _____ Class _____

The Verb Phrase

A **verb phrase** consists of a main verb and at least one **helping verb** (also called an **auxiliary verb**). Some commonly used helping verbs are forms of the verbs *be, have,* and *do,* as well as *may, might, must, can, shall, will, could, should,* and *would.*

    I **should have brought** an umbrella.   **Did** you **listen** to the weather forecast?

    I **was sleeping** by then.

NOTE: The word *not* and its contraction *(–n't)* are never part of a verb phrase. Instead, they are adverbs telling *to what extent.*

Exercise A   On the line provided, write the verb phrase from each of the following sentences. Then underline the helping verb(s) in the phrase.

              EXAMPLE: 1. <u>Did</u> you see the newspaper today? *Did see*

1. I have been reading about the author Amy Tan.   _____

2. Her book *The Kitchen God's Wife* will certainly delight most readers.   _____

3. Didn't Amy Tan consider a career as an artist at one time?   _____

4. I know that she did do some kind of work with children.   _____

5. According to her parents, she could have easily been a neurosurgeon or a concert pianist.   _____

6. Tan's mother, a Chinese immigrant, must have shared many stories of her heritage with her daughter.   _____

7. Could her mother have inspired one of the characters in Tan's novels?   _____

8. What an interesting childhood Tan must have had!   _____

9. Is *The Kitchen God's Wife* her only book, or has she written others? _____

10. No, do check the card catalog for other titles.   _____

Exercise B   Underline the five verb phrases in the following paragraph. Be sure to include all helping verbs.

             EXAMPLE: What <u>are</u> we <u>doing</u> in class today?

      Several students are writing a poem about famous people; other students have not chosen famous people. After much thought, I have finally selected an African American woman whom I admire. My choice is Barbara Brandon, whose cartoons were syndicated in the mainstream press in 1991; she is the first African American woman cartoonist with that distinction. Brandon's cartoon strip depicts life from the perspective of an African American woman. Brandon pictures only the heads and, occasionally, the hands of her characters, all of whom are women; for she believes that women's bodies have been displayed enough in the media.

GRAMMAR/USAGE

Name _____ Date _____ Class _____

 **WORKSHEET 8**   *The Adverb*

An **adverb** is a word used to modify a verb, an adjective, or another adverb by telling *how, when, where,* or *to what extent (how long* or *how much).*

A pale moon **slowly** rose over the water. [*Slowly* modifies the verb *rose* and tells *how.*]

The test seemed **too** easy. [*Too* modifies the adjective *easy* and tells *to what extent.*]

We are **almost** home. [*Almost* modifies the adverb *home* and tells *to what extent.*]

Exercise   Underline once the adverbs in the following sentences. Underline twice the verb, verb phrase, adjective, or adverb that each adverb modifies. A sentence may have more than one adverb.

EXAMPLE: 1. We were quite pleased with the results.

1. American physicist Rosalyn Yalow helped develop an extremely sensitive biological technique.

2. Radioimmunoassay, which is now used in laboratories worldwide, readily detects antibodies and hormones.

3. Yalow writes, "If you ever have a new idea, and it's really new, you have to expect that it will not be widely accepted immediately."

4. So, most scientists do not leap excitedly from the bath crying "Eureka!" as Archimedes supposedly did after discovering a new idea.

5. Yalow and her colleague discovered radioimmunoassay accidentally while observing two patients.

6. After they carefully interpreted their observations, they arrived at their exciting discovery.

7. In 1977, though Yalow's collaborator had died, the Nobel Prize Committee awarded Yalow the undeniably prestigious Nobel Prize for medicine.

8. Radioimmunoassay eventually became a basic diagnostic tool in widely different areas of medicine.

9. According to Yalow, the technique was not quickly accepted because people ordinarily resist change.

10. She believes that progress cannot be impeded forever and that good ideas are eventually accepted.

Name _____ Date _____ Class _____

The Preposition

A **preposition** is a word used to show the relationship of a noun or pronoun to another word. A preposition introduces a *prepositional phrase*. A **prepositional phrase** consists of the preposition, a noun or pronoun called the **object of the preposition,** and any modifiers of the object.

> Take me **to** your leader. [*To* is the preposition; *leader* is the object of the preposition, and *your* modifies *leader*.]

A preposition that consists of more than one word is called a **compound preposition**.

> **Except for** the first act, the play went well.

Exercise A   In each of the following sentences, underline each preposition once and the object of the preposition twice. Some sentences have more than one prepositional phrase.

> EXAMPLE: 1. Everyone <u>except</u> <u><u>Al</u></u> waited <u>for</u> the <u><u>bell</u></u>.

1. According to this note, all suggestions were considered by the committee.

2. The top of the table in the hallway is always covered with mail.

3. Behind the door lay the answers to our questions.

4. Leave the film in the developer for three minutes.

5. Through squalls and heavy winds, the sailboat made its way into the harbor.

Exercise B   Add prepositional phrases to the following sentences to make them more interesting. Write your phrases on the lines provided. Underline the prepositions you use.

> EXAMPLE: 1. Wait there <u>*for me*</u> .

1. Rob collects postcards _____ .

2. _____ we collapsed.

3. We first heard the rumor _____ .

4. _____ people had gathered to hear the concert.

5. Exhausted _____ , the explorers pitched their tents

_____ and planned the next day's work.

GRAMMAR/USAGE

Name _____ Date _____ Class _____

The Conjunction and the Interjection

A **conjunction** is a word used to join words or groups of words. A **coordinating conjunction** connects words or groups of words used in the same way. **Correlative conjunctions** are pairs of conjunctions that connect words or groups of words in the same way. A **subordinating conjunction** begins a subordinate clause and connects it to an independent clause. A subordinating conjunction may come at the beginning of a sentence.

COORDINATING CONJUNCTION: The alarm sounded, **but** we could find no problem.

CORRELATIVE CONJUNCTIONS: Why do you wear **both** a belt **and** suspenders?

SUBORDINATING CONJUNCTION: **If** the train is delayed, call me.

An **interjection** is a word used to express emotion. It is set off from the rest of the sentence by an exclamation point or a comma.

Hey! That's my foot!   **Well,** that's okay.

Exercise A   Underline the conjunctions in the following sentences. Then, on the line provided, classify each conjunction as *coordinating*, *correlative*, or *subordinating*.

EXAMPLE: 1. I'm late because I had to feed the cat. *subordinating*

1. Our old car needs either a valve job or a new engine.   _____

2. Before you write your paper, you must submit an outline.   _____

3. Workers here pay city, state, and federal income taxes.   _____

4. When Liberia was founded in 1821, thousands of free African
   Americans moved there.   _____

5. Are you going to the movies or to the concert?   _____

6. Thomas Hardy found a publisher for his poetry only after he had
   published more than a dozen novels.   _____

7. We'll have to hurry if we want to catch the bus.   _____

8. The new factory opened, but employment has not yet risen.   _____

9. Opinion is divided, yet a decision must be made.   _____

10. We must not only dig a hole but also pour the concrete.   _____

Exercise B   Underline the interjection in each of the following sentences.

1. Ouch! That was my finger, not a nail!

2. Well, either you get ready quickly or we'll have to leave without you.

3. Hey! You forgot your lunch!

4. All I can say is, Hooray!

5. I'm enjoying this novel, but , oh, is it long!

Chapter 1: Parts of Speech

WORKSHEET 11 *Review*

Exercise A The following passage contains twenty numbered and italicized words. On the line provided, identify the part of speech of each italicized word. Base your answer on the way the word is used in the sentence. Use the following abbreviations:

N for noun	**ADV** for adverb
P for pronoun	**PREP** for preposition
ADJ for adjective	**CON** for conjunction
V for verb	**INT** for interjection

EXAMPLE: Read the passage [1] *carefully* __ADV__ .

From 1853 to 1857, Nathaniel Hawthorne was a United States [1] *consul* _____ [2] *in*

_____ England. He traveled extensively [3] *and* _____ kept a series of journals in which

he commented [4] *shrewdly* _____ on the English landscape and [5] *English* _____

character. After his return to America, he gathered together a number of excerpts from

these journals and [6] *published* _____ them as a [7] *book* _____ . [8] *One* _____ excerpt

recounts an experience he had [9] *while* _____ he was journeying in the Lake District of

England. He was traveling [10] *between* _____ the villages of Grasmere and Windermere in

a stagecoach that was greatly overloaded; there were fifteen [11] *outside* _____ passengers,

[12] *besides* _____ the four inside passengers. The road was rough and [13] *hilly* _____ ,

and [14] *Hawthorne* _____ expected that the coach would topple any minute, since [15] *it*

_____ was creaking and swaying [16] *dangerously* _____ . He [17] *became* _____

convinced that he was going to be thrown headlong from the coach against the high stone

fence that [18] *bordered* _____ the road. [19] *Ouch* _____ ! He determined that at the

moment of catastrophe he would fling his heavy shawl [20] *about* _____ his head to give

himself some protection. With this decision, he settled back to await his fate.

Chapter 1, Worksheet 11, continued

Exercise B Each of the following sentences contains either one word or two words of the kind specified before the sentence. Find these words and write them on the line provided. Base your answers on the way each word is used in the sentence.

EXAMPLES: 1. *noun*   Who was it that spread that rumor? *rumor*

2. *conjunction* Did you see any Broadway plays or musicals when you were in New York? *or, when*

1. *preposition*   European schools usually place more emphasis on foreign-language training than American schools do.   _____

2. *adverb*   Many seventeen-year-olds in French and Italian schools are expected to be able to write grammatically perfect compositions in the foreign languages that they are studying.   _____

3. *pronoun*   These students are usually required, too, to take oral examinations in their foreign-language courses.   _____

4. *adverb*   Few American seventeen-year-olds would feel adequately prepared to take oral and written examinations that demanded fluent command of a foreign language.   _____

5. *preposition*   This does not mean that European students are brighter than American students; it merely shows that European schools devote more time to foreign-language studies than American schools do.   _____

Exercise C Each of the following sentences contains an italicized word that is used twice. This word may function as more than one part of speech. On the lines provided, indicate the part of speech for each use of this word. Use the following abbreviations:

N for noun   ADV for adverb
P for pronoun   PREP for preposition
ADJ for adjective   CON for conjunction
V for verb   INT for interjection

EXAMPLE: 1. As you (a) *near* ___V___ Branch Street, you will see the drugstore (b) *near* _PREP_ there.

1. (a) *Well* _____ , you certainly play the clarinet very (b) *well* _____ .

2. No, the (a) *latch* _____ is not broken, but we couldn't (b) *latch* _____ the door.

3. I thought I was (a) *so* _____ smart, (b) *so* _____ I didn't listen to anyone.

4. Put your bicycle (a) *in* _____ the garage, then come (b) *in* _____ .

5. (a) *This* _____ is the first time that Lorinda has been to (b) *this* _____ part of the country.

Chapter 1, Worksheet 11, continued

Exercise D The following passage contains ten numbered and italicized words. On the line provided, identify the part of speech of each italicized word. Base your answer on the way the word is used in the sentence. Use these abbreviations: **N, P, ADJ, V, ADV, PREP, CON, INT.**

Diego Rivera is [1] *chiefly* _____ famous for his murals. However, he was a prolific

artist who [2] *worked* _____ in a wide variety of styles. Rivera, who was born in

Guanajuato, Mexico, in 1886, entered the [3] *San Carlos Academy of Fine Arts* _____ in

Mexico City when he was only eleven. In 1907, with the proceeds from his first art show, he

made the first of [4] *several* _____ lengthy visits to Europe. There he experimented with

different approaches until he realized it was the fresco process, the art of painting [5] *on*

_____ wet plaster, that best suited his artistic vision.

Two of Rivera's lifelong interests were Mexican history [6] *and* _____ machinery. His

murals in the [7] *former* _____ palace of Hernán Cortés in Cuernavaca, in the state of

Morelos, depict the history of Morelos from before the conquest by Spain until after the

Mexican Revolution of 1910. [8] *One* _____ of the works that Rivera created in the United

States was a series of twenty-seven murals that the Detroit Arts Commission asked him to

paint on subjects related to Detroit and the general theme of industrialization.

Rivera was [9] *controversial* _____ in the United States because he included political

themes in his work. Ironically, capitalists attacked him for his affiliation with Communists,

and, [10] *well* _____ , Communists attacked him for accepting commissions from

capitalists.

Exercise E Each of the following sentences contains either one word or two words of the kind specified before the sentence. Find these words and write them on the lines provided. Base your answers on the way each word is used in the sentence.

EXAMPLE: 1. *adverb* I've really improved my skills with a camera lately.
really, lately

1. *verb*   Last year my school gave two photography
                 courses, neither of which had ever been offered
                 before.   _____

2. *adjective*   The course that I took dealt with the ways in which
                 most people perceive their environment.   _____

3. *noun*   Many of us block out much in our everyday
                 surroundings.   _____

4. *preposition* You can demonstrate how unaware of our
                 surroundings nearly all of us are.   _____

5. *noun*   Which of you, just back from a trip, hasn't noticed
                 how different your home looks to you?   _____

6. *interjection* Some of your possessions may seem unfamiliar to
                   you, and a few of them may appear, well, quite
                   peculiar.   _____

7. *conjunction* Eventually the sensation fades, and your
                  surroundings assume their usual background role.   _____

8. *adverb*   Each of us can regain the ability to see freshly if we
                  learn to make full use of our sense of sight.   _____

9. *pronoun*   We can train ourselves to perceive the objects as
                  shapes instead of thinking about their function.   _____

10. *adjective*   As the French Impressionist painter Claude Monet
                  observed, we must forget the names of the things
                  that we observe.   _____

Name _____ Date _____ Class _____

Agreement of Subject and Verb A

A verb agrees with its subject in **number**. Singular subjects take singular verbs, and plural subjects take plural verbs.

> SINGULAR: His **idea sounds** interesting.

> PLURAL: Their **ideas sound** interesting.

Verb phrases must also agree in number with their subjects. The number of a verb phrase is indicated by the form of its first helping (auxiliary) verb.

> SINGULAR: **She has** been working hard.

> PLURAL: **They have** been debating the plan.

Exercise A   For each of the following sentences, underline the verb or helping verb in parentheses that agrees in number with the subject. On the line provided, write the subject of each sentence.

> EXAMPLE: 1. Thanks to modern technology, scientists (has, <u>have</u>) been able to explain causes of earthquakes. *scientists*

1. The theory of plate tectonics (has, have) explained causes of earthquake activity throughout the world. _____

2. Enormous plates of rock (is, are) shifting constantly far beneath the earth's surface. _____

3. In addition to the pressure of molten rock, these movements (causes, cause) the plates to collide. _____

4. The cause of most earthquakes (is, are) the sudden release of stress along a fault. _____

5. A ridge of these breaks (is, are) called a fault. _____

Exercise B   For each of the following sentences, circle the subject of the verb in parentheses. Then underline the verb form that agrees in number with the subject.

> EXAMPLE: 1. In an earthquake, the rock (layers) in a fault line (fractures, <u>fracture</u>).

1. The pressure of colliding plates (forces, force) the rock to bend until it breaks.

2. The Richter scale, as well as other measurements, (has, have) been used to record the magnitude of earthquakes.

3. The tremors of the great San Francisco earthquake that occurred in 1906 (was, were) estimated to have measured 8.3 on the Richter scale.

4. California, with two major fault lines, (has, have) about ten times the world average of earthquake activity.

5. Maps of the earth's plates, which are available in most libraries, (gives, give) you a pretty good idea of why California has so many earthquakes.

GRAMMAR/USAGE

Name _____ Date _____ Class _____

Agreement of Subject and Verb B

The following **indefinite pronouns** are always singular: *anybody, anyone, each, either, everybody, everyone, neither, nobody, no one, one, somebody,* and *someone.*

SINGULAR SUBJECT AND VERB: **Neither** of those films **is** available on video.

The following indefinite pronouns are always plural: *both, few, many,* and *several.*

PLURAL SUBJECT AND VERB: **Few** who have seen that film **praise** it.

The following indefinite pronouns may be either singular or plural: *all, any, most, none,* and *some.* These pronouns are singular when they refer to singular words and plural when they refer to plural words.

SINGULAR: **Most** of the film **is** exciting. [*Most* refers to the singular noun *film.*]

PLURAL: **Most** of the action scenes **are** exciting. [*Most* refers to the plural noun *scenes.*]

Exercise A   For each of the following sentences, underline the subject. Then underline the verb form that agrees in number with the subject.

EXAMPLE: 1. <u>One</u> of my friends (play, <u>plays</u>) the tuba.

1. Each of the pictures (was, were) in a silver frame.

2. All of our belongings (is, are) carefully unpacked.

3. Some of these rare books (has, have) leather covers.

4. None of the people in the theater (was, were) sitting in the first two rows.

5. Every one of these computer games (is, are) on sale.

Exercise B: Proofreading   Most of the following sentences contain verbs that do not agree with their subjects. If the verb does not agree with its subject, write the correct form on the line provided. If the verb agrees with its subject, write *C.*

EXAMPLE: 1. Anyone without shoes are refused admittance. __*is*__

1. A few students in my class was asked to help out. _____

2. Neither of these issues present a problem. _____

3. Everybody living in Lewis Heights go to George Washington Carver High School. _____

4. Several on the team also attend these computer classes. _____

5. Most of the meal were prepared by my father. _____

Name _____ Date _____ Class _____

WORKSHEET 3

Other Problems in Agreement A

A **compound subject** is two or more subjects that have the same verb. A compound subject joined by *and* usually takes a plural verb.

> **Hume Cronyn** and **Jessica Tandy are** actors.

However, some compound subjects joined by *and* name only one person or thing. Such compound subjects take singular verbs.

> The **producer** and **director** of the movie **was** Penny Marshall.

Two singular subjects joined by *or* or *nor* take a singular verb.

> Neither **Tom Cruise** nor **Nick Nolte has** won an Academy Award.

When a singular subject and a plural subject are joined by *or* or *nor,* the verb agrees with the subject that is nearer to the verb.

> Neither the **coach** nor the team **members have** been to the Super Bowl.
> Neither the team **members** nor the **coach has** been to the Super Bowl.

Exercise A   For each of the following sentences, circle the compound subject of the verb in parentheses. Then underline the verb or helping verb that agrees with the subject.

1. Macaroni and cheese (is, are) the only thing the child will eat.

2. Neither the sales tax nor property taxes (seem, seems) to be producing enough revenue.

3. Either Tina or her parents (pick, picks) us up after school.

4. I was surprised to hear that you and your sister (was, were) moving.

5. The spark plugs and the distributor both (need, needs) to be replaced.

Exercise B: Proofreading   Most of the following sentences contain verbs that do not agree with their subjects. If the verb does not agree with its subject, write the correct form of the verb on the line provided. If the verb agrees with its subject, write *C*.

1. Del Rio and San Angelo is two Texas cities that have names of Spanish origin.   _____

2. My books and tennis racket barely fits in the locker.   _____

3. Either my cat or the raccoons always eats all the food by morning.   _____

4. That blouse and scarf are a good combination.   _____

5. Neither Mariah Carey nor Gloria Estefan, I believe, sings that song.   _____

GRAMMAR/USAGE

Chapter 2: Agreement

WORKSHEET 4

Other Problems in Agreement B

In a question, or in a sentence beginning with *Here, Where,* or *There,* the subject usually follows the verb. Make sure that the subject and the verb agree.

Here **is** your **coat**.   There **are** your **shoes**.   Where**'s** that **bus**?

A **collective noun** is singular in form but names a group of persons or things. Use a singular verb with a collective noun when the noun refers to the group as a unit. Use a plural verb when the collective noun refers to the parts or members of the group.

The **club meets** on Tuesday. [The club meets together as a unit.]

The **club have** cast their votes. [Each member of the club has cast one vote.]

An expression of an amount is singular when the amount is thought of as a unit. It is plural when the amount is thought of as many parts.

Five dollars is the price of the buffet lunch. [The amount is a unit.]

Five dollars were in the bag. [The dollars were separate bills.]

A fraction or percentage is singular when it refers to a singular word and plural when it refers to a plural word.

The first **half** of the book **was** interesting.

Half of the singers **were** singing the wrong note.

Expressions of measurement (length, weight, and so on) are usually singular.

Five yards is the amount of cloth I need to buy.

Three feet equals one yard.

Exercise   For each of the following sentences, underline the verb in parentheses that agrees with the subject.

1. Forty dollars (is, are) too much to pay for those jeans.

2. (Where's, Where are) my coat and boots?

3. Here (comes, come) our band!

4. The newspaper staff (has, have) turned in all their stories.

5. One half of the receipts (was, were) found in a shoe box.

6. (Here's, Here are) the notes you took about the history of Japanese pagodas.

7. Two thirds of the students (intend, intends) to go to trade school or college.

8. The orchestra (specialize, specializes) in the Big Band music of Count Basie and Duke Ellington.

9. In the fall, the flock (flies, fly) south for the winter.

10. Fifty miles (is, are) a long way to drive to work every day.

Name _____ Date _____ Class _____

WORKSHEET 5

Other Problems in Agreement C

The title of a creative work, the name of an organization, or the name of a country or city takes a singular verb.

> ***The Potato Eaters* is** a painting by Vincent van Gogh.
>
> The **United States produces** large quantities of wheat.

Some nouns, such as *civics, measles,* and *physics,* are plural in form but singular in meaning.

> The **news** from the doctor **is** discouraging. **Mumps is** her diagnosis.

Nouns that refer to pairs, such as *binoculars* and *scissors,* always take plural verbs.

> Here **are** the **scissors**. Where **are** the **pliers**?

A subject that is a phrase or clause always takes a singular verb.

> **How to raise goldfish was** the topic of the film.
>
> **Swimming laps is** good exercise.

Exercise: Proofreading   Most of the following sentences contain verbs that do not agree with their subjects. If the verb does not agree with its subject, write the correct form on the line provided. If the verb agrees with its subject, write C.

1. Before breakfast are a good time to exercise. _____

2. Hilda thought that *The Ambassadors* were an extremely boring movie, but I didn't. _____

3. Many critics agree that *Boyz N the Hood* offer movie watchers a realistic look at inner-city life. _____

4. The Chicago Cubs is a team that rally in the late innings. _____

5. Civics are supposed to be his best subject. _____

6. The Society of Procrastinators have postponed its annual meeting. _____

7. Whatever you order is fine with me. _____

8. The kitchen scissors were not on the counter this morning. _____

9. Your clothes is lying on the floor again. _____

10. Twin Oaks Mall sponsor an art festival on the first day of spring. _____

GRAMMAR/USAGE

Chapter 2: Agreement

Other Problems
in Agreement D

A verb agrees with its subject, not with its predicate nominative.

One cool-weather **crop is** peas. **Peas are** a cool-weather crop.

Subjects preceded by *every* or *many a(n)* take singular verbs.

Every student and teacher **is** here. Many a seat **remains** empty, though.

Use *doesn't* with all singular subjects except the pronouns *I* and *you*. Use *don't* with all plural subjects and with the pronouns *I* and *you*.

She **doesn't** need a ride. I **don't** need a ride, either.

When a relative pronoun is the subject of an adjective clause, the verb in the clause should agree with the word that the relative pronoun refers to.

We need reforms **that ease** the burdens of taxpayers.

Exercise A: Proofreading   Most of the following sentences contain verbs that do not agree with their subjects. If the verb does not agree with its subject, write the correct form on the line provided. If the verb agrees with its subject, write C.

1. By now, every car have left the parking lot.   _____

2. My favorite part of the movie were the mountain scenes.   _____

3. The men who was responsible received a medal.   _____

4. Modern conveniences, which sometimes cost a great deal of
   money, are often left unused.   _____

5. Many a gymnast dream of winning an Olympic medal.   _____

6. The thing that I most wanted to get were copies of the revised
   bus schedules.   _____

7. That was one of those jokes that offend everyone.   _____

8. My major agricultural interest is tropical crops.   _____

9. Libraries, as Mr. Wu noted, is an important community resource.   _____

10. Every volunteer in the hospitals are being honored tonight.   _____

Exercise B   Write *doesn't* or *don't* in the space provided to make the sentence correct.

1. Bao _____ remember when her grandparents visited Vietnam.

2. We _____ know where they are.

3. No, he _____ care about things like that.

4. Sorry, the item you requested _____ appear to be here.

5. When snowfall is heavy, the schools _____ open.

Chapter 2: Agreement

Agreement of Pronoun and Antecedent A

A pronoun usually refers to a noun or another pronoun. The word a pronoun refers to is called its **antecedent**. A pronoun agrees with its antecedent in number, gender, and person.

Theodore Roethke won the Pulitzer Prize for one of **his** books of poetry.

The **trees** have shed **their** leaves.

Jaime and **Inés** are still making plans for **their** party.

Use singular pronouns to refer to indefinite pronouns such as *anybody, each, either, everybody, everyone, everything, neither, no one, nothing, one,* and *something.* Use plural pronouns to refer to the indefinite pronouns *both, few, many,* and *several.* Use singular or plural pronouns to refer to the indefinite pronouns *all, any, most, none,* and *some.*

SINGULAR: **Most** of the **painting** retained **its** original color.

PLURAL: **Most** of the **musicians** have memorized **their** parts.

Exercise A: Proofreading   Most of the following sentences contain pronouns that do not agree with their antecedents. If the pronoun does not agree with its antecedent, write the correct form on the line provided. If the pronoun agrees with its antecedent, write C.

1. Weren't you told that several of the new members did not receive their membership cards?   _____

2. Everyone in the women's group brought their camera to the party.   _____

3. Both of the male soloists pronounced his words clearly.   _____

4. Each of the men says that they will help pack the books.   _____

5. Did any of the newborn kittens seem steady on its feet?   _____

Exercise B   Complete each of the following sentences by supplying at least one pronoun that agrees with its antecedent. Use standard formal English.

EXAMPLE: 1. All of us should be free to express _*our*_ opinions.

1. All of the senior citizens enjoyed their trip to Boston, where many made

   _____ way along the Freedom Trail.

2. Most of the reporters at the press conference asked _____ questions too quickly.

3. Each woman on the tour knew she could use _____ map if she got separated from the group.

4. As far as I could see, each of the men made a mistake while presenting

   _____ argument during the debate.

5. The factory of the future will have robots working on _____ assembly line.

GRAMMAR/USAGE

Name _____ Date _____ Class _____

Agreement of Pronoun and Antecedent B

Use a plural pronoun to refer to two or more singular antecedents joined by *and*. Use a singular pronoun to refer to two or more singular antecedents joined by *or* or *nor*. When a singular and a plural antecedent are joined by *or* or *nor*, the pronoun usually agrees with the nearer antecedent.

> When **Rafael** and **Dave** sang, **their** lyrics were hard to understand.
>
> Either **Mrs. Wells** or the **Chases** will bring **their** grill.

If a singular antecedent may be either masculine or feminine, use both the masculine and feminine pronouns to refer to it.

> Each **student** told what **he or she** wanted to do.
>
> Every **member** of the club contributed **his or her** time to the project.

Collective nouns may act as either singular or plural antecedents.

> The **platoon** won an award for **its** excellent performance. [The platoon is thought of as a unit.]
>
> The **platoon** received **their** paychecks today. [The members received individual paychecks.]

The title of a creative work or the name of a country, city, or organization takes a singular pronoun.

> When did the **United Nations** hold **its** first meeting?

Some words, such as *civics*, *measles*, and *physics*, are plural in form but singular in meaning. These words take singular pronouns. Nouns that refer to pairs, such as *shorts* and *pliers*, always take plural pronouns. Nouns preceded by *every* or *many a(n)* take singular pronouns.

Exercise Complete each of the following sentences by supplying at least one pronoun that agrees with its antecedent. Use standard formal English.

1. Every citizen of Los Angeles and the surrounding areas must do

   _____ part to prevent traffic problems.

2. Copies, Inc., and thousands of other companies like _____ will be forced to change as technology changes.

3. Either María or her sisters will visit _____ best friend this summer.

4. According to the newspaper, the band will take _____ place in the parade just after the float.

5. Mumps may often be harder on adults than _____ is on children.

Chapter 2: Agreement

WORKSHEET 9 *Review*

Exercise A: Proofreading   Most of the following sentences contain verbs that do not agree with their subjects. If the verb does not agree with its subject, write the correct form on the line provided. If the verb agrees with its subject, write C.

EXAMPLE: 1. The Hawaiian Islands has a rich past that long predates American statehood in 1959. *have*

1. The history of the Hawaiian Islands tell of some interesting rulers. _____

2. Of course, none of these rulers is more amazing than King Kamehameha I. _____

3. This powerful leader, together with his followers, are credited with uniting the numerous islands into a kingdom in 1795. _____

4. Kamehameha I, whose family ruled the islands until 1872, was sometimes called the Napoleon of the Pacific. _____

5. Few of his descendants was more influential than King Kamehameha III. _____

6. No one deny that he helped the common people by permitting them to own land and by issuing a democratic constitution. _____

7. The musical interest of Hawaii's last two royal rulers, King Kalakaua I and Queen Liliuokalani, are a fascinating fact. _____

8. Both of these monarchs was known as songwriters. _____

9. The queen, whose regal bearing is legendary, has several claims to fame. _____

10. One of these are having written the famous song "Aloha Oe" ("Farewell to Thee"). _____

Exercise B   Complete each of the following sentences by supplying at least one pronoun that agrees with its antecedent. Use standard formal English.

EXAMPLE: 1. Nobody has come to claim *his or her* lost umbrella.

1. Every house in the neighborhood had _____ lawn mowed recently.

2. Both Jason and Maggie bought _____ shoes before the sale started.

3. Neither Mr. Kelly nor Mr. Arcaro accepted _____ award without gratitude.

4. I stopped several of the men marching in the band, but _____ could not talk to me.

GRAMMAR/USAGE

5. Many of the local artists displayed _____ paintings during the festival.

6. Many a member of the Rotary Club expressed _____ appreciation to the speaker.

7. The ski team always waxed _____ skis every morning before leaving the lodge.

8. Has anyone on the bus lost _____ ski boots?

9. The state has always stressed _____ highway safety record.

10. If someone asks for me, please tell _____ I will be back soon.

Exercise C: Proofreading   Most of the following sentences contain errors in agreement. If the sentence contains an error or errors in agreement, underline the incorrect verb(s) or pronoun(s), and supply the correct form(s). If the sentence is correct, write *C*.

> EXAMPLE: [1] Not all war poetry <u>glorify</u> battle and combat.
> 1. *glorifies*

[1] One of the great descriptions of modern warfare are contained in Randall Jarrell's poem "The Death of the Ball Turret Gunner." [2] Shaped by Jarrell's skill, the poem's five matter-of-fact lines becomes a moving narration of the last minutes of a man's life. [3] Glamour and glory does not appear in this stark poem. [4] Yet, something more enduring emerge—the gunner himself. [5] The voice of the gunner, with force and cool objectivity, narrate their own story. [6] In a sense, not all of his life were ended; some of his feelings and thoughts seems to live on. [7] Because few who reads these lines fails to be touched, this poem remains, long after Jarrell's own death, one of the most distinguished poems of World War II. [8] During that war, Jarrell was both a pilot and an instructor of celestial navigation. [9] He, like most good poets, shaped their experiences into art. [10] Either *Little Friend, Little Friend* or *Losses* make a good introduction to his works.

1. _____   6. _____

2. _____   7. _____

3. _____   8. _____

4. _____   9. _____

5. _____   10. _____

Name _____ Date _____ Class _____

Principal Parts of Regular Verbs

Every verb has four basic forms called the **principal parts**: the *base form*, the *present participle*, the *past*, and the *past participle*. A **regular verb** is one that forms its past and past participle by adding *–d* or *–ed* to the base form. A few regular verbs have alternative past and past participle forms that end in *–t*.

Base Form	Present Participle	Past	Past Participle
work	working	worked	(have) worked
sew	sewing	sewed	(have) sewed
burn	burning	burned *or* burnt	(have) burned *or* burnt

Exercise A   In each space provided, write the past or past participle of the verb shown in parentheses.

1. Last weekend Fatima, Joseph, and I _____ breaded chicken rolls. (cook)

2. We first _____ all the recipe ingredients. (purchase)

3. We were _____ to mince the garlic and parsley. (suppose)

4. Then we _____ the bread crumbs, garlic, parsley, and cheese. (combine)

5. With a mallet, I _____ the chicken to make it easy to roll. (pound)

6. Joseph had _____ lemon juice and oil into the crumb mixture. (pour)

7. Each piece of chicken was _____ with the moistened crumbs. (coat)

8. Then we rolled and _____ each piece of chicken with a toothpick. (secure)

9. When we had _____ the chicken in a pan, we baked it. (arrange)

10. I _____ to think cooking was hard, but our cooking experience was fun and easy. (use)

Exercise B: Revising   Revise each sentence below, using the past form of the verb instead of the present form. Write your revision on the line provided.

1. Ms. Woods works for the school board here in Baker County.

_____

2. At the first mention of a hurricane, everyone prepares well in advance.

_____

GRAMMAR/USAGE

Name _____ Date _____ Class _____

Principal Parts of Irregular Verbs A

An **irregular verb** forms its past and past participle in some way other than by adding –*d* or –*ed* to the base form. Such verbs form the past or past participle many ways:

CHANGING VOWELS *OR* CONSONANTS: drink, drank, drunk; send, sent, sent

CHANGING VOWELS *AND* CONSONANTS: see, saw, seen; go, went, gone

MAKING NO CHANGE: cost, cost, cost

Exercise A   On the line provided, write the past or past participle form of the verb in parentheses.

EXAMPLE: 1. Haven't you _*said*_ enough? (say)

1. Before the festival last Sunday, the Conchero dancers had _____ behind the church to practice. (meet)

2. By some unlucky chance, I _____ the door prize—a full-grown Leghorn rooster. (win)

3. The accomplishments of Maggie Lena Walker, the first female bank president in the

    United States, _____ a firm financial foundation for the African

    American community of Richmond, Virginia. (lay)

4. After a few hesitant steps, we _____ into the rhythm of the fox trot. (swing)

5. For all those years, the old man had _____ the dog-eared photograph of his childhood home in Hawaii. (keep)

Exercise B: Proofreading   The following sentences contain errors in the use of tenses. Underline each error. Then write the correct form of the verb on the line provided.

1. While in Arizona, Uncle Arthur boughten a magnificent storm-pattern Navajo rug by Shirley Tsinnie.   _____

2. How could you have spended all of your allowance before Saturday afternoon!   _____

3. A green velvet ribbon binded the large white box on the dining room table.   _____

4. The cool skin of the chameleon feeled dry, not wet.   _____

5. That colorful painting by the Haitian artist Euguerrand Gourgue lended a cheery touch to the room.   _____

Name _____ Date _____ Class _____

WORKSHEET 3

Principal Parts of Irregular Verbs B

When forming the past and the past participle of irregular verbs, avoid these common errors:

(1) using the past form with a helping verb

NONSTANDARD: I have never went to Mexico.

STANDARD: I never **went** to Mexico.

(2) using the past participle form without a helping verb

NONSTANDARD: He done his best.

STANDARD: He **had done** his best.

(3) adding *–d*, *–ed*, or *–t* to the base form

NONSTANDARD: Who **letted** the dog out?

STANDARD: Who **let** the dog out?

Exercise   For each sentence in the following paragraphs, underline the correct verb in the parentheses.

[1] Years ago in Africa, languages like Bantu had no alphabet; therefore, nothing was (wrote, written) in these languages. [2] In fact, the musical quality of many African languages (gived, gave) them an intricacy unsuitable for written alphabets. [3] Consequently, drums (sung, sang) these languages throughout equatorial and southern Africa, and these songs acted as a kind of musical writing. [4] According to Janheinz Jahn, the use of drums (arose, arisen) for communication at a distance. [5] Young Africans learned to read the different sounds of the drums and (knew, known) the meanings of these sounds in combinations, just as you were taught to read using the alphabet.

[6] The wide acoustic range of drums like the Yorubas' *dundun* (gived, gave) quick and easy access to a complex language. [7] By varying tone, pitch, and modulation, a skillful drummer (striven, strove) to re-create the sounds of his language. [8] With this meaningful music, he (wove, woven) the news of the day into an informative report. [9] At the speed of sound, his warnings, invitations, and other messages (flew, flown) over miles of jungle and plain. [10] With drum scripts that had been (beat, beaten) for decades, he sent information to interested listeners. [11] Many of the drum scripts eventually (became, become) classic epics. [12] As you can see, drummers were not just musicians; they (been, were) also teachers and historians. [13] Through them, generations of young Africans (drank, drunk) in the history of their ancestors.

[14] When European missionaries came to Africa, however, they (forbidden, forbade) the playing of drums. [15] Their prohibitions (struck, stricken) at the hearts of many African cultures. [16] Today, through disuse, almost all of the old drum scripts have been (forgot, forgotten). [17] Scholars, however, have (maked, made) recordings of many of the remaining scripts. [18] Sadly, many listeners have never (spoke, spoken) their traditional languages; consequently, even verbal translations of the drum songs are meaningless to many Africans. [19] The power of the drums has (went, gone). [20] Like so much of ancient knowledge and wisdom, this marvelous system of communication has been (forsaken, forsook).

Chapter 3: Using Verbs

WORKSHEET 4

Principal Parts of Irregular Verbs C

The best way to learn the principal parts of irregular verbs is to memorize them. No single usage rule applies to the different ways that these verbs form their past and past participle forms. Remember that there are some general guidelines you can use. Irregular verbs form the past and past participle by

- changing vowels or consonants
- changing vowels and consonants
- making no change

Exercise: Proofreading   Most of the following sentences contain incorrect verb forms. If a verb form is incorrect, write the correct past form on the line provided. If a sentence is correct, write C.

1. During the freeze last March, the water pipes at school bursted.   _____

2. That dog would not have hurted a fly.   _____

3. Yesterday evening, I had just putted dinner on the table when the phone rang.   _____

4. Shaka led his Zulu warriors into battle, and soon news of Shaka's victory had spreaded throughout Zululand.   _____

5. Have you ever cutted out a pattern before?   _____

6. Have you read the assignment yet?   _____

7. After art class, Jeremy and I setted our pottery out in the sun to dry.   _____

8. The drought hitted the spring crops hard.   _____

9. One chance remark had costed her the election.   _____

10. Wisely, Francisca Henrique de Ribera letted the Andean natives treat her malaria attack with a powerful bark, now known as quinine.   _____

Chapter 3: Using Verbs

WORKSHEET 5 *Troublesome Verbs*

Certain verbs are troublesome because they are so similar. Study the following verbs:

Lie: The verb *lie (lying, lay, lain)* means "to rest, stay, or recline." *Lie* never takes an object.

Lay: The verb *lay (laying, laid, laid)* means "to put [something] in a place." *Lay* usually takes an object.

Sit: The verb *sit (sitting, sat, sat)* means "to rest in an upright seated position." *Sit* seldom takes an object.

Set: The verb *set (setting, set, set)* usually means "to put [something] in a place." *Set* usually takes an object.

Rise: The verb *rise (rising, rose, risen)* means "to go up" or "to get up." *Rise* almost never takes an object.

Raise: The verb *raise (raising, raised, raised)* means "to cause [something] to rise" or "to lift up." *Raise* usually takes an object.

Exercise A   For each of the following sentences, underline the correct verb in parentheses.

1. All week that box has (lain, laid) unopened on the desk.

2. Our applications were (lying, laying) in front of the file.

3. Would you like to (sit, set) with us at the powwow?

4. I always (lie, lay) the phone book on this table.

5. If you (sit, set) the pie on the ledge, it may vanish.

6. Kathy sang as she (lay, laid) the baby in the crib.

7. Last night's victory really (rose, raised) the team's spirit and confidence.

8. Tempers (rose, raised) as the debate progressed.

9. Mrs. Nasser (sat, set) the tabbouleh and kibbe next to other traditional Lebanese foods.

10. Billows of dust (rose, raised) from the field.

Exercise B   Each of the following sayings lacks a verb. Choose the correct verb in parentheses and write it on the line provided.

1. You have made your bed; now, you must _____ in it. (lie, lay)

2. Humpty Dumpty _____ on a wall. (set, sat)

3. Whoever _____ down with dogs gets up with fleas. (lies, lays)

4. She thinks the sun _____ and sets on him. (rises, raises)

GRAMMAR/USAGE

Chapter 3: Using Verbs

WORKSHEET 6 ## *Verb Tense*

The **tense** of a verb indicates the time of the action or the state of being expressed by the verb. Every verb has six tenses that are formed from the four principal parts of a verb.

PRESENT: Ruby **sings** a familiar song.

PAST: Carmen **sang,** too.

FUTURE: Ruby **will sing** with Carmen.

PRESENT PERFECT: Carmen **has sung** for school concerts.

PAST PERFECT: Before she sang with Carmen, Ruby **had sung** in a group.

FUTURE PERFECT: By next year, Ruby and Carmen will **have sung** as a duo at many dances and parties.

Exercise A   On the line provided, write the tense of each verb in italics.

1. I *have read* the poem "Dusting" by Julia Alvarez. _____

2. The poem *reveals* something about the poet's relationship with her mother. _____

3. The poem's speaker *felt* anonymous within her family. _____

4. There are times, I think, when all children *feel* that way. _____

5. Julia Alvarez was only ten when she *moved* to the United States with her family. _____

6. Before that, she *had lived* in the Dominican Republic. _____

7. Ms. Alvarez *has taught* creative writing at George Washington University. _____

8. She *based* her poetry and short stories on her childhood experiences. _____

9. By the end of the term, we *will have studied* several poems from her book *Homecoming*. _____

10. Next term, we *will read* selections from her first book of fiction, *How the García Girls Lost Their Accents*. _____

Exercise B   On the lines provided, write five original sentences about a movie you have seen or would like to see. Use five different verbs in at least three different tenses in your sentences.

_____

_____

_____

_____

_____

Name _____ Date _____ Class _____

WORKSHEET 7

Special Problems in the Use of Tenses

Use tense forms carefully to show the correct relationship between verbs in a sentence. When describing events that occur at the same time, use verbs of the same tense. When describing events that occur at different times, use verbs in different tenses to show the order of events.

SAME TIME: The telephone **rang,** so I **answered** it. [past]

DIFFERENT TIMES: I **picked** up the receiver, but the person **had** already **hung** up. [two different points in the past]

Exercise A   Decide if the italicized verbs in each sentence below tell about the same time or different times. On the lines provided, write *S* for same or *D* for different.

_____ 1. He *delivers* the mail when the regular letter carrier *is* sick.

_____ 2. If the rain *had stopped*, we *would have eaten* outdoors.

_____ 3. The train *approached* and all the cars *stopped*.

_____ 4. I already *knew* that mushrooms *are* spore-bearing fungi.

_____ 5. When you *arrived*, we *had been waiting* only a few minutes.

Exercise B: Proofreading   Each of the following sentences contains an error in the use of tenses. Cross out each error, and write your corrections above the sentence.

had forgotten
EXAMPLE: 1. If she ~~forgot~~ the directions, we could have been lost.

1. Pam finally appreciated the old saying that every cloud had a silver lining.

2. By the time we graduate in June, Ms. Vargas will be teaching Spanish for twenty-four years.

3. Although Denny's skill was demonstrated during the season, he was not chosen to play in the All-Star game.

4. When Jeremy finally got to the dentist, his tooth already stopped hurting.

5. The company hired Ms. Littmann because she lived for many years in Japan.

6. By the time I presented my report before the committee, the members have already studied several other reports on nuclear waste disposal.

7. The clerk remembered that the manager has ordered the new shipment last Tuesday.

8. When we reviewed the videotapes of the game, we saw that the other team committed the foul.

9. If they had enough money, they could have taken a taxi home.

10. As I thought about our argument, I had been sure you lost your temper first.

GRAMMAR/USAGE

Chapter 3: Using Verbs

Progressive and Emphatic Forms

Each verb tense has an additional form called the **progressive form,** which expresses a continuing action or state of being. In each tense, the progressive form consists of the appropriate tense of *be* plus the present participle of the main verb. Some forms also include additional helping verbs.

PRESENT PROGRESSIVE: is dancing

PAST PROGRESSIVE: was dancing

FUTURE PROGRESSIVE: will be dancing

PRESENT PERFECT PROGRESSIVE: has been dancing

PAST PERFECT PROGRESSIVE: had been dancing

FUTURE PERFECT PROGRESSIVE: will have been dancing

The **emphatic form** of a verb is used to express emphasis. This form consists of the present or the past tense of *do* with the base form of the main verb. Only present tense and past tense verbs have emphatic forms.

PRESENT EMPHATIC: The car **does need** an oil change.

PAST EMPHATIC: Waiter, I **did ask** for a side of cole slaw.

The emphatic form is also used in questions and in negative statements.

QUESTION: **Do** you **know** the city well?

NEGATIVE STATEMENT: No, I **don't have** an extra pen.

Exercise   On the line provided, identify the tense and form of the verb in each of the following sentences as either *present, past,* or *future progressive; present perfect, past perfect,* or *future perfect progressive;* or *present emphatic* or *past emphatic.*

1. In June, Mr. Taylor will have been working for thirty years. _____

2. Do tell us your news! _____

3. The whole neighborhood had been searching for the dog all afternoon. _____

4. She is talking on the phone at the moment. _____

5. The company has been manufacturing staples for fifty years. _____

6. No, Roger, don't give us another one of your lectures. _____

7. Three wires were hanging loosely from the back of the stereo. _____

8. Nicole will be moving next month. _____

9. Did you get the license number? _____

10. A dark cloud was gathering in the distance. _____

Name _____ Date _____ Class _____

Active and Passive Voice

Voice is the form a transitive verb takes to indicate whether the subject of the verb performs or receives the action. When the subject of a verb performs the action, the verb is in the **active voice**. When the subject receives the action, the verb is in the **passive voice.**

ACTIVE: A group of ecologists **visited** the Amazon rain forest. [The subject *(ecologists)* performs the action.]

PASSIVE: The Amazon rain forest **was visited** by a group of ecologists. [The subject of the sentence is *rain forest.* It receives the action.]

In general, the passive voice is less direct, less forceful, and less concise than the active voice. Use the passive voice when you do not know or do not want to reveal the performer of an action or when you want to emphasize the receiver of an action.

AWKWARD PASSIVE: Specific areas of the forest have been studied by ecologists.

DELIBERATE PASSIVE: Specific areas of the forest have been studied. [The performer is not mentioned and the emphasis is on the areas of the forest.]

Exercise A   Decide if each italicized verb below is in the active or passive voice. On the line provided, write *A* for active or *P* for passive.

_____ 1. Chico Mendes *was raised* in Brazil, deep in the Amazon rain forest.

_____ 2. As an adult, Chico Mendes and his fellow workers *were angered* by the devastation of the Amazon rain forest by ranchers.

_____ 3. Chico's voice *was heard* by environmentalists and ecologists all over the world.

_____ 4. The Brazilian government eventually *declared* millions of acres in the Amazon protected.

_____ 5. Chico's murder by two local ranchers in 1988 *overshadowed* his victory.

Exercise B: Revising   On the lines provided, revise the following sentences by changing the passive voice to active voice wherever the change is desirable.

1. After the new computers had been installed by the service representatives, a training session was given to us by them.

_____

2. A community meeting was held by the area homeowners to discuss the landfill project, which had been proposed by the city council.

_____

3. Shinae Chun is admired and respected by her colleagues.

_____

4. The grass was mowed and the leaves were raked by me.

_____

GRAMMAR/USAGE

Chapter 3: Using Verbs

WORKSHEET 10 *Mood*

Mood is the form a verb takes to indicate the attitude of the person using the verb. Verbs may be in one of three moods. The **indicative mood** is used to express a fact, an opinion, or a question.

> INDICATIVE MOOD: Sweden **claims** one of the world's highest per capita incomes.

The **imperative mood** is used to express a direct command or request.

> IMPERATIVE MOOD: **Tell** me where you learned that information.

The **subjunctive mood** has different uses in the past and present tenses. The present subjunctive is used to express a suggestion or a necessity. The past subjunctive is used to express a condition contrary to fact, or to express a wish.

> PRESENT SUBJUNCTIVE: Herbert asked that he **be** allowed to participate.

> PAST SUBJUNCTIVE: Canditha wishes that her computer skills **were** stronger.

Exercise A   Identify the mood of the italicized verbs below. On the lines provided, write *IND* for indicative, *IMP* for imperative, or *SUB* for subjunctive.

_____ 1. I wish I *were able* to go to the sneak preview of the new Spike Lee movie, but I have to work.

_____ 2. *Let* me know how you are doing.

_____ 3. The manual recommends that the system *be cleaned* every six months.

_____ 4. *Were* the fluids and oil *checked*?

_____ 5. *Be* there!

Exercise B: Revising   Most of the following sentences contain errors in the use of verbs. Rewrite those sentences correctly on the lines provided. If a sentence is correct, write C.

1. Willis had insisted that every employee is invited to the company's annual picnic.

   _____

2. I'd be a lobster fisher if I was living on Cape Cod.

   _____

3. Gloria was confused all day because it seemed as though it was Friday, but it was only Thursday.

   _____

4. Striking out again, Kevin moaned, "I wish I was a better hitter!"

   _____

5. Vernon lost many of his friends when he began acting as if he were better than they.

   _____

Name _____ Date _____ Class _____

Using Verbals Correctly

The **present participle** or the **past participle** is used to express an action or a state of being that occurs at the same time as that of the main verb. The **present perfect participle** is used to express an action or a state of being that happens before that of the main verb.

PRESENT PARTICIPLE: **Swimming in the bay,** I noticed a triangular fin. [The action expressed by *swimming* occurs at the same time as the action expressed by *noticed*.]

PAST PARTICIPLE: **Alarmed by the sight,** I quickly swam to shore. [The action expressed by *alarmed* occurs at the same time as the action expressed by *swam*.]

PRESENT PERFECT PARTICIPLE: **Having been torn** only at the seams, the shirt was easily mended. [The action expressed by *having been torn* precedes the action expressed by *mended*.]

The **present infinitive** is used to express an action or a state of being that follows that of the main verb. The **present perfect infinitive** is used to express an action or a state of being that precedes that of the main verb.

PRESENT INFINITIVE: The team hoped **to win.** [The action expressed by *to win* follows the action expressed by *hoped*.]

PRESENT PERFECT INFINITIVE: Paula wanted **to have received** an invitation. [The action expressed by *to have received* precedes the action expressed by *wanted*.]

Exercise: Proofreading   Most of the following sentences contain errors in the use of verbals. Underline each error. Then write the correct form of the verbal on the line provided.

1. Native Arctic peoples learned to have survived in a harsh environment.

_____

2. Standing in line for more than two hours, Tamisha finally got tickets to the Hammer concert.

_____

3. Making weekend plans earlier, I declined the invitation.

_____

4. No one said a word as the big yellow arrow was spun to have determined who would take the first turn.

_____

5. We wanted to have avoided any controversy.

_____

GRAMMAR/USAGE

Chapter 3: Using Verbs

WORKSHEET 12 **Review**

Exercise A For each of the following sentences, give the correct form (past or past participle) of the verb in parentheses.

EXAMPLE: 1. The Americas have _given_ the world a rich larder. (give)

1. Have you ever _____ anything about the origin of foods? (read)

2. Many of the foods you have _____ have a long history. (eat)

3. Like naturalized citizens, many food products have _____ vital, even characteristic, parts of their adopted nations. (become)

4. Consequently, most people have _____ that key ingredients, such as tomato sauce on pizza, came from the Americas. (forget)

5. Reports from early explorers _____ cooks all over Europe into a creative frenzy. (put)

6. When the explorers returned home, dozens of strange and exotic foods were suddenly _____ available to Europeans. (make)

7. Some of the foods that the explorers _____ home included sweet potatoes, white potatoes, corn, peppers, tomatoes, avocados, vanilla, maple sugar, chocolate, peanuts, all sorts of beans (kidney, lima, snap, string, butter, pole, and navy), and a host of other welcome additions to a chef's larder. (send)

8. So many new spices, fruits, vegetables, meats, and grains _____ the market that this period in history can be called a "Food Revolution." (hit)

9. In these unfamiliar foods, many peoples also _____ new hope against famine. (find)

10. The Chinese, for example, _____ experienced severe famine for years. (have)

11. Countless lives had been _____ due to the failure of rice crops. (lose)

12. However, with the introduction of the sweet potato, an alternative to rice _____ . (arise)

13. Sweet potatoes _____ little and did well in poor soil. (cost)

14. Soon, cooks had _____ sweet-potato flour into Chinese dumplings, noodles, and many other dishes. (put)

15. Because of the continuing popularity of the sweet potato in China, Chinese farmers have _____ more sweet potatoes than farmers in any other country. (grow)

16. Europe, too, often had been _____ by famine due to poor weather conditions. (strike)

17. For Europeans, their salvation _____ in the Andean potato. (lay)

18. With harvest after harvest of potatoes, Europeans _____ famine and also created a whole new menu. (fight)

19. In soups, stews, pancakes, and pies, the potato _____ its substance and nutrition to a host of European dishes. (lend)

20. Who in the time of Christopher Columbus could have _____ of the vast variety of American food sources or of the vital roles they would play in the world's fight against famine? (think)

Exercise B Underline the correct form of the verb in parentheses.

1. At the tribal council meeting, someone (rose, raised) the issue of land ownership within reservation boundaries.

2. If you are sick, you should be (lying, laying) down.

3. They were (sitting, setting) placemats on the table.

4. The men (lain, laid) the heavy crate on the handcart.

5. I left my gloves (lying, laying) on the counter.

6. Lucia's mother has always (lain, laid) a great deal of emphasis on bilingual education.

7. Mist was (rising, raising) from the ground.

8. In Japan people often (sit, set) on tatami, or floor mats, instead of chairs.

9. I may never know who (sat, set) on my glasses.

10. To make traditional challah, braid the bread dough after it has (risen, raised) for an hour.

Exercise C: Proofreading Each of the following sentences contains an error in the use of verbs. Underline the error. Then give the correct form of the verb on the line provided.

1. Spending three hours on a review of chemistry, we then worked on irregular French verbs. _____

2. Having attempted to travel across the African continent, the explorers encountered both vast deserts and dense swamp forests. _____

3. If I was Luís, I would have argued with the umpire. _____

4. Cindy retraced her steps and found the café at which she left her credit card. _____

5. I never realized that hurricanes and typhoons were really the same thing. _____

6. As he slowly turned the key, the door suddenly swings wide
open.   _____

7. Last week, the school newspaper has printed Kim's story.   _____

8. Winning the medal, she revised her practice schedule and gave
herself more free time.   _____

9. By the time the next presidential election comes up, I will be in
the United States for six years.   _____

10. Mr. Washington wanted to shown them his collection of African
sculptures, but he was suddenly called away on business.   _____

Exercise D: Proofreading   Most of the sentences in the following paragraphs contain errors in the use of verbs. Identify each error. Then supply the correct verb form above the sentence.

EXAMPLE: [1] Have you ever wanted to ~~have celebrated~~ *celebrate* growing up?

[1] Many cultures have not forsaked their traditional ceremonies that mark the significant stages in a person's life. [2] For instance, when an Apache girl has came of age, she may receive a Sunrise Ceremonial. [3] Through this ceremony, the young woman is forever separated from her girlhood and lead into womanhood. [4] Everything in the ceremony is suppose to have remind the young woman of the deep spiritual meaning of her life. [5] Perhaps part of that meaning can be founded in the glad hearts of her many friends and family members who come to participate in the ceremony.

[6] Not long ago, a young woman named Carla and her mother seeked the blessings of a traditional Sunrise Ceremonial. [7] During Carla's ceremonial, many traditional songs were sang, thirty-two of them by one group of dancers alone. [8] Having stood for seemingly endless hours in the burning sun, Carla danced for six hours at a time, wearing a hot, heavy buckskin dress. [9] If Carla was a young woman of a century ago, she would have danced all night. [10] Surely, these tests of self-discipline have teached Carla and everyone who attended the ceremony something about the endurance and strength that a woman needs to live as a proper Apache.

Name _____ Date _____ Class _____

 **WORKSHEET 1** *Pronoun Case*

Case is the form of a noun or pronoun that shows how it is used. In English, there are three cases: **nominative, objective,** and **possessive**. Personal pronouns change form in the different cases, as the chart below indicates.

		Nominative	Objective	Possessive
SINGULAR	FIRST PERSON:	I	me	my, mine
	SECOND PERSON:	you	you	your, yours
	THIRD PERSON:	he, she, it	him, her, it	his, her, hers, its
PLURAL	FIRST PERSON:	we	us	our, ours
	SECOND PERSON:	you	you	your, yours
	THIRD PERSON:	they	them	their, theirs

Exercise A Each of the following sentences contains an italicized personal pronoun. On the line before the sentence, write *1* if the pronoun is first person, *2* if it is second person, or *3* if it is third person. Then write *N* if the pronoun is in the nominative case; *O* if it is in the objective case; or *P* if it is in the possessive case.

EXAMPLE: _1—N_   1. Deniz and *I* went to the Rose Bowl in Pasadena.

_____ 1. The clerk was very helpful to Ms. Ayala and *me*.

_____ 2. Was it *he* who called while I was at the recycling center?

_____ 3. I didn't know that *their* mother was a published poet.

_____ 4. I've decided that I thoroughly support *your* point of view.

_____ 5. Please provide *them* with your new address and phone number.

Exercise B On the line following each sentence, write the pronoun that completes the sentence correctly. A description of the pronoun appears in parentheses.

1. I gave Gino and *(third person, plural, objective)* copies of my speech. _____

2. The coach hasn't seen *(first person singular, possessive)* best effort yet. _____

3. *(First person plural, nominative)* have donated funds to the relief effort. _____

4. Do *(second person singular, nominative)* understand this poem? _____

5. The riders have mounted *(third person plural, possessive)* horses. _____

GRAMMAR/USAGE

Chapter 4: Using Pronouns

 **WORKSHEET 2** | *The Nominative Case*

Personal pronouns in the **nominative case**—*I, you, he, she, it, we,* and *they*—are used as *subjects of verbs* and as *predicate nominatives.* A **predicate nominative** is a noun or pronoun that follows a linking verb and explains or identifies the subject of the verb. A pronoun that is used as a predicate nominative always follows a form of the verb *be: am, is, are, was, were, be,* or *been.*

SUBJECT: Sudi and **I** particularly liked Sylvia Plath's poem "Mushrooms."

PREDICATE NOMINATIVE: The candidate with the most votes is **she**.

Exercise A Each sentence contains two personal pronouns in parentheses. Underline the pronoun that correctly completes the sentence. Then, on the line before the sentence, write *S* if the pronoun is the subject of the verb or *PN* if it is a predicate nominative.

_____ 1. Vince and (he, him) are playing bridge tonight.

_____ 2. Either Theo or (I, me) will be the punter for the football team.

_____ 3. I'm sure that the woman who painted the portrait was (her, she).

_____ 4. It may have been (we, us) who left the gate unlocked.

_____ 5. Neither Han-Ling nor (he, him) has taken a course in calligraphy.

_____ 6. The partners with the highest scores were (us, we).

_____ 7. Was it (they, them) who requested my address?

_____ 8. Angelo knew that the people in the horse costume were (them, they).

_____ 9. You and (her, she) deserve a lot of credit.

_____10. (He, Him) and Marianne became finalists in the tennis tournament.

Exercise B: Proofreading The following paragraph contains five errors in the case forms of personal pronouns. Identify each error, and correct it.

Rosebud Yellow Robe Frantz was born in Rapid City, South Dakota. It was her who wrote the book *Album of the American Indian.* Her was the daughter of Chauncey Yellow Robe. Him was the chief of the Lakota. It may have been him or two other ancestors, Iron Plume and Sitting Bull, who were the inspiration for Rosebud Yellow Robe's many books about Native Americans and their cultures. My brother and me have enjoyed reading these interesting books.

Name _____ Date _____ Class _____

 **WORKSHEET 3** *The Objective Case A*

Personal pronouns that are used as **objects of verbs**—*me, you, him, her, it, us,* and *them*—are in the **objective case**. A **direct object** follows an action verb and tells *whom* or *what*.

      DIRECT OBJECT: We saw **her** and **them** at the concert.

An **indirect object** comes between an action verb and a direct object. It tells *to whom, to what, for whom,* or *for what* the action of the verb is done.

      INDIRECT OBJECT: Critics have awarded **them** many honors.

Exercise A   For each of the following sentences, underline the correct form of the pronoun in parentheses.

  1. Did you tell the superintendent or (her, she)?

  2. (She, Her) and (he, him) I would never doubt.

  3. Leave (me, I) alone for a while.

  4. Carmen will be inviting both you and (I, me) to the recital.

  5. Did you see Lois or (him, he) today?

  6. I sent the admissions director and (her, she) a letter.

  7. The coach chose Joan and (we, us).

  8. The principal should have notified (he, him) and Gail.

  9. Ron just passed Tina and (me, I) in the hall.

10. Please don't ask (they, them) about today's game.

Exercise B   On the line provided, write the pronoun that could be used in place of the italicized word or words in the sentence.

  1. Have you read the new biography about *Carl Lewis*?   _____

  2. Please notify *Mr. and Mrs. Sanchez* about the meeting.   _____

  3. After *the presentation,* the moderator gave a summation.   _____

  4. Most of *the science and math classes* have prerequisites.   _____

  5. Frank lent *Joanna* his guidebook of the Sierras.   _____

GRAMMAR/USAGE

Name _____ Date _____ Class _____

The Objective Case B

A **prepositional phrase** consists of a preposition, a noun or pronoun called the **object of the preposition,** and any modifiers of that object. A personal pronoun that is used as the object of a preposition is in the **objective case**.

OBJECT OF A PREPOSITION: Between **you** and **me,** I didn't like that movie.

A **verbal** is a verb form that is used as another part of speech. **Participles, gerunds,** and **infinitives** are verbals. A personal pronoun in the objective case is used as the object of a verbal.

OBJECT OF A PARTICIPLE: Watching Kyle and **them,** I have learned a lot about guitar.

OBJECT OF A GERUND: Sally's dream is one day meeting the president and **her**.

OBJECT OF AN INFINITIVE: Didn't you promise to help **me** with the chores?

Exercise For each of the following sentences, underline the correct form of the pronoun in parentheses.

1. The chess team sent a challenge to Don and (he, him).

2. The slide show was presented by my sister and (I, me).

3. We are planning to leave with (they, them) and Alice.

4. I dedicated my poem to both Marcia and (she, her).

5. The matter is strictly between Ms. James and (they, them).

6. Would you draw a cartoon for the girls and (we, us)?

7. Would you please stop bothering Simon and (I, me)?

8. Baby-sitting my brother and (she, her) is not the easiest job in the world.

9. I wanted to see (they, them) before I left.

10. Greeting the Bakers and (I, me) at the door, our host graciously led us to the living room.

Name _____ Date _____ Class _____

WORKSHEET 5 *Possessive Case*

The personal pronouns in the **possessive case**—*my, mine, your, yours, his, her, hers, its, our, ours,* and *theirs*—are used to show ownership or relationship. The possessive pronouns *mine, yours, his, hers, its, ours,* and *theirs* are used in the same ways that the pronouns in the nominative and objective cases are used.

SUBJECT: **Yours** was the best performance.

PREDICATE NOMINATIVE: That opinion is **hers**.

OBJECT OF VERB: I got **mine** at a department store.

OBJECT OF PREPOSITION: Ted's dog will be friendly to **yours**.

The possessive pronouns *my, your, his, her, its, our,* and *their* are used as adjectives before nouns.

Your poem is beautiful. **Its** imagery is outstanding.

A noun or pronoun that precedes a **gerund** must be in the possessive case to modify the gerund. Do not confuse a gerund with a **present participle**. Although both end in *–ing,* a gerund acts as a noun, whereas a present participle serves as an adjective. A noun or pronoun that is modified by a present participle should *not* be in the possessive case.

GERUND: **His listening** helped. [*Listening* acts as a noun.]

PARTICIPLE: I appreciated **him listening**. [*Listening* acts as an adjective.]

Exercise A   For each of the following sentences, underline the correct pronoun form in parentheses.

1. Their parents have become close friends with (our, ours).

2. That old coat of (my, mine) really needs a good cleaning.

3. I've got my racquet; please get (your, yours).

4. If (their, theirs) is the green car, then the Daleys must own the red car.

5. The buzzer will go off when (our, ours) is ready.

Exercise B   Each sentence below contains an italicized word that is either a gerund or a present participle. Before each italicized word, two pronouns appear in parentheses. Underline the pronoun that completes the sentence correctly.

1. Keep (them, their) *listening* by adding a little humor to your speech.

2. (You, Your) *whispering* is disrupting the class.

3. Sakima has worked hard to improve (his, him) *skiing*.

4. We saw (them, their) *putting* up campaign posters all over town.

5. We regretted (our, us) *jumping* to the wrong conclusions.

GRAMMAR/USAGE

Appositives and Elliptical Constructions

WORKSHEET 6

An **appositive** is a noun or pronoun placed next to another noun or pronoun to explain or identify it.

N APP	PRO APP

The **singers, Leo and she,** won the prize.   **We singers** won the prize.

A **pronoun** used as an appositive is in the same case as the word to which it refers.

> The judges chose the **singers,** Leo and **her**. [The pronoun *her* is in the nominative case because it is an appositive of the direct object *singers*.]

An **elliptical construction** is a phrase or clause from which words have been omitted. The words *than* and *as* often begin elliptical constructions. A pronoun following *than* or *as* in an elliptical construction is in the same case that it would be in if the construction were completed.

> They know Jill better than **her**. [They know Jill better than *they know her*.]
>
> They know Jill better than **she**. [They know Jill better than *she knows Jill*.]

Exercise A   Cross out any incorrect pronouns in the following sentences. On the line provided, write the correct form. If a sentence is correct, write C.

1. The bus driver greeted we students with a smile.   _____

2. The basketball team elected co-captains, Mario and him.   _____

3. Two students, Angela and her, toured the Capitol.   _____

4. Should we members of the fitness club sponsor the walk-a-thon? _____

5. The cafeteria was painted by two seniors, Chad and he.   _____

Exercise B: Revising   For each sentence, complete the elliptical clause, including the appropriate pronoun form. Tell whether the pronoun is a *subject* or an *object*. For each sentence, you need to give only one revision.

> EXAMPLE: 1. Eva is shorter than (I, me). *than I am—subject*

1. Have you and the rest of your family lived in this area as long as (they, them)?

   _____

2. Can Ms. Edwards tutor Paula as well as (I, me)?

   _____

3. The senior class scored higher than (they, them).

   _____

4. I understand him better than (she, her).

   _____

5. The field trip next week will probably benefit Roger more than (I, me).

   _____

Name _____ Date _____ Class _____

WORKSHEET 7

Reflexive and Intensive Pronouns

Reflexive pronouns and **intensive pronouns** (sometimes called **compound personal pronouns**) end in *–self* or *–selves*. Reflexive and intensive pronouns are identical in form, but they are used differently. A **reflexive pronoun** refers to another word that indicates the same individual(s) or thing(s).

> Rick hurt **himself**. [*Himself* refers to *Rick*.]

An **intensive pronoun** emphasizes another word that indicates the same individual(s) or thing(s).

> I **myself** must take full responsibility. [*Myself* emphasizes *I*.]

A pronoun ending in *–self* or *–selves* should not be used in place of a simple personal pronoun.

> NONSTANDARD: Sid and myself went to the art museum.
>
> STANDARD: Sid and **I** went to the art museum.

Exercise A   For each of the following sentences, label the italicized pronoun as intensive *(I)* or reflexive *(R)* on the line provided. Also, write the word or words that the pronoun refers to or emphasizes. [Note: If the sentence is imperative, the word that the pronoun refers to may be understood.]

> EXAMPLE: 1.   Aunt Flo should take better care of *herself*. *Aunt Flo—R*

1. Will the principal *himself* preside at the awards ceremony?   _____

2. I bought *myself* a Scottish kilt at the import store.   _____

3. Mark and Jo should be ashamed of *themselves* for missing your birthday.   _____

4. You'll just have to take care of the problem *yourself*.   _____

5. We should give *ourselves* credit for a job well-done.   _____

Exercise B   In each of the following sentences, cross out any pronouns that are used incorrectly. On the line provided, write the correct form of the pronoun.

1. My choices for the editors of the paper are Eula and yourself.   _____

2. Thanks to ourselves, the publicity for the drama festival had great results.   _____

3. Lilith introduced herself and myself to the visiting delegates.   _____

4. The winners were myself and my friend.   _____

5. This journal is for myself alone.   _____

GRAMMAR/USAGE

Chapter 4: Using Pronouns

Who *and* Whom

Like most personal pronouns, the pronoun *who (whoever)* has three cases. When *who* and *whoever* are used to form questions, they are called **interrogative pronouns**. The case of an interrogative pronoun depends on its use in the question.

  NOMINATIVE CASE: **Who** is that? [*Who* is the subject.]

  OBJECTIVE CASE: **Whom** are you inviting? [*Whom* is the direct object.]

  POSSESSIVE CASE: **Whose** car is that? [*Whose* modifies *car*.]

When these pronouns are used to introduce a subordinate clause, they are called **relative pronouns**. To choose between *who* and *whom* in a subordinate clause, determine how the pronoun is used in the clause.

  The man **who called** was Dr. Tehrani. [*Who* is the subject of the clause.]

  The man **whom I called** was Dr. Tehrani. [*Whom* is the direct object of the verb *called*.]

Exercise A   For each of the following sentences, underline the correct form of the pronoun in parentheses.

  1. I wondered (who, whom) the next volunteer would be.

  2. We can't remember (who, whom) played the leading role.

  3. (Whoever, Whomever) receives the most votes will be the team captain.

  4. To (who, whom) should I send my application form?

  5. Ms. Quarles, (who, whom) I met at the trial, is a reporter.

Exercise B   For each of the following sentences, underline the correct form of the pronoun in parentheses. Then identify its use in the subordinate clause—as a subject *(S)*, a predicate nominative *(PN)*, a direct object *(DO)*, or an object of the preposition *(OP)*.

_____ 1. The two people (who, whom) I like most are Will and Rosa.

_____ 2. Someone called, but I don't know (who, whom) she was.

_____ 3. With (who, whom) do you intend to go to the play?

_____ 4. Several of the women (who, whom) had served on other committees were considered for the position.

_____ 5. (Whoever, Whomever) the committee chooses will receive a large scholarship.

Name _____ Date _____ Class _____

WORSHEET 9

Ambiguous and General Reference

A **pronoun** should always refer clearly to its **antecedent**. Avoid **ambiguous references,** which occur when a pronoun refers to either of two antecedents.

> AMBIGUOUS: Rosa phoned Lois while **she** was in Miami. [Who was in Miami?]
>
> CLEAR: While Rosa was in Miami, she phoned Lois.

Similarly, avoid **general references,** which occur when a pronoun such as *it, this, that, which,* or *such* refers to a general idea rather than to a specific noun.

> GENERAL: Hank sang beautifully. **This** impressed the audience. [no specific antecedent for *this*]
>
> CLEAR: Hank impressed the audience by singing beautifully.

Exercise: Revising Most of the following sentences contain ambiguous or general pronoun references. On the lines provided, revise each faulty sentence. [Note: You need to give only one revision for each sentence.]

> EXAMPLE: 1. Benito Pablo Juárez, who was of Zapotec ancestry, was a serious man, which is evident in photographs.
>
> *Photographs show that Benito Pablo Juárez, who was of Zapotec ancestry, was a serious man.*

1. Juárez was a liberal reformer and president of Mexico during the 1860s and early 1870s, and he helped mold Mexico into a nation. That established Juárez as a national hero.

   _____

   _____

2. Juárez, Oaxaca's governor in 1853, was opposed to the dictator General Santa Anna, and he was exiled. _____

   _____

3. Juárez later returned to Mexico and joined the movement to overthrow Santa Anna. It was a brave and risky endeavor. _____

   _____

4. Juárez's presidency was interrupted when France installed Maximilian as emperor of Mexico in 1864, but he was not popular. _____

   _____

5. Maximilian's government collapsed in 1867, which opened the way for Juárez to return and be reelected president. _____

   _____

GRAMMAR/USAGE

Chapter 4: Using Pronouns

WORKSHEET 10 | Weak and Indefinite Reference

A pronoun must always refer clearly to its antecedent. Avoid a **weak reference,** which occurs when a pronoun refers to an antecedent that has not been expressed.

> WEAK: I want to be a playwright, but **it** isn't offered at my school.
>
> CLEAR: I want to be a playwright, but a course in playwriting isn't offered at my school.

Similarly, avoid an **indefinite reference,** which occurs when a pronoun such as *it, they,* or *you* refers to no particular person or thing.

> INDEFINITE: In Mexico City, **they** have a huge festival on May 5. [*They* does not refer to any specific people.]
>
> CLEAR: Mexico City has a huge festival on May 5.

Exercise: Revising   Most of the following sentences contain weak and indefinite pronoun references. On the lines provided, revise each faulty sentence. [Note: Although sentences can be corrected in more than one way, you need to give only one revision.]

> EXAMPLE: 1. I take many photographs with my camera and consider it an enjoyable hobby.
>
> *I consider photography an enjoyable hobby, and I take many pictures with my camera.*

1. In many households in India, they serve a flat, pancake-like bread called *chapati.*

   _____

   _____

2. In large cities you often don't feel comfortable calling the mayor about problems.

   _____

   _____

3. In the newspaper article, it calls this election the closest race in many years.

   _____

   _____

4. Being neighborly is important because you may need their help someday in an emergency.

   _____

   _____

5. Nguyen has become a virtuoso violinist, but he has never owned a valuable one.

   _____

   _____

Name _____ Date _____ Class _____

WORKSHEET 11 *Review*

Exercise A   For each sentence in the following paragraph, underline the correct form of the pronoun in parentheses.

At the start of track season, our coach told Sarah and [1] (I, me) the story of famous sprinter Evelyn Ashford. During high school, Ashford had started running races against the boys at lunch time, and eventually she beat [2] (they, them). Later, champion coach Pat Connolly recognized the young runner as a great talent when [3] (she, her) saw Ashford race at the University of California at Los Angeles in 1976. In 1983 and 1984, Ashford set records in the women's 100-meter event, and [4] (she, her) became the fastest woman in the world. Our coach said that Ashford's speed—10.76 seconds for the 100-meter dash in 1984—amazed even [5] (he, him). At the 1988 Olympic Games, Ashford hoped that [6] (she, her) could better her record time. The other competitors knew that the runner to beat that year was [7] (she, her). Ashford's talent, hard work, and determination earned [8] (she, her) a gold and a silver medal, but set no new records at those games. The crowd cheered for [9] (she, her) as she carried the flag for the American team at the 1988 Olympics. [10] She certainly has been an inspiration to all of (we, us).

Exercise B   Most of the following sentences contain incorrect pronoun forms. Underline each error, and then write the correct form on the line provided. If a sentence is correct, write *C*.

EXAMPLE: 1. This art book about sculpture belongs to my father and <u>myself</u>. __*me*__

1. Satoshi Yabuuchi is a modern Japanese sculptor whom works with wood. _____

2. Critics generally agree that few sculptors today are as inventive as him. _____

3. For example, one of my favorite works by he has some very interesting subjects. _____

4. Them are children's heads representing the days of the week. _____

5. Working with simple tools, Yabuuchi created they out of cypress. _____

6. Who do you know that could resist his engaging faces? _____

7. Yabuuchi's sense of humor is important to himself. _____

8. Other modern Japanese wood sculptors and him use techniques that date back more than fifteen hundred years. _____

9. Yabuuchi, whom was born in 1953, first studied European art but then became interested in wood carving and sculpture. _____

10. A number of works by himself also incorporate elements of American pop art. _____

Exercise C: Revising   Revise each of the following sentences, correcting the pronoun reference. [Note: Although these sentences can be corrected in more than one way, you need to give only one revision.]

1. Irish author Christy Brown (1932–1981) was extremely talented, but he had to overcome great physical challenges for it to be recognized. _____

    _____

2. In Brown's autobiography, *My Left Foot*, it tells about his lifelong struggle with cerebral palsy. _____

    _____

3. In some biographies, you don't become emotionally involved, but Brown's autobiography is very personal. _____

    _____

4. The public likes accurate film biographies, and that is a strong point of the movie *My Left Foot*. _____

    _____

5. In many moving scenes of the movie, it shows actor Daniel Day-Lewis portraying Christy Brown. _____

    _____

6. In the movie, they show how Brown learned to write and type with his only functioning limb—his left foot. _____

    _____

7. Brown married in 1972, and her help contributed to Brown's improved muscular control.

    _____

    _____

8. Brown excelled as a writer, but it is sometimes difficult to locate them in libraries and bookstores in the United States. _____

    _____

9. Brown was acclaimed as a poet and as a novelist, but I have never read one.

    _____

    _____

10. In the card catalog it lists these books by Brown: *My Left Foot, Down All the Days, A Shadow on Summer,* and *Wild Grow the Lilies.* _____

    _____

Name _____ Date _____ Class _____

Adjectives and Adverbs

An **adjective** limits the meaning of a noun or a pronoun. An adjective may also limit the meaning of a gerund—a verbal used as a noun. An **adverb** limits the meaning of a verb or a verbal, an adjective, or another adverb.

> ADJECTIVE: An attack would be a **strategic** disaster. [*Strategic* limits *disaster*.]
>
> ADVERB: Akoni sings **beautifully**. [*Beautifully* limits *sings*.]

Linking verbs, especially the forms of the verb *to be* and verbs of sense (*taste, smell, feel,* etc.), are often followed by adjectives that modify the subject of the verb. Action verbs are often followed by adverbs.

> The **chili** was **spicy**. [The adjective *spicy* follows the linking verb *was* and modifies the subject *chili*.]
>
> Linda **drove slowly**. [The adverb *slowly* modifies the action verb *drove*.]

Exercise   For each of the following sentences, underline the correct modifier in parentheses. Then circle the word that it modifies.

1. You may have seen Debbie Allen dancing (energetic, energetically) on the TV series *Fame*.

2. Most observers agree that Allen feels (comfortable, comfortably) with her own fame.

3. Allen, who grew up in Houston, Texas, has danced (continual, continually) since the age of three.

4. She attended the Houston Ballet School, graduated from Howard University, and then headed (confident, confidently) to New York City.

5. On Broadway, she was (triumphant, triumphantly) in the revivals of the musicals *West Side Story* and *Sweet Charity*.

6. Later, she (successful, successfully) choreographed *Fame* and won two Emmy Awards for her work on that show.

7. Allen looks (natural, naturally) in a director's chair, too, and has directed episodes of such TV shows as *A Different World* and *Quantum Leap*.

8. Through the years, she has worked (diligent, diligently) and has battled racism and sexism to succeed.

9. Never one to accept second best, Allen has risen (steady, steadily) to the top in her profession.

10. In interviews, Debbie Allen seems (proud, proudly) of her achievements but ready for new challenges, too.

GRAMMAR/USAGE

Chapter 5: Using Modifiers

 **WORKSHEET 2** *Comparison*

Comparison refers to the change in the form of an adjective or adverb to show increasing or decreasing degrees in the quality the modifier expresses. The three degrees of comparison are **positive, comparative,** and **superlative.** Most one-syllable modifiers form the comparative and superlative degrees by adding *–er* and *–est*. Some two-syllable modifiers form the comparative and superlative degrees by adding *–er* and *–est*. Other two-syllable modifiers form the comparative and superlative degrees by using *more* and *most*. Modifiers of more than two syllables form the comparative and superlative degrees by using *more* and *most*.

> COMPARATIVE FORMS: smaller, harder, more restless, more wisely
>
> SUPERLATIVE FORMS: smallest, hardest, most restless, most wisely

To show a decrease in the qualities they express, all modifiers form the comparative and superlative degrees by using *less* and *least*.

> less important, least important; less exciting, least exciting

Some modifiers, such as those listed below, do not follow the regular methods of forming the comparative and superlative degrees.

> bad, worse, worst   little, less, least   good, better, best   much, more, most

Exercise   On the line provided, write the comparative and the superlative forms of each of the following modifiers.

> EXAMPLE: 1. modest *more (less) modest; most (least) modest*

1. tiny _____

2. wistful _____

3. curious _____

4. thin _____

5. gently _____

6. ill _____

7. much _____

8. proudly _____

9. friendly _____

10. abruptly _____

Chapter 5: Using Modifiers

WORKSHEET 3

Uses of Comparative and Superlative Forms

Use the **comparative degree** when comparing two things. Use the **superlative degree** when comparing more than two things.

COMPARING TWO: Shane is the **taller** of my two brothers.

COMPARING MORE
THAN TWO: Of all my relatives, Casey is the **most** musical.

Exercise A   Complete each of the sentences below by giving the correct form of the modifier on the left. Write the correct form on the line provided.

1. large   That tapestry is the _____ I've ever seen.

2. far   Tanya disappeared behind the _____ of the
          two doors.

3. good   Try to select the _____ tomatoes on display.

4. bright   Set your course by the _____ star in the sky.

5. bad   Traffic will be _____ during rush hour.

Exercise B   On the line provided, write the correct form of the modifier shown in italics in each sentence below. If a sentence is correct, write *C*.

1. Of all the puppies in the litter, the smallest puppy barks
   more loudly.   _____

2. Both twins, Holly and Julie, have brown eyes, but Holly's
   are *darkest*.   _____

3. Could you show me the *less expensive* watch that you have?   _____

4. Thomas Jefferson is generally regarded as one of the *more
   important* Americans in United States history.   _____

5. That is the *more foolish* thing I've ever heard you say.   _____

6. Will the contest officials give a prize for the kite that flies
   the *farthest*?   _____

7. Take your time, and paint the chair *most carefully* than you
   painted the porch.   _____

8. After his operation, Grandfather walked *least painfully* than
   he had before.   _____

9. Dividing the pumpkin pie in two, Felicia gave me the *largest*
   portion.   _____

10. What could be *more exciting* than a game of golf?   _____

GRAMMAR/USAGE

Name _____ Date _____ Class _____

Problems with Comparative and Superlative Forms

A **double comparison** is the use of two comparative forms (usually *–er* and *more*) or two superlative forms (usually *–est* and *most*) to modify the same word. Avoid using double comparisons.

> DOUBLE COMPARISON: The river route is more safer than the mountain trail.
>
> STANDARD: The river route is **safer** than the mountain trail.

Include the word *other* or *else* when comparing one member of a group with the rest of the group.

> ILLOGICAL: Melissa is more ambitious than anyone in the class. [Melissa is a member of the class. Logically, Melissa cannot be more ambitious than herself.]
>
> LOGICAL: Melissa is more ambitious than anyone **else** in the class.
>
> LOGICAL: Melissa is more ambitious than any **other** person in the class.

Avoid comparing items that cannot logically be compared.

> ILLOGICAL: William's design is more complicated than Vincent.
>
> LOGICAL: William's design is more complicated than Vincent**'s design**.

Exercise: Revising   On the lines provided, revise the following sentences by correcting the errors in the use of modifiers.

> EXAMPLE: 1. In each graduating class, the valedictorian is the student whose academic average is higher than that of any senior.
>
> *In each graduating class, the valedictorian is the student whose academic average is higher than that of any other senior.*

1. That was the most highest grade Oscar ever earned on a Spanish test.

_____

2. To gain a more clearer understanding of the problems in the Middle East, people need to learn more about the history of that region.

_____

3. Performing better than all the gymnasts, Mary Lou Retton was the first U.S. gymnast to win an Olympic gold medal in her sport.

_____

4. Your cooking is much better than my mom.

_____

5. To finish painting the eyes, take your most smallest brush, and paint the pupils.

_____

Chapter 5: Using Modifiers

More Problems with Comparative and Superlative Forms

An **incomplete comparison** results when the second part of a comparison can be understood in two ways. State both parts of a comparison completely.

> INCOMPLETE: I tutored Kaley more often than Lori. [The elliptical clause *than Lori* may be completed in more than one way.]
>
> COMPLETE: I tutored Kaley more often than I tutored Lori.
>
> COMPLETE: I tutored Kaley more often than Lori tutored Kaley.

A **compound comparison** uses both the positive and comparative degrees of a modifier. Include all the words necessary to complete a compound comparison.

> NONSTANDARD: My brother can cook as well, if not better than, my mother.
>
> STANDARD: My brother can cook **as well as,** if not better than, my mother.

Absolute adjectives (such as *complete, equal, perfect, infinite,* and *unique*) express qualities that either exist completely or don't exist at all. These adjectives have no comparative or superlative forms because they do not vary in degree. Absolute adjectives may be used in comparisons if the absolute is accompanied by *more nearly* or *most nearly*.

> NONSTANDARD: That was the most perfect example of a swan dive that I've ever seen.
>
> STANDARD: That was the **most nearly** perfect example of a high dive that I've ever seen.
>
> STANDARD: That was the **best** high dive that I've ever seen.

Exercise: Revising Each of the following sentences contains an error in the use of a comparison. On the line provided, revise each sentence to correct the error.

> EXAMPLE: 1. Which department store has the most complete line of household items?
>
> *Which department store has the most nearly complete line of household items?*

1. These boots fit as well, if not better than, the black ones.

   _____

2. He thinks he is the most perfect person in the world.

   _____

3. I hear from my brother more often than my sister.

   _____

4. Make sure that you give the most complete answer to each of the questions.

   _____

5. Jim speaks Portuguese as easily, if not more easily than, English.

   _____

GRAMMAR/USAGE

Chapter 5: Using Modifiers

 **Placement of Modifiers**

Place one-word modifiers, such as *even, hardly, just, merely, nearly, only,* and *scarcely,* immediately before the words they modify.

Only we saw her.   I **hardly** knew anyone there.

We saw **only** her.   I knew **hardly** anyone there.

A modifying word, phrase, or clause that sounds awkward because it modifies the wrong word or word group is called a **misplaced modifier**. To correct a misplaced modifier, place the word, phrase, or clause as close as possible to the word or words it modifies.

MISPLACED: Ms. Steinberg, the explorer, described her trips through the jungle in our social studies class.

CLEAR: **In our social studies class,** Ms. Steinberg, the explorer, described her trips through the jungle.

Avoid placing a word, phrase, or clause so that it seems to modify either of two words. Such a misplaced modifier is called a **two-way modifier** or a **squinting modifier**.

TWO-WAY: Remind Michelle before lunch we have a meeting.

CLEAR: **Before lunch,** remind Michelle we have a meeting.

CLEAR: Remind Michelle we have a meeting **before lunch.**

Exercise A   On the first line below, write a sentence using one of the following modifiers: *even, hardly, just, merely, nearly, only,* or *scarcely.* Then, on the next line, rewrite the sentence, changing its meaning by moving the modifier.

EXAMPLE: 1. *Even Carl could not finish the obstacle course.*

2. *Carl could not even finish the obstacle course.*

1. _____

2. _____

Exercise B: Revising   The following sentences contain misplaced and two-way modifiers. Correct each sentence by circling the faulty modifier and drawing an arrow to show where it should go in the sentence.

EXAMPLE: 1. One of our observers sighted a plane (through binoculars) that she could not identify.

1. Captain André Callioux was one of many heroic African American soldiers who fought during the Civil War in the Union Army.

2. Mr. Rodriguez said at the end of class he would make the students a Mexican meal.

3. We only finished half of the pizza.

4. Please tell Terry when he gets home from the mall Mom wants him to make dinner.

5. At Tuesday's meeting, the mayor discussed the enormous cost of draining Buskill Swamp with city council members.

Name _____ Date _____ Class _____

WORKSHEET 7   *Dangling Modifiers*

A modifying word, phrase, or clause that does not sensibly modify any word or words in a sentence is called a **dangling modifier**.

> DANGLING: To be healthy, good nutrition is necessary. [Who needs good nutrition?]
>
> CLEAR: To be healthy, a person needs good nutrition.
>
> CLEAR: Good nutrition is necessary for good health.

Exercise A   Read each sentence below and decide if it is correct or if it contains a dangling modifier. On the line provided, write *C* for correct or *DM* for dangling modifier.

_____ 1. Before moving to San Angelo, Miami had been their home.

_____ 2. When selecting a college, a number of factors should be considered.

_____ 3. Riding in the glass-bottomed boat, we could see hundreds of beautiful tropical fish.

_____ 4. While talking with some friends of mine, the topic of careers in dentistry came up.

_____ 5. To understand many of the allusions in modern literature, a knowledge of Greek and Roman myths is essential.

Exercise B: Revising   The following sentences contain dangling modifiers. On the line provided, revise each sentence so that its meaning is clear and correct.

> EXAMPLE: 1. After working in the fields all day, little energy was left.
>
> *After working in the fields all day, we had little energy left.*

1. Listening to his grandfather's stories, it was amazing to learn that several of their ancestors had worked with the Underground Railroad.

_____

2. Architecturally striking, everyone is impressed by the building's size and elegance.

_____

3. After searching all over the bookstore, Amy Tan's novel was found in the "bestseller" section.

_____

4. To keep the guacamole dip from turning brown, its surface should be covered with a thin layer of lemon juice.

_____

5. Having promised to be home by midnight, Mom was still waiting up when the door opened at two o'clock.

_____

GRAMMAR/USAGE

Chapter 5: Using Modifiers

WORKSHEET 8   *Review*

Exercise A: Proofreading   Proofread the following paragraph, and correct any errors in the use of modifiers. If a sentence is correct, circle its number.

biggest
EXAMPLE: [1] I'm the ~~biggest~~ fan of foreign films in my whole family.

[1] Of all the world's movie directors, Akira Kurosawa of Japan is considered one of the greater. [2] He is certainly best known in the United States than any other Japanese director. [3] In addition to directing, the multitalented Kurosawa has edited and written many of his films. [4] Acclaimed by critics, his films not only look beautifully, but they also contain serious moral themes. [5] Among the more popular of his dozens of films is *Ran*, which blends Shakespeare's *King Lear* with a Japanese folk tale. [6] Kurosawa made the story more stronger emotionally for his Japanese audience by having the conflict be between a father and three sons rather than between a father and three daughters. [7] That conflict is apparent in many scenes from *Ran*. [8] Moviegoers in the United States also enjoyed Kurosawa's film *Dersu Uzala*, which won an Academy Award for bestest foreign film. [9] The stark scenery in that film certainly shows how fiercely the Siberian wilderness can be. [10] If you have the chance to see these two films, you can decide which one you like best.

Exercise B: Proofreading   Read each of the following sentences to see if it contains an error in the use of modifiers. Draw a line through any incorrect words, and write the correct word or words on the line provided. If a sentence needs an additional word or words, write them on the line, and use a caret (∧) to show where the added word or words belong. If a sentence is correct, write C.

EXAMPLES: 1. After a long rehearsal, the dance troupe performed ~~good~~.
well

2. This was easier than any ∧ test I've ever taken! *other*

1. Doesn't the official explanation of the budget cut sound incredibly to you?   _____

2. Mike smiled proud when he told us about his West African heritage.   _____

3. Neka embroidered the rain-bird symbol perfect, checking each stitch as she worked.   _____

4. Why is the sled going so slow?   _____

5. I read the shorter of the three books for my report.   _____

6. I have narrowed my choice to two colleges, and I want to visit them to see which I like best. _____

7. The picture looks much more clearer on this television set than on that one. _____

8. We thought Patti was the most talented of all the actors in the community play. _____

9. Modeling her mother's silk kimono, Toshi seemed even gracefuller than usual. _____

10. "Life can't be treating you all that bad," I told Walker. _____

11. Chen tried to teach me to use chopsticks, but the lesson didn't go very good. _____

12. "I'm positive I did good on that test," Anzu confidently remarked. _____

13. "Remember to speak slow when you give your speech," Mr. Schmidt advised the nervous candidate. _____

14. Ms. Stein is a good teacher who listens to students better than any teacher at school. _____

15. I paid twelve dollars for this map, but it was worth the money because it is the most complete map of the city that I have seen. _____

16. My beagle Buster knows more tricks than any dog I know. _____

17. How could today have been more perfect? _____

18. Why don't you like the piano as much as your brother? _____

19. She was as athletic, if not more athletic, than her sister was. _____

20. Her horse has a smoother gait than Karen. _____

Exercise C: Revising   Most of the following sentences contain errors in the placement of modifiers. On the line provided, revise each faulty sentence so that its meaning is clear. If a sentence is correct, write C.

EXAMPLE: 1. I have made a study of the cultures of Native American peoples for several years.

For several years, I have made a study of the cultures of
Native American peoples.

1. I found a fascinating book at the library book sale that includes a map showing where Native Americans traditionally lived on the Plains.

_____

_____

2. You can see the homelands of the major Plains peoples looking at the map.

_____

3. The size of the Great Plains especially surprised me, extending farther north and south than I had thought.

_____

_____

4. While thumbing through the book, a picture of a Sioux encampment caught my attention.

_____

_____

5. Living much of the year in villages, farming was the main activity of most of these peoples.

_____

_____

6. However, I read during the summer they hunted buffalo.

_____

7. They followed the buffalo across the Plains, which provided them with food and clothing.

_____

_____

8. Characterized by a strong sense of independence, a form of democracy has been practiced by the Plains peoples.

_____

_____

9. To make key decisions, votes are cast at council meetings.

_____

10. I'm going to find out more about such peoples as the Crow and the Cheyenne, having read this fascinating book about the peoples of the Plains.

_____

_____

Chapter 6: Phrases

The Adjective Phrase

A **phrase** is a group of related words that is used as a single part of speech and does not contain both a verb and its subject. A **prepositional phrase** consists of a preposition; a noun, pronoun, or verbal called the **object of the preposition;** and any modifiers of that object.

> **Along with cooking and sewing,** my mother taught my brothers to do laundry and to vacuum. [*Cooking and sewing* is the compound object of the compound preposition *along with.*]

An **adjective phrase** is a prepositional phrase that modifies a noun or a pronoun.

> The irises **of her eyes** are flecked with gold. [The prepositional phrase modifies the noun *irises.*]

An adjective phrase always follows the word it modifies.

> She can give you information **about camping in the park**. [*About camping* modifies the direct object *information. In the park* modifies *camping,* which serves as the object of the preposition *about.*]

More than one adjective phrase may modify the same word.

> Where did I put that book **about psychology by Carl Jung**? [The two phrases *about psychology* and *by Carl Jung* modify the noun *book.*]

Exercise A   In the following sentences, underline each adjective phrase once and the word it modifies twice.

1. New Guinea rivers are popular areas for rafting enthusiasts.

2. A series of nearly continuous rapids criss-crosses jungles of primeval beauty.

3. The twenty-eight major rapids on the Tua River make it a course for rafters with experience and courage.

4. Brilliantly colored butterflies brighten the riverbanks, and the metallic whine of cicadas almost drowns out the roar of the river.

5. The banks are a chaos of tumbled boulders and uprooted trees.

Exercise B   Expand each of the following sentences by adding an adjective phrase on the line provided.

> EXAMPLE: 1. Fog *on the bridge* obscured our view.

1. The ice _____ made the drivers uneasy.

2. A large group _____ descended on the playground.

3. Do you have any books _____ ?

4. The crane _____ lifted the girder upwards.

5. The student _____ usually wins the debate match.

SENTENCES

Chapter 6: Phrases

WORKSHEET 2

The Adverb Phrase and the Noun Phrase

Like an adjective phrase, an **adverb phrase** is a prepositional phrase. While an adjective phrase modifies a noun or a pronoun, an adverb phrase modifies a verb, an adjective, or an adverb. More than one adverb phrase can modify the same word. Unlike an adjective phrase, an adverb phrase can precede the word it modifies.

> **With animation,** the candidate **from our district** talked **for two hours**. [The adverb phrases *with animation* and *for two hours* both modify the verb *talked*. The adjective phrase *from our district* modifies the noun *candidate*.]

Occasionally a prepositional phrase may function as a noun.

> **Before breakfast** is when I like to jog. [*Before breakfast* is the subject of the verb *is*.]

Exercise Circle each prepositional phrase in the following sentences. On the line provided, identify each prepositional phrase as an adjective *(ADJ)*, an adverb *(ADV)*, or a noun *(N)*. Be sure to include any prepositional phrase that modifies the object of another preposition.

EXAMPLE: 1. (On any map), the function (of the Panama Canal) is obvious.
    ADV, ADJ

1. The canal, which is fifty-one miles long, links the Pacific Ocean to the Atlantic Ocean. _____

2. Ships can travel from ocean to ocean using the canal's elaborate series of locks that raise and lower the water levels. _____

3. Construction of the canal, an engineering marvel, began in 1904 and continued until 1914. _____

4. The builders faced many obstacles during the canal's construction. _____

5. Mosquitoes posed a major health risk throughout the area and had to be eliminated. _____

6. For the duration of the canal project, Dr. William C. Gorgas, an army surgeon, fought the mosquitoes. _____

7. With great efficiency, he drained swamps, fumigated buildings, and installed a pure water supply. _____

8. After the resignation of two chief engineers, President Theodore Roosevelt appointed Army Lieutenant Colonel George W. Goethals chief engineer in 1907. _____

9. Goethals, active in all phases of the canal's construction, quickly gained the respect of workers. _____

10. The workers who dug through the mountains along the Continental Divide finished the job with hard work and the loss of many lives. _____

Name _____ Date _____ Class _____

Participles and Participial Phrases

WORKSHEET 3

A **verbal** is a form of a verb used as a noun, an adjective, or an adverb. One kind of verbal is called a **participle,** a verb form that is used as an adjective. There are two kinds of participles—**present participles** and **past participles**. Present participles end in *–ing,* while most past participles end in *–d* or *–ed.*

> The **trembling** swimmer clambered out of the **frozen** waters. [The present participle *trembling* modifies the noun *swimmer*. The past participle *frozen* modifies the noun *waters*.]

A **participial phrase** consists of a participle and all of the words related to the participle. Don't confuse a participle used as an adjective with a participle that is part of a verb phrase.

> PARTICIPIAL PHRASE: **Marked with paw prints,** the script arrived at the producer's office. [*Marked with paw prints* modifies the noun *script*.]
>
> VERB PHRASE: The kitten **was marking** the manuscript with paw prints.

An **absolute phrase** consists of a participle and the noun or pronoun it modifies. The entire phrase is used to modify an independent clause.

> **Class ended,** we all headed for the assembly hall. [The absolute phrase *class ended* modifies the independent clause by telling *when*.]

Exercise A Each sentence below contains an italicized participial phrase. Underline the noun or pronoun that each phrase modifies.

1. *Living far from the city,* I developed an interest in nature at an early age.

2. Today's newspaper, *printed last night,* made no mention of the president's speech.

3. *Looking through the catalog*, Earl found a Cajun cookbook.

4. We saw a group of riders *galloping over the knoll.*

5. *Addressing the senior class,* the principal praised their clean-up campaign.

Exercise B Each of the following sentences contains at least one participial phrase. Underline each participial phrase. On the line provided, identify the word or words the phrase modifies. If the participial is part of an absolute phrase, write *absolute.*

1. All of the students trying out for the soccer team have heard from the coach or her assistant. _____

2. Thanking us several times, the piano teacher returned the chairs borrowed for the recital. _____

3. The tree being the oldest one in the county, the county commission passed a law protecting it. _____

4. Cheered by the crowd, the Special Olympics team took a bow. _____

5. The movies showing tonight are old ones released before 1940. _____

SENTENCES

Chapter 6: Phrases

WORKSHEET 4

Gerunds and Gerund Phrases

A **gerund** is a verb form that ends in *–ing*. Unlike the present participle, which also ends in *–ing*, a gerund acts as a noun.

SUBJECT: **Canoeing** is good exercise for the mind and body.

PREDICATE NOMINATIVE: My favorite form of exercise is **canoeing**.

DIRECT OBJECT: I take **canoeing** seriously.

INDIRECT OBJECT: I give **canoeing** a high priority in my life.

OBJECT OF PREPOSITION: I find in **canoeing** an escape from stress.

A **gerund phrase** consists of a gerund and all of the words related to the gerund.

Jeffra's traveling in Africa has been an enlightening experience. [The gerund phrase is the subject of the verb *has been*. The possessive *Jeffra's* and the prepositional phrase *in Africa* modify the gerund *traveling*.]

Exercise A   Underline the gerund phrase in the following sentences. On the line provided, identify each gerund as subject *(S)*, direct object *(DO)*, indirect object *(IO)*, predicate nominative *(PN)*, or object of a preposition *(OP)*.

EXAMPLE: __*S*__ 1. <u>Learning to type</u> has been one of my most practical accomplishments.

_____ 1. One of the most interesting characteristics of bees is their dancing to communicate the location of food sources.

_____ 2. My grandparents enjoy practicing their square-dance routines with the Nicholsons.

_____ 3. Hector earns money on the weekends by giving guitar lessons.

_____ 4. Producing a movie for Mr. Matsuyama's cinematography course requires the ability to organize and communicate.

_____ 5. Sylvia's method of making decisions reveals a great deal about her.

Exercise B   Underline the verbal phrase or phrases in each of the following sentences. On the line provided, identify each phrase as a participial phrase *(P)* or gerund phrase *(G)*.

_____ 1. Solving crossword puzzles is one of Geraldo's favorite pastimes.

_____ 2. Before making any changes, please notify our secretary, Ms. Erikson.

_____ 3. Having studied hard, Karen wasn't surprised that she did well on the Spanish test.

_____ 4. Early every morning, almost everyone in the house is awakened by my brother's singing in the shower.

_____ 5. I don't mind him singing, but the early morning tap-dancing can be too much!

Name _____ Date _____ Class _____

Infinitives and Infinitive Phrases

An **infinitive** is a verb form that can be used as a noun, an adjective, or an adverb. An infinitive usually begins with *to*.

NOUN: The hyena began **to laugh**. [*To laugh* is used as a direct object.]

ADJECTIVE: Toyoko is the runner **to watch**. [*To watch* modifies *runner*.]

ADVERB: Rodrigo said that he came **to dance**. [*To dance* modifies *came*.]

An **infinitive phrase** consists of an infinitive and all of the words related to the infinitive. The entire infinitive phrase can be used as a noun, an adjective, or an adverb.

> INFINITIVE PHRASE: I want **to watch the film again**. [The infinitive phrase *to watch the film again* is used as a noun that is the object of the verb *want*. The infinitive *to watch* is modified by the adverb *again*.]

Exercise A   Underline the infinitive in each of the following sentences. On the line provided, identify it as a noun *(N)*, an adjective *(ADJ)*, or an adverb *(ADV)*. If the infinitive is used as a noun, identify it as a subject *(S)*, a direct object *(DO)*, or a predicate nominative *(PN)*. If the infinitive is used as a modifier, underline the word it modifies twice.

> EXAMPLE: _N—DO_ 1. I like to compose music for the guitar.

_____ 1. To win an Olympic medal is the hope of every member of the ski team.

_____ 2. The candidate had the courage to speak on a controversial issue.

_____ 3. We went to Italy to see Michelangelo's statue *David*.

_____ 4. The Latin and French clubs try to work together on projects.

_____ 5. The dream of Martin Luther King, Jr., was that all Americans should be free to exercise their rights as citizens.

Exercise B   Complete each of the following phrases or sentences by adding an infinitive or infinitive phrase that serves as the part of speech indicated in parentheses. Use the appropriate end marks.

> EXAMPLE: 1. Every weekend Tom calls home *(adverb)*
>
> *Every weekend Tom calls home to talk to his family.*

1. Everyone on the committee has his or her own job *(adjective)*

_____

2. After I graduate, my goal is *(noun)*

_____

3. When we heard the crash, we ran quickly *(adverb)*

_____

4. On a hunch, the detective decided *(noun)*

_____

SENTENCES

Name _____ Date _____ Class _____

Appositives and Appositive Phrases

Types of Phrases:

PREPOSITIONAL PHRASE: Red and yellow roses grew **along the fence**.

PARTICIPIAL PHRASE: **Standing on the dock,** we saw several porpoises approach.

GERUND PHRASE: **Setting the table** is my brother's job.

INFINITIVE PHRASE: The commission had planned **to make the announcement today**.

Another kind of phrase is the *appositive phrase*. An **appositive** is a noun or a pronoun placed beside another noun or pronoun to identify or explain it. An **appositive phrase** consists of an appositive and its modifiers.

APPOSITIVE: My sister, **Akela,** wants to become a trapeze artist.

APPOSITIVE PHRASE: Akela, **the youngest in our family,** joined the circus.

APPOSITIVE PHRASE: **A native of Haiti,** the man was a skilled woodworker.

APPOSITIVE PHRASE: Community schools offer a variety of courses: **landscaping, art, computer skills, and many more**.

Exercise A   Underline the appositive phrase in each sentence below.

1. Yori's letter, a poem about our friendship, made my birthday unforgettable.

2. Those overalls, my favorites, have been mended and patched dozens of times.

3. Helen's collage was composed of everyday items: cloth, paper, and bits of cartons.

4. A hardy perennial, the grape hyacinth comes from a bulb.

5. Lanelle's favorite song, "Moondance," is a jazz-rock tune sung by Van Morrison.

Exercise B   On the line provided, identify each italicized phrase in the following paragraph as a prepositional phrase *(PREP)*, a participial phrase *(PART)*, a gerund phrase *(GER)*, an infinitive phrase *(INF)*, or an appositive phrase *(APP)*. Do not separately identify a phrase that is part of a larger phrase.

Marlee Matlin, [1] *an actress whom you may have seen* _____ , has gained attention for championing the rights of people with hearing impairments. Matlin has never let her deafness stand in her way. [2] *Learning to sign, to read lips, and to speak* _____ helped Matlin [3] *to communicate effectively with a wide range of people* _____ . [4] *Interested in acting* _____ , she was soon performing in a children's theater group. After high school, she started on the road [5] *to Hollywood and stardom* _____ by [6] *winning a supporting role in a Chicago revival of the play* _____ [7] *Children of a Lesser God* _____ . Producers saw Matlin's performance and wanted her [8] *to audition for a starring role* _____ . [9] *Praised by critics and the public alike* _____ , Matlin's portrayal of a proud and independent woman with a hearing impairment was magnificent. [10] *For her stellar performance* _____ , Matlin won an Oscar.

Chapter 6: Phrases

WORKSHEET 7 *Review*

Exercise A Each of the following sentences contains a prepositional phrase. First, underline the phrase. Then, on the line provided, tell how the phrase is used. Write *ADJ* for an adjective phrase or *ADV* for an adverb phrase.

> EXAMPLE: _ADV_ 1. Few names <u>among American writers</u> rival that of Henry David Thoreau.

_____ 1. Not ambitious for fame, Thoreau wanted most to live life fully.

_____ 2. Nature and its preservation were central to Thoreau's life.

_____ 3. His days on Walden Pond prompted his great work, *Walden,* which describes the spirit that Thoreau believed nature embodied.

_____ 4. Never one to content himself with intellectual achievements, Thoreau acted on his humanitarian beliefs.

_____ 5. One of his most worthy acts was the assistance he gave fugitive slaves.

Exercise B On the line provided, identify each italicized phrase in the following sentences. Write *PREP* for a prepositional phrase or *PART* for a participial phrase. Then give the word or words each phrase modifies. Do not separately identify a prepositional phrase that is part of a participial phrase.

> EXAMPLE: 1. *Visiting friends in Los Angeles last year,* I became interested *in low-riders.* PART—I; PREP—interested

1. My friend Jorge told me that this unique form *of folk art* has been popular *for forty years or more.* _____

2. He said the term "low-rider" refers *to the automobile, its driver, and any passengers.* _____

3. *Making artistic statements with their automobiles,* many young Mexican American men in the Southwest spend both time and money *on their cars.* _____

4. First, a car is lowered *by several methods* so that its chassis just skims the pavement. _____

5. *After the height adjustment,* the car is embellished with exterior paint and trim work. _____

6. *Decorated elaborately,* Jorge's car, *painted metallic brown with elegant pin-striping,* is a good example of a low-rider. _____

7. When their cars are finished and spotlessly cleaned, riders drive slowly *through their communities.* _____

8. *Relaxing behind the steering wheel of his car,* Jorge is proud when people admire the results *of his hard work.* _____

SENTENCES

9. On sunny days, long caravans of low-riders may drive *for hours through the neighborhood*. _____

10. Low-riders *in some cities* have even formed clubs that work *with charitable organizations*. _____

Exercise C On the line provided, identify each italicized phrase in the following sentences. Write *PREP* for a prepositional phrase, *PART* for a participial phrase, *GER* for a gerund phrase, or *INF* for an infinitive phrase. Do not separately identify a prepositional phrase that is part of a larger phrase.

EXAMPLE: 1. The ability *to speak distinctly* is an advantage *in job interviews.* <u>INF, PREP</u>

1. *For many years,* Louis Pasteur experimented *to discover a method for preventing rabies.* _____

2. *To open the box* required a hammer and a crowbar as well as two people *lifting the lid.* _____

3. Alana's hobby is *developing original computer programs* for preschool children *to use.* _____

4. *Gaining the vote for women* was Susan B. Anthony's mission *in life.* _____

5. *Finished with her paper,* Ms. Sanapaw turned *to the bibliography.* _____

Exercise D Each of the following sentences contains an italicized phrase. On the line provided, identify each phrase. Write the correct abbreviation from the following list:

PREP = prepositional phrase   **GER** = gerund phrase   **APP** = appositive phrase
PART = participial phrase   **INF** = infinitive phrase

_____ 1. Altamont Pass, *an area of grassy hills* surrounding San Francisco Bay, is producing a new cash crop.

_____ 2. Energy entrepreneurs are hurrying *to lease acreage throughout the Altamont.*

_____ 3. One rancher owns several hundred acres *dotted with tall white wind machines.*

_____ 4. *Standing in rows on the windswept hills,* these machines are expected to produce electricity.

_____ 5. The wind-power industry may soon spread *to other parts of the country.*

_____ 6. The temperature differences between the cool coast and the hot valley can create air surges funneling inland *through natural gaps like the Altamont.*

_____ 7. According to some energy experts, wind machines will soon produce thirty million kilowatts per year, *the power used by 4,800 homes.*

_____ 8. An economist and a trained engineer, John Eckland has advocated *generating electricity by using these updated windmills.*

_____ 9. Not until the oil shortages of the 1970s did a serious effort begin in the United States *to develop a wind industry.*

_____10. *Harnessing the wind* may someday make wind turbines as numerous in the United States as windmills were in Holland.

Name _____ Date _____ Class _____

WORKSHEET 1

Independent Clauses and Subordinate Clauses

A **clause** is a group of words that contains a verb and its subject and that is used as part of a sentence. An **independent** (or **main**) **clause** expresses a complete thought and can stand by itself as a sentence.

S   V

INDEPENDENT CLAUSE: Chandra makes delicious curry.

S V   S   V

INDEPENDENT CLAUSE: I make a nice salad, but Chandra makes delicious curry.

Independent clauses may sometimes be split by dependent clauses.

S   V

The vegetables, which Ray grew from seeds, were delicious.

A **subordinate** (or **dependent**) **clause** does not express a complete thought and cannot stand alone as a sentence.

SUBORDINATE CLAUSE: The parts **that we ordered** have not arrived.

SUBORDINATE CLAUSE: **What I say,** you do.

Exercise On the line provided, identify each italicized word group in the following paragraph as an independent clause *(I)* or a subordinate clause *(S)*.

[1] _____ Egyptology is the branch of learning *that is concerned with the language and culture of ancient Egypt.* [2] _____ *Until the Rosetta Stone was discovered in 1799,* the ancient Egyptian language was a mystery to scholars. [3] _____ A man named Bouchard, *who was a captain under Napoleon,* and some of his men found the stone in the trenches near Rosetta, a city near the mouth of the Nile. [4] _____ Photographs of the Rosetta Stone often show *that it has three different kinds of writing inscribed on it.* [5] _____ Because the same message was written on the stone in two kinds of Egyptian writing and in Greek script, *it provided the needed key for deciphering the Egyptian language.* [6] _____ *When the Rosetta Stone was found,* part of the hieroglyphic portion was missing. [7] _____ Scholars could easily read the Greek inscription, *which was nearly complete.* [8] _____ *In 1818, Thomas Young isolated several hieroglyphics* that he took to represent names. [9] _____ *The message* that was inscribed on the stone *was not very exciting.* [10] _____ Since the priests of Egypt were grateful for benefits from the king, *they were commemorating the crowning of Ptolemy V.*

SENTENCES

Chapter 7: Clauses

WORKSHEET 2   *The Adjective Clause*

An **adjective clause** is a subordinate clause that modifies a noun or a pronoun. Usually, an adjective clause begins with a *relative pronoun,* such as *who, whom, whose, which,* or *that.* This pronoun relates the clause to the word or words that the clause modifies.

> ADJECTIVE CLAUSE: The Inca, **who were great weavers,** often used threads spun of gold. [The relative pronoun *who* relates the adjective clause to the noun *Inca. Who* also serves as the subject of *were.*]

An adjective clause may begin with a relative adverb, such as *when* or *where.*

> ADJECTIVE CLAUSE: At the time **when the Spanish conqueror Francisco Pizarro arrived,** the Inca had just concluded a bloody civil war. [The adjective clause modifies the noun *time.*]

Exercise A   Underline the adjective clause in each of the following sentences. Then draw an arrow to the word that each clause modifies.

> EXAMPLE: 1. Have you ever studied the planet that hangs red in the sky?

1. To the nonscientist, Mars is a planet of the imagination, where maps blossom with romantic place names like Utopia Planitia and Elysium.

2. "Earthlings" looked on Mars as a home for creatures who might someday cross cosmic barriers and visit planet Earth.

3. Such thinking was encouraged by an Italian astronomer who observed the planet through a telescope and saw a series of fine lines that crisscrossed its surface.

4. He called the lines *canali,* which was wrongly translated into English as "canals."

5. A planet where there are canals must, of course, be inhabited by people who are capable of building not only canals but also, presumably, cities.

Exercise B   Underline each adjective clause below. On the line provided, tell whether the relative pronoun is used as the *subject, direct object,* or *object of a preposition.*

1. Percival Lowell, the astronomer who founded the Lowell Observatory, brought new life to old myths about life on Mars with nonscientific observations that most astronomers disputed.   _____

2. Lowell reported hundreds of Martian canals, of which many were discovered by his own team of astronomers.   _____

3. One writer who developed an interest in Mars was Edgar Rice Burroughs, the creator of Tarzan.   _____

4. In his Martian books, Burroughs recounts the adventures of John Carter, who could get to Mars by standing in a field and wishing.   _____

5. Burroughs' best-known literary successor is Ray Bradbury, who wrote *The Martian Chronicles,* published in 1950.   _____

Chapter 7: Clauses

WORKSHEET 3 *The Noun Clause*

A **noun clause** is a subordinate clause used as a noun. A noun clause may be used as a subject, a predicate nominative, a direct object, an indirect object, the object of a preposition, or an object of a verbal.

SUBJECT:	**How the pyramids were built** fascinates me.
PREDICATE NOMINATIVE:	Is this **what you wanted**?
DIRECT OBJECT:	I know **who will win the award**.
INDIRECT OBJECT:	Give **whoever comes first** the best seat.
OBJECT OF A PREPOSITION:	These are the laws by **which we live**.
OBJECT OF A VERBAL:	Painting **whatever would sit still** was her passion.

Noun clauses are usually introduced by *that, what, when, where, whether, who, whoever, whom, whomever, whose, why,* and *how*. The word that introduces a noun clause may or may not have another function in the clause.

Exercise A   Underline the noun clause or clauses in each of the following sentences.

1. What I like most about Harriet is that she never complains.

2. Sometimes I am amused and sometimes I am amazed by what I read in the newspaper's advice column.

3. I don't know how they made that decision.

4. Can you please tell me where the Museum of African Art is located and when it opens?

5. Through scientific research, psychologists have learned that everyone dreams during sleep.

Exercise B   Underline the noun clause in each sentence. Then identify how the clause is used. On the line provided, write *S* (subject), *DO* (direct object), *IO* (indirect object), *OP* (object of a preposition), or *PN* (predicate nominative).

EXAMPLE: __DO__   1. Marie Curie discovered <u>that radium is an element</u>.

_____ 1. The problem is that my finances don't allow me to live in style; in fact, I'm broke!

_____ 2. The radio station will give whoever can answer the next question one hundred dollars.

_____ 3. What the dancers Agnes De Mille and Martha Graham did was to create a new form of American dance.

_____ 4. Scientists disagree about why dinosaurs became extinct.

_____ 5. Do you know what the referee says to the opponents at the start of a boxing match?

SENTENCES

Chapter 7: Clauses

WORKSHEET 4 *The Adverb Clause*

An **adverb clause** is a subordinate clause that modifies a verb, an adjective, an adverb, or a verbal. An adverb clause tells *how, when, where, why, to what extent,* or *under what condition.* Adverb clauses are introduced by **subordinating conjunctions,** such as *after, although, before, if, since, so, then, unless,* or *while.*

MODIFYING MAIN VERB: **Before you leave Japan,** take a picture of the family with whom you are staying. [The adverb clause modifies the verb *take*. The subordinating conjunction is *before*.]

MODIFYING ADJECTIVE: The rice paddies were dry **because the rains had not come.** [The adverb clause modifies the adjective *dry*. The subordinating conjunction is *because*.]

Part of a clause may be left out when the meaning can be understood from the context of the sentence. Such a clause is called an **elliptical clause**.

ELLIPTICAL CLAUSE: **While** [it was] **interesting,** the sequel was not as thrilling as the previous movie.

Exercise A Underline the adverb clause in each of the following sentences.

1. Because Keith was born in Tokyo, his parents gave him a Japanese middle name.

2. This hat is prettier than the one you bought in Sicily.

3. If you like the music of Mozart, you might enjoy the movie *Amadeus*.

4. George Bernard Shaw did not write a play until he was thirty-five years old.

Exercise B Underline the adverb clause in each of the following sentences. On the line provided, state whether the cause tells *how, when, where, why, to what extent,* or *under what condition*. [Note: If a clause is elliptical, be prepared to supply the omitted word or words.]

EXAMPLE: 1. Because company was coming for dinner, Lola Gómez and her father prepared a special treat of Cuban-style black beans, one of their specialties. _why_

1. After Lola had soaked a pound of black beans overnight, she drained them and covered them with fresh water to make the beans more easily digestible. _____

2. Lola peeled the onions under running water because they often make her cry. _____

3. While the beans were simmering, Mr. Gómez prepared the *sofrito*, which is a characteristic ingredient in many Latin American dishes. _____

4. He then crushed some of the beans against the side of the pot so that the bean mixture would become thicker. _____

5. No one at the dinner table was more eager than I to enjoy a large helping of the Gómezes' special black beans. _____

Name _____ Date _____ Class _____

WORKSHEET 5 *Review*

Exercise A   Each of the following sentences contains an italicized clause. On the line provided, identify the italicized clause as *IND* (independent) or *SUB* (subordinate).

_____ 1. Do you know *who George Sand was*?

_____ 2. *I learned* that she was born Amandine-Aurore-Lucile Dupin.

_____ 3. *She created a pen name* that became one of the most famous pseudonyms in the history of literature.

_____ 4. *When a person chooses a pseudonym,* he or she does so for a variety of reasons.

_____ 5. *A pseudonym, or fictitious name, is not always one* that conceals a person's identity.

Exercise B   Each of the following sentences contains a subordinate clause. First find this clause and underline it. Then, on the line provided, identify the kind of subordinate clause it is. Write *ADJ* (adjective), *ADV* (adverb), or *N* (noun).

_____ 1. When a group of scholars first applied computer science to the study of literature, their colleagues expressed what can only be described as polite skepticism.

_____ 2. What, they asked, would the computer do?

_____ 3. Scornful scholars argued that measuring the length of Hemingway's sentences was dreary enough when it was done without computers.

_____ 4. Would precise mathematical analyses of style determine whether Sir Thomas More wrote one of Shakespeare's plays?

_____ 5. Initial studies made along these lines fueled controversy that raged for years.

_____ 6. Researchers now use computers whenever their projects involve such mechanical tasks as compiling an index or a bibliography.

_____ 7. Since all of ancient Greek is now stored on computers, scholars can make analyses that shed light on etymology.

_____ 8. There are some features of literary works that computers can identify faster than human readers can.

_____ 9. Of course, nowadays many students take advantage of computer technology when they write research papers about literature.

_____10. After they write their first drafts, students may then revise their papers using software programs that check spelling, grammar, and style.

SENTENCES

Exercise C   Each of the following sentences contains a subordinate clause. First, find this clause and underline it. Then, on the line provided, identify the kind of subordinate clause it is. Write *ADJ* (adjective), *ADV* (adverb), or *N* (noun).

_____   1.   Could you tell me when I should take the bread out of the oven?

_____   2.   It will be ready when the top has turned brown.

_____   3.   Fast and accurate, the new spreadsheet program is also much easier than the older editions were.

_____   4.   Oh no! One of the pieces that you made exploded in the kiln.

_____   5.   For me, wherever I hang my hat is home.

Exercise D   Underline the subordinate clause or clauses in each of the following sentences. On the line provided, tell whether the subordinate clause is used as an *adjective* or a *noun*. Then state whether each noun clause is used as a *subject*, a *direct object*, an *object of a preposition*, or a *predicate nominative*.

EXAMPLE: 1.   Do you think <u>you are too old for toys?</u> *noun, direct object*

1.   Athelstan Spilhaus found that toys are not meant only for children. _____

2.   Spilhaus, an oceanographer, admits he has sometimes been unable to distinguish between his work and his play. _____

3.   Some of the toys he collects are simply to be admired; his favorites are those that can be put into action. _____

4.   Some of his collectibles are put into intensive care, where he skillfully replaces parts that have been damaged or lost. _____

5.   Dr. Spilhaus says that a toy is anything that enables us to stop and refresh ourselves during our hectic lives. _____

6.   What is appealing about some toys is that they can make us laugh. _____

7.   I have read that many mechanical principles were first applied to playthings. _____

8.   For example, one toy monkey is activated by squeezing a rubber bulb that uses the same principle as a jackhammer that digs up our streets. _____

9.   Only those who have lost touch with childhood question what a toy can be worth to a young boy or girl. _____

10.   Ask someone who knows toys what their enchantment is worth. _____

Name _____ Date _____ Class _____

WORKSHEET 1 *The Sentence*

A **sentence** is a group of words that expresses a complete thought. A sentence begins with a capital letter and ends with a period, a question mark, or an exclamation point. Do not be misled by a group of words that looks like a sentence; it may not make sense by itself. Such a word group is called a **sentence fragment**.

> SENTENCE FRAGMENT: With their sirens screaming.

> SENTENCE: With their sirens screaming, the fire engines raced off.

Exercise A   Decide if the following groups of words are sentence fragments or complete sentences. On the line provided, write *F* if an item is a fragment or *S* if an item is a sentence.

_____ 1. Found on the Hopi reservation in Arizona.

_____ 2. A remarkable description about the life of the Hopi people.

_____ 3. The Hopi reservation is surrounded by the Navajo reservation.

_____ 4. Those baskets, pottery, and jewelry over there?

_____ 5. Read about the ceremonial Snake Dance and other religious ceremonies.

Exercise B: Revising   Decide whether the following items are sentences or fragments. If an item contains only complete sentences, write *C* on the line provided. If an item contains fragments, rewrite the item as one or two complete sentences.

1. Chief Paulinho Paiakan of the Kayapó people of Brazil appealing to his people and the rest of the world to help him save his homeland in the rain forest.

_____

_____

2. Loggers had been coming in and buying the land, but Chief Paiakan refused to sell his village land.

_____

_____

3. He worked, instead, with a major cosmetics company. To have his villagers harvest and sell Brazil nuts. Which can be used in the manufacture of hair products.

_____

_____

4. Chief Paiakan demonstrated to his people. Earning a living from the rain forest without contributing to its destruction.

_____

_____

SENTENCES

Chapter 8: Sentence Structure

 **WORKSHEET 2** *Subject and Predicate*

A sentence consists of two parts: a **subject** and a **predicate**. The **subject** tells *whom* or *what* the sentence is about. The **predicate** tells something about the subject.

> SUBJECT   PREDICATE
> The Gulf of Mexico | serves as an important shipping area.

> PREDICATE SUBJECT   PREDICATE
> When will | they | be notified about the results?

In these examples, all words labeled *subject* make up the **complete subject,** and all the words labeled *predicate* make up the **complete predicate**.

A **simple subject** is the main word or group of words that tells *whom* or *what* the sentence is about. A **simple predicate** is a verb or verb phrase that tells something about the subject.

> SIMPLE SUBJECT: The rugged western **coast** of England will provide the setting for the story.

> SIMPLE PREDICATE: **Should** you really **have been** out so late?

Exercise For each of the following sentences, underline the simple subject once and the simple predicate twice. Be sure to include all words in a verb phrase.

> EXAMPLE: 1. <u>Have</u> <u>you</u> ever <u>seen</u> the miniature Japanese sculptures called *netsuke*?

1. This exquisite art form originated as a practical solution to an everyday problem.

2. During Japan's Tokugawa period (1603–1867), an important part of the traditional costume of the new merchant class was a set of lacquerware boxes for medicines and spices.

3. The boxes were threaded onto the sash of the kimono and served as pockets for the otherwise pocketless garment.

4. Originally just small, plain toggles of lightweight ivory or wood, the *netsuke* held the boxes in place along the sash.

5. Under the feudal system then in effect, there were strict laws against any display of wealth by persons below the rank of *samurai*.

6. However, wealthy merchants had often wanted some observable symbol of their success.

7. Over time, increasingly elaborate *netsuke* from the nation's finest artisans became that symbol.

8. Eventually, the Japanese adopted Western clothing, with pockets.

9. As a result, the *netsuke* became obsolete.

10. Today, collectors all over the world will gladly pay large sums for these beautiful objects with humble origins.

Name _____ Date _____ Class _____

Compound Subjects and Verbs

A **compound subject** consists of two or more subjects that are joined by a conjunction and that have the same verb. A **compound verb** consists of two or more verbs that are joined by a conjunction and that have the same subject.

COMPOUND SUBJECT: **Romeo** and **Juliet** are characters in a play by William Shakespeare.

COMPOUND VERB: The two **fall** in love but **are kept** apart by their families.

Exercise A   Underline the compound parts in each of the following sentences. Then, on the line provided, write *CS* for compound subject or *CV* for compound verb.

_____ 1. Flight 623 has arrived and is boarding at Gate 5.

_____ 2. A good driving record and a driver's education course can keep your insurance rates low.

_____ 3. The cattle spotted the truck, turned, and slowly ambled toward it.

_____ 4. Grandmother did not speak but sat silently awaiting our explanation.

_____ 5. Did Mary Shelley and her husband Percy let peacocks roam their house?

Exercise B: Revising   Combine each set of sentences to create one sentence with a compound subject or a compound verb. Write each new sentence on the line provided.

1. The Maricopa people of Arizona mold clay. They shape it into beautiful and unusual pottery. _____

   _____

2. The Chinese practice the art of growing bonsai. The Japanese do also.

   _____

3. In the Southeast, the Gullah women weave baskets out of marsh grasses. The women sell the baskets in open-air markets. _____

   _____

4. For skill with horses, few peoples rival the Arabs. However, the Cossacks are famed for their skill as well. _____

   _____

5. In Mexico, skilled silversmiths make intricate silver objects. They display them in shop windows to attract tourists. _____

   _____

SENTENCES

Chapter 8: Sentence Structure

WORKSHEET 4 *Finding the Subject*

To find the subject of a sentence, ask *Who?* or *What?* before the verb.

Mr. Kinney coached the team. [*Who* coached? Mr. Kinney coached.]

(1) The subject of a sentence expressing a command or request is always understood to be *you*, although *you* may not appear in the sentence. The subject of a command or a request is *you* even when the sentence contains a **noun of direct address**—a word naming the one or ones spoken to.

REQUEST: [*You*] Please get the rake out of the garage.

COMMAND: Jason, [*you*] bring in some more firewood.

(2) The subject of the sentence is never in a prepositional phrase.

Many of these magic tricks are actually quite simple. [*Tricks* is the object of the preposition *of. Many* is the subject of the sentence.]

(3) The subject of a sentence expressing a question usually follows the verb or part of the verb phrase. Turning the question into a statement will often help you find the subject.

What time shall **I** pick you up? [*I* shall pick you up at noon.]

(4) The words *there* and *here* are never the subject of a sentence.

Here are the **photographs** of the party. [*What* are? *Photographs* are.]

Exercise A   Underline the subject once and the verb twice in the following sentences. If the subject is understood to be *you*, write *you* on the line provided.

_____ 1. There is the sign for the turnoff to Illinois.

_____ 2. Hey, some of these landmarks look familiar to me.

_____ 3. Do you recognize that old store with the tractor in front?

_____ 4. Hand me that map, please.

_____ 5. Uh, oh, whose directions have we been following anyway?

Exercise B   Decide if the underlined word in each of the following sentences is the subject. If it is, write *C* on the line provided. If it is not, find the subject and write it on the line provided.

1. Isn't Mabel Jones the <u>architect</u> for the new office building?   _____

2. <u>There</u> aren't many more of these old classic records left.   _____

3. <u>Vince</u>, did you put the ad in today's paper?   _____

4. Should <u>some</u> of these vegetables go in the freezer?   _____

5. Here's my first-grade class <u>photo</u>!   _____

Chapter 8: Sentence Structure

Direct and Indirect Objects

A **complement** is a word or a group of words that completes the meaning of a verb. *Direct objects* and *indirect objects* are two types of complements. A **direct object** is a word or word group that receives the action of a verb or that shows the result of the action. A direct object tells *whom* or *what* after a transitive verb. An **indirect object** is a word or word group that comes between a transitive verb and a direct object and that tells *to whom* or *to what* or *for whom* or *for what* the action of the verb is done.

           IO   DO
  I gave the **baby** a plastic **jar** with a ball in it.

                  IO   DO
  Suddenly, the baby gave **me** a brilliant **smile**.

A verbal may have complements.

  Grandfather enjoyed **writing** his **grandson** a **letter**. [*Letter* is the direct object of the gerund *writing*, and *grandson* is the indirect object.]

Exercise A   Decide whether the underlined words in the following sentences are direct objects or indirect objects. On the line provided, write *DO* for a direct object or *IO* for an indirect object.

_____ 1. John Le Carré writes suspenseful spy <u>stories</u>.

_____ 2. Give your <u>voice</u> more depth and strength for that part.

_____ 3. Maria taught the <u>dogs</u> some clever tricks.

_____ 4. On returning from his vacation in Spain, Juan entertained <u>Sam</u> and <u>me</u> with an account of his adventures.

_____ 5. Andrés Segovia has transcribed an enormous <u>amount</u> of classical music for the guitar.

Exercise B   In the following sentences, underline the indirect objects once and the direct objects twice.

1. This course offers students an introduction to contemporary art.

2. Our guide showed us the school of porpoises to the left of us and the coral reef to the right.

3. Bernise eventually offered me an explanation and an apology for her weird behavior last night.

4. Coach Nicks gave Tim and Nathan key positions on the team.

5. At the banquet, the principal presented the senior-class debate team the first-place trophy.

SENTENCES

Name _____ Date _____ Class _____

 **WORKSHEET 6** *Objective Complements*

A **direct object** receives or shows the result of the action of a verb. A direct object tells *whom* or *what* after a transitive verb. An **indirect object** comes between a transitive verb and a direct object and tells *to whom, to what, for whom,* or *for what* the action of the verb is done.

> IO   DO
> Last night, I bought my **sister** a **ticket** to the circus.

Another type of complement is an *objective complement*. An **objective complement** is a word or word group that helps complete the meaning of a transitive verb by identifying or modifying the direct object. Only a few verbs take objective complements: *consider, make,* and verbs that can be replaced by *consider* or *make,* such as *appoint, call, choose, dye, elect, keep, name,* and *sweep.* An objective complement may be a noun, an adjective, or a participle.

> I consider Jane my best **friend**. [The noun *friend* identifies the direct object *Jane.*]
>
> The article called Andrew Jackson **energetic** and **motivated**. [The adjective *energetic* and the participle *motivated* modify the direct object *Andrew Jackson.*]

A verbal can take an objective complement.

> Shawn decided to call the **puppy Kid**. [*Puppy* is the direct object of the infinitive *to name,* and the objective complement *Kid* identifies the direct object.]

Exercise A Underline the objective complements in the following sentences.

1. I consider African American writer Toni Morrison one of the most important living authors.

2. Ms. Morrison makes her characters powerful and honest.

3. A newspaper article called her writing a "compelling blend of heart and language."

4. Judges named her 1987 novel, *Beloved,* winner of the 1988 Pulitzer Prize for fiction.

5. Whom do you consider her equal among today's writers?

Exercise B Underline each complement in the following sentences. Then, in the space above each sentence, identify each complement as a direct object *(DO),* an indirect object *(IO),* or an objective complement *(OC).*

1. Recent advances in technology have made interactive television systems a reality.

2. A remote-control converter box with a computer inside gives viewers several options for the content of a program.

3. During a football game, for example, viewers can order the network's choice of camera angle, an alternate shot, an instant replay, or the scores of other games.

4. The computer records each response made by the viewer.

5. Viewers can also select exercise workouts suited to their needs and can tailor news and comedy shows to their interests.

Name _____ Date _____ Class _____

 **WORKSHEET 7** *Subject Complements*

A **subject complement** is a word or word group that completes the meaning of a linking verb and that identifies or modifies the subject. There are two kinds of subject complements: the **predicate nominative** and the **predicate adjective**. A **predicate nominative** is a word or group of words that follows a linking verb and that refers to the same person or thing as the subject of the verb. A **predicate adjective** is an adjective that follows a linking verb and that modifies the subject of the verb.

PREDICATE NOMINATIVES: A college degree is a great **achievement** and a lifelong **asset**.

PREDICATE ADJECTIVES: This week has been unusually **chilly** and **rainy**.

NOTE: Do not confuse a verbal used as a predicate nominative with a participle used as the main verb in a verb phrase.

PREDICATE NOMINATIVE: The thing I hate most is **waiting for a bus**.

VERB: They **are waiting** for the bus.

Exercise A   Underline the linking verb twice and the subject complement(s) once in each of the following sentences. On the line provided, indicate whether the complement is a *predicate nominative* or a *predicate adjective*.

1. The candidate's campaign speech at last night's rally was both
   effective and persuasive.   _____

2. Do these strawberries look ripe?   _____

3. Mexican president Porfirio Díaz became dictatorial.   _____

4. Very sleek, very red, and incredibly powerful is Nina's dream car. _____

5. The dog grew restless just before the storm.   _____

6. Pablo Casals was a brilliant cellist and conductor.   _____

7. The sea spray tasted salty.   _____

8. How musty the rooms in this empty house smell!   _____

9. In 1992, Bill Clinton became president.   _____

10. Kicking Bear was a Sioux warrior, artist, and prophet.   _____

Exercise B   On the line provided, add a subject complement to each group of words below to make a complete sentence.

1. After walking all day, my feet felt _____ .

2. When I graduate from college, I may become a _____ .

3. This test is _____ .

4. In his younger days, my father was a _____ .

SENTENCES

Name _____ Date _____ Class _____

Classifying Sentences by Structure

According to their structure, sentences are classified as *simple, compound, complex,* or *compound-complex.* A **simple sentence** has one independent clause and no subordinate clauses. However, it may have a compound subject or a compound verb. A **compound sentence** has two or more independent clauses but no subordinate clauses.

SIMPLE: This English crystal is handmade.

COMPOUND: This English crystal is handmade, and it is quite valuable.

A **complex sentence** has one independent clause and at least one subordinate clause. A **compound-complex sentence** has two or more independent clauses and at least one subordinate clause.

COMPLEX: When he played, the entire room grew silent.

COMPOUND-COMPLEX: Everyone was transfixed, and time seemed to stand still as we listened to his music.

Exercise   On the line provided, classify each of the following sentences as simple *(S)*, compound *(CD)*, complex *(CX)*, or compound-complex *(CC)*.

EXAMPLE: ___*S*___ 1. H. J. (Henry Jackson) Lewis is generally regarded as the first African American political cartoonist.

_____ 1. During the late 1800s, H. J. Lewis drew political cartoons for *The Freeman*, which was the first illustrated African American newspaper.

_____ 2. Through his cartoons, Lewis frequently criticized the U.S. government's racial policies; however, he also produced nonpolitical ink drawings, sketches, and chalk plates.

_____ 3. If you examine any of his self-portraits, you can see evidence of his artistic versatility, and you can get a sense of the atmosphere in which he worked.

_____ 4. Lewis had to overcome many difficulties to achieve success as an artist, and parts of his life are shrouded in mystery.

_____ 5. Lewis was born into slavery in Mississippi and was badly burned and blinded in one eye when he was a toddler.

_____ 6. As a young man, he worked at various menial jobs until a Little Rock newspaper artist taught him how to draw.

_____ 7. It is known that Lewis made sketches for archaeological studies in Arkansas, Mississippi, Tennessee, and Louisiana in 1882 and 1883.

_____ 8. The Smithsonian Institution now has most of these sketches, which include drawings of prehistoric Native American burial mounds.

_____ 9. Throughout his life, Lewis produced drawings for various publications.

_____ 10. Upon Lewis' death in 1891, *The Freeman*, the newspaper that had made him famous, praised his talent and mourned his loss.

Chapter 8: Sentence Structure

WORKSHEET 9

Classifying Sentences by Purpose

Sentences may be classified according to purpose. A **declarative sentence** makes a statement. It is followed by a period. An **interrogative sentence** asks a question. It is followed by a question mark. An **imperative sentence** makes a request or gives a command. It is usually followed by a period. A very strong command, however, is followed by an exclamation point. An **exclamatory sentence** expresses strong feeling or shows excitement. It is followed by an exclamation point.

DECLARATIVE: Equal access laws benefit everyone**.**

INTERROGATIVE: Why doesn't your building have ramps**?**

IMPERATIVE: Please install ramps and handrails as soon as possible.

EXCLAMATORY: This is a wonderful surprise!

Exercise   On the line provided, identify each of the following sentences. Write *D* for declarative, *INT* for interrogative, *IMP* for imperative, or *E* for exclamatory. Then supply the appropriate end mark after the last word in each sentence.

EXAMPLE: _*IMP*_   1. Look at these beautiful butterflies*!*

_____ 1. Are you aware that there is a huge worldwide demand for butterflies

_____ 2. Millions are caught and sold each year to entomologists, museums, private collectors, and factories

_____ 3. The plastic-encased butterflies that are used to decorate ornamental objects such as trays, tabletops, and screens are usually common varieties, many of which come from Taiwan, Korea, and Malaysia

_____ 4. Keep in mind, though, that there is a difference between collection practices there and what goes on in Papua New Guinea

_____ 5. Papua New Guinea, which was administered by Australia until 1975, has taken advantage of a growing interest in tropical butterflies

_____ 6. Butterfly ranchers gather, raise, and market high-quality specimens, which are accompanied by scientific data

_____ 7. Because biologists have not yet determined the life cycles of all of these butterflies, local villagers have become the experts; as a result, butterfly ranching has improved the country's economy

_____ 8. Did you know that some butterfly specimens are quite small, but others are larger than an adult human hand

_____ 9. Imagine butterflies emerging from cocoons that a rancher had gathered

_____10. What rich, vibrant colors these butterflies have

SENTENCES

Chapter 8: Sentence Structure

Review

Exercise A On the line after each sentence, write the simple subject and the verb. Be sure to include all parts of a verb phrase and all parts of a compound subject or verb.

EXAMPLE: 1. The small, isolated nation of Iceland is a republic with a long history.

Subject: _nation_   Verb: ___is___

1. Before the tenth century, few people had visited Iceland.

   Subject: _____   Verb: _____

2. One of the early Norse settlers was Eric the Red.

   Subject: _____   Verb: _____

3. A kind of parliament, the Althing, was established in 930.

   Subject: _____   Verb: _____

4. Even so, there was much turmoil in the early days of Iceland's history.

   Subject: _____   Verb: _____

5. English, Spanish, and Algerian pirates raided the coast and ruined trade.

   Subject: _____   Verb: _____

6. Not until the late 1700s did a measure of stability return to the island.

   Subject: _____   Verb: _____

7. Iceland remained for centuries under the Danish crown.

   Subject: _____   Verb: _____

8. During World War II Great Britain and the United States sent troops to Iceland in case of German attack.

   Subject: _____   Verb: _____

9. Toward the end of the war came an almost unanimous Icelandic vote for independence from Denmark.

   Subject: _____   Verb: _____

10. Today the people of Iceland, nearly all of them literate, read more books per capita than any other people on earth.

    Subject: _____   Verb: _____

Exercise B   On the line provided, identify the sentence part or parts indicated in parentheses. Be sure to include all parts of a compound subject or verb.

> EXAMPLE: 1. Arabesques are complex, elaborate designs of flowers, foliage, calligraphy, and geometric patterns. *(predicate nominative)* _designs, patterns_

1. The arabesques from the fortress-palace of the Alhambra in Granada, Spain, and the ones from the king's palace in Fez, Morocco, illustrate a historic link between two cultures. *(complete subject)* _____

2. In 711, Arabs and Muslim Berbers from North Africa invaded and occupied Spain. *(complete predicate)* _____

3. They launched the invasion from Morocco and as a result were called Moors. *(direct object)*
    _____

4. The Moors' encouragement of commerce made Spain's major cities wealthy. *(objective complement)* _____

5. Meanwhile, the Moors' patronage of art, literature, and science rendered the cities centers of learning for Christian, Jewish, and Muslim scholars. *(direct object, objective complement)*
    _____

6. Through reconquest, parts of Spain became Christian again as early as 1085. *(predicate adjective)* _____

7. At the end of the fifteenth century, Granada remained the Moors' last stronghold, until finally, in 1492, it too fell to the forces of Ferdinand V and Isabella I. *(verb)*
    _____

8. Spain gave the Moors the choice of conversion to Christianity or expulsion from the country. *(indirect object)* _____

9. Nearly all of them rejected the idea of conversion and left. *(simple subject)*
    _____

10. Yet traces of their rich heritage still survive in the architecture, poetry, and music of Spain. *(simple predicate)* _____

Exercise C   Write the proper punctuation at the end of each sentence. Then, on the line provided, write *D* for declarative, *INT* for interrogative, *IMP* for imperative, or *E* for exclamatory. There may be more than one correct answer for some sentences.

_____ 1. What a mess you've made

_____ 2. The drought has killed all my flowers

_____ 3. Could you keep my dog over the weekend

Chapter 8, Worksheet 10, continued

_____ 4. Do not let the bird out of its cage

_____ 5. Look out for that snake

Exercise D On the line provided before each of the following sentences, identify the type of sentence it is. Write *S* for simple, *CD* for compound, *CX* for complex, or *CC* for compound-complex.

_____ 1. Cattle raisers have long used the technique of crossbreeding to produce animals that combine the best qualities of two different breeds.

_____ 2. The Hereford breed, for instance, originated in England in the eighteenth century as a cross between native Herefordshire cattle and cattle brought from the Netherlands.

_____ 3. More recently, American breeders have crossed Herefords and Brahmans to produce a breed called Brafords.

_____ 4. The Hereford is a beef breed, and the Brahman, a breed native to India, is noted for its resistance to heat and to disease.

_____ 5. One of the most unusual animals that American breeders have produced is the cattalo; it is a cross between a buffalo and a cow.

Name _____ Date _____ Class _____

Coordinating Ideas

Ideas of equal weight in a sentence are called **coordinate ideas**. To give equal emphasis to two or more **independent clauses**—clauses that express complete thoughts—link them with a connecting word, appropriate punctuation, or both. The result is a **compound sentence**.

> Moles have eaten most of the carrots, **but** the tomatoes seem fine.
>
> Insects have eaten a few of the beans; **however,** we have plenty left.
>
> We take care of our garden; it takes care of us.

Different connectives show different kinds of relationships between independent clauses.

ADDITION	CONTRAST	CHOICE	RESULT
also	but	either . . . or	accordingly
and	however	neither . . . nor	consequently
as well as	nevertheless	nor	hence
both . . . and	still	or	therefore
likewise	yet	otherwise	thus

You can also use connecting words to coordinate words or phrases in a sentence. The result is a compound element in your sentence.

> **Music and laughter** filled the room. [compound subject]
>
> He neither **smiled nor spoke** for a whole hour. [compound predicate]

Exercise On the line provided, use an appropriate connecting word and punctuation to join each of the following items.

1. Matthew Henson was a famous African American navigator
   _____ explorer.

2. Henson had very little formal education or other advantages _____
   he overcame these limitations and became the first explorer to reach the North Pole.

3. Admiral Robert E. Peary led the 1909 expedition to the Pole _____
   Henson, his assistant, was actually the first to set foot on the Pole.

4. Radio and satellite communications had not yet been invented
   _____ the world did not learn of the expedition's success until
   months after the event.

5. Peary and Henson met in 1888 _____ they worked and traveled
   together for over twenty-three years.

SENTENCES

Chapter 9: Sentence Style

WORKSHEET 2

Subordinating Ideas in Adverb Clauses

You can express ideas so that one is grammatically subordinate to another. A **subordinate clause** is a group of words that has a subject and a verb and that depends on the sentence's main clause for its full meaning. An **adverb clause** is a subordinate clause that modifies a verb, an adjective, or an adverb in a sentence. A subordinating conjunction introduces an adverb clause. The list below shows subordinating conjunctions you can use to express the following relationships between the main clause and the adverb clause: *time or place, cause or reason, purpose or result,* or *condition.*

TIME OR PLACE: after, as, before, since, until, when, whenever, where, wherever, while

CAUSE OR REASON: as, because, even though, if, since, that, unless, whereas, while

PURPOSE OR RESULT: so that, in order that

CONDITION: although, even though, if, provided that, unless, while

Exercise   For each of the following sentences, write an appropriate subordinating conjunction in the blank. The hint in parentheses tells you what kind of relationship the conjunction should express. Do not use the same conjunction twice.

1. _____ you buy a rare manuscript, make sure it's authentic. *(time)*

2. William Henry Ireland was a highly successful forger _____ he was only a teenager at the height of his exploits. *(condition)*

3. Ireland started forging Shakespeare manuscripts _____ his father had a keen interest in them. *(cause or reason)*

4. _____ he forged a document, Ireland had to do careful research on the details that would make it look genuine. *(time)*

5. He used special blends of ink _____ the forged manuscript would look older than it really was. *(purpose)*

6. _____ he trusted his son, Ireland's father published a collection of the forged manuscripts. *(cause or reason)*

7. Scholars became more and more skeptical _____ Ireland could no longer defend himself against their accusations. *(time)*

8. Ireland published a confession _____ the documents were proven to be fraudulent, and his father's health declined. *(time)*

9. _____ Ireland tried to ease his father's disappointment, the older man died in disgrace in the middle of the scandal. *(condition)*

10. _____ Ireland himself died in 1835, the art of forgery obviously did not die with him. *(condition)*

Chapter 9: Sentence Style

Subordinating Ideas in Adjective Clauses

You can subordinate an idea in a sentence by putting the idea in an adjective clause. An **adjective clause** modifies a noun or pronoun in a sentence. An adjective clause usually begins with *who, whom, whose, which, that, when,* or *where.*

Before you use an adjective clause in a sentence, decide which idea you want to emphasize. Then put the idea you want to emphasize in the independent clause and the other information in an adjective clause.

> The Navajos, who lived in the Southwest, were among the first Native Americans to have horses. [This sentence emphasizes that the Navajos were among the first Native Americans to have horses.]
>
> The Navajos, who were among the first Native Americans to have horses, lived in the Southwest. [This sentence emphasizes that the Navajos lived in the Southwest.]

Exercise: Revising   Change the emphasis in each of the following sentences. Emphasize the idea that is now in the adjective clause, and subordinate the idea that is now in the independent clause. You may have to delete some words, change the word order, or use a different word to begin the new subordinate clause.

1. The word *alphabet,* which comes from the Greek letters *alpha* and *beta,* refers to a series of

   signs used to write a language. _____

   _____

2. The Egyptians, who developed their alphabet around 3000 B.C., had several hundred signs

   for words and syllables. _____

   _____

3. The Greeks, who borrowed symbols from the Phoenician alphabet, improved on earlier

   alphabets by using separate signs for vowel sounds. _____

   _____

4. The Roman alphabet, which is the one we use to write English today, comes from the Greek

   alphabet. _____

   _____

5. Roman stonecutters, who had to make the alphabet practical for carving, simplified the

   letters and added graceful finishing strokes called serifs. _____

   _____

SENTENCES

Chapter 9: Sentence Style

WORKSHEET 4 *Weak Coordination*

In writing, it's important to show the relative importance of ideas and their logical connections. If you overuse coordination, you end up with **weak coordination**. One symptom of weak coordination is *weak focus,* or poor definition of the main point or details. Another is *weak connections,* or fuzzy bridges between ideas.

> WEAK: The car was old, and it had recently been painted, and it had recently been overhauled. [What is the main idea of the sentence: Are all three clauses equally important?]

> BETTER: Although the car was old, it had recently been painted and overhauled.

Avoid weak coordination. Check each compound sentence to be sure that every clause is equally important and therefore best linked by the coordinating conjunctions *and, but, for, nor, or, so,* or *yet.* If not, subordinate an idea by placing it in a subordinate clause or phrase.

Exercise: Revising Each of the following sentences contains weak coordination. On the lines provided, correct the sentences. You may move, add, or delete words as needed.

> EXAMPLE: 1. Some of my most picturesque memories are of Mackinac Island, and we vacationed there one year.
>
> *Some of my most picturesque memories are of Mackinac Island, where we vacationed one year.*

1. Mackinac Island is located in a channel between Michigan and Lake Huron, and it is my favorite place to visit. _____

    _____

2. People get around mostly by bicycle and by horse and carriage, and automobiles are not permitted on the island. _____

    _____

3. It was the first morning of our visit, and we woke to the click-clack of horses' hooves on the street below. _____

    _____

4. I had some mechanical problems with my bike, but I still enjoyed my ride, and the ride was around the island. _____

    _____

5. Mackinac Island's Grand Hotel is one of the oldest hotels in the United States, and the movie *Somewhere in Time* was filmed there. _____

    _____

Chapter 9: Sentence Style

WORKSHEET 5 *Parallel Structure*

Use the same grammatical form to express equal, or parallel, ideas. Applying the same form to equal ideas creates **parallel structure,** used to link coordinate ideas.

>NOT PARALLEL: I like reading and to swim. [gerund paired with an infinitive]
>
>PARALLEL: I like to read and to swim. [infinitive paired with an infinitive]

Use parallel structure when you compare or contrast ideas.

>NOT PARALLEL: The reduction of waste materials is as important as disposing of them properly. [noun compared with a gerund]
>
>PARALLEL: The reduction of waste materials is as important as proper disposal. [noun compared with a noun]

Use parallel structure when you link ideas with correlative conjunctions (*both . . . and, either . . . or, neither . . . nor, not only . . . but also*).

>NOT PARALLEL: Vanessa was admired not only for her intelligence, but she had excellent business sense as well.
>
>PARALLEL: Vanessa was admired not only for her intelligence but also for her excellent business sense. [Note that the correlative conjunctions are placed directly before the parallel phrases.]

Exercise: Revising Make the following sentences parallel by putting the ideas in parallel form. You may delete, add, or move some words.

1. When Thomas "Fats" Waller was a child, his favorite pastimes were singing for his family and to pretend to play the piano. _____

   _____

2. At the suggestion of Waller's older brother and because an uncle helped to finance it, the family finally got a real piano at home. _____

   _____

3. His parents hired a music teacher for him, but Fats was more interested in learning by ear than to take lessons. _____

   _____

4. After his tour with a vaudeville group and writing the hit tune "Boston Blues," Fats got a job playing the organ at the Lincoln Theater in New York. _____

   _____

5. He became a favorite there, not only for his musical talents but also because he had a sense of humor. _____

   _____

SENTENCES

Chapter 9: Sentence Style

WORKSHEET 6   *Sentence Fragments*

A sentence should express a complete thought. When you punctuate a part of a sentence as if it were a complete sentence, you create a **sentence fragment**. In general, avoid using sentence fragments.

A **phrase** is a group of related words that doesn't contain a subject and a verb. Because a phrase doesn't express a complete thought, it can't stand on its own as a sentence.

> FRAGMENT: Was planning on finishing the chores after dinner.
>
> SENTENCE: I was planning on finishing the chores after dinner.
>
> FRAGMENT: To make time for all his activities.
>
> SENTENCE: To make time for all his activities, Ben works out a weekly schedule every Saturday morning.

A **subordinate clause** contains a subject and a predicate but doesn't express a complete thought and can't stand alone as a sentence.

> FRAGMENT: If only she had remembered to take the lens cap off.
>
> SENTENCE: The photographs would have been great if only she had remembered to take the lens cap off.

Exercise: Revising   The following items contain fragments. Revise each item to include the fragment in a complete sentence.

1. Elizabeth Blackwell was born in 1821. And died in 1910. _____

   _____

2. In 1832, her parents immigrated with their eight children to New York. To escape an

   unpleasant social and political situation in Bristol, England. _____

   _____

3. Troubled by the financial plight of her family. Blackwell established a school for girls a few

   years later. _____

   _____

4. Although a friend of Blackwell's encouraged her to become a doctor. At first, Blackwell

   totally rejected this suggestion. _____

   _____

5. Eventually, she became the first woman in the United States to earn an M.D. degree. When

   she graduated in 1849 at the head of her class. _____

   _____

Name _____ Date _____ Class _____

WORKSHEET 7 *Run-on Sentences*

Two or more sentences that run together as if they were a single thought create a **run-on sentence**. There are two kinds of run-on sentences: the *fused sentence* and the *comma splice*. A **fused sentence** has no punctuation at all between the two complete thoughts. A **comma splice** has just a comma between them. The following is a list of several ways to correct a run-on sentence:

1. You can make two sentences.
2. You can use a comma and a coordinating conjunction.
3. You can change one independent clause to a subordinate clause.
4. You can use a semicolon, with or without a conjunctive adverb.

Exercise: Revising   The following items are confusing because they're run-on sentences. On the lines provided, revise each run-on sentence by using one of the methods listed above. Use each of the four methods at least once.

1. Some friends and I are making a movie, it will be on videotape.

   _____

   _____

2. We saved up our money then we rented a camcorder from an electronics store.

   _____

   _____

3. We're still revising some parts of the script, we've already written most of the scenes.

   _____

   _____

4. The sets will be simple most of the scenes will be shot in Joe's back yard.

   _____

   _____

5. We want to shoot a pool-party scene at the neighborhood swimming pool, we'll need to recruit some of our friends as "pool-party extras."

   _____

   _____

SENTENCES

Chapter 9: Sentence Style

WORSHEET 8 *Unnecessary Shifts*

Avoid making unnecessary shifts in sentences. Sometimes, a shift in subject is necessary to express the meaning you intend.

Do invite Jan to the party, or everyone will be disappointed.

Often, though, a shift in subject, tense, or voice in mid-sentence can create an awkward or confusing sentence.

AWKWARD: Students must file appropriate forms, or you will be denied transportation on the charter bus. [unnecessary shift in subject]

BETTER: Students must file appropriate forms or be denied transportation on the charter bus.

AWKWARD: The train pulled into the station where dozens of passengers wait. [unnecessary shift in tense]

BETTER: The train pulled into the station where dozens of passengers waited.

AWKWARD: High storm winds swept through the city and several roofs were blown off. [unnecessary shift from active voice to passive voice]

BETTER: High storm winds swept through the city and blew several roofs off.

Exercise: Revising   On the line provided, revise each of the following sentences to correct any unnecessary shifts in tense or subject. If the sentence contains a shift that is necessary to express its meaning, write *C*.

1. *Windwalker* is a film that portrayed the cultures of the Cheyenne and Crow people.

   _____

2. The film is set in the late 1700s, and the viewer learns about traditional Native American

   values. _____

   _____

3. In the film, which debuted in 1980, a warrior tells his grandchildren his life story.

   _____

4. Before he can die, he must find his long-lost son, and the telling of his story must be

   finished. _____

   _____

5. A Crow warrior, who said he considers Windwalker an enemy for life, had kidnapped

   Windwalker's son. _____

   _____

Name _____ Date _____ Class _____

Varying Sentence Beginnings

Varied sentence beginnings hold a reader's attention.

USE A SINGLE-WORD MODIFIER: **Finally,** we crawled into our sleeping bags. [adverb]

USE A PHRASE MODIFIER: **Without warning,** the tent collapsed. [prepositional phrase]

Jumping up, we all became entangled in tent poles and nylon. [verbal phrase]

USE A CLAUSE MODIFIER: **Although we all were a bit startled,** no one was hurt. [adverb clause]

Exercise: Revising   On the lines provided, revise the following sentences by varying their beginnings. The hint in parentheses after each sentence will tell you which type of beginning to use. You may add or delete words or change word forms as needed.

1. Michael Jordan, darting aggressively past defensive players and scoring basket after basket, was one of the most exciting players in the National Basketball Association. *(phrase)*

   _____

   _____

2. He was embarrassed by his awkwardness and rarely dated in high school. *(phrase)*

   _____

   _____

3. Jordan was named All-American Player and College Player of the Year during his years at the University of North Carolina. *(phrase)*

   _____

   _____

4. Jordan acknowledges that his knowledge and ability seemed to come together at the pro level, although his college career was outstanding. *(clause)*

   _____

   _____

5. Jordan, smiling, agrees that he has traveled a long way from his days as a gawky teenager. *(single-word modifier)*

   _____

   _____

SENTENCES

Chapter 9: Sentence Style

WORKSHEET 10 *Varying Sentence Structure*

You can improve your style by varying the structure of your sentences. Use a mix of simple, compound, complex, and compound-complex sentences in your writing.

Besides Chinese New Year, there are many important holidays in China. [*simple*] One Chinese festival/ritual involves a visit to family graves where participants clear away old leaves and pull weeds. [*complex*] After this is done, they pour some wine on the ground, they bow, and they make an offering of three kinds of food: chicken, fish, and pork. [*compound-complex*] Then they burn incense, and they complete the ceremony by burning spiritual money. [*compound*]

Exercise: Revising   On the lines provided, revise the following paragraph to create variety in sentence structure. Continue your revision on an additional sheet of paper if necessary.

I learned recently that companies can pay filmmakers to display name-brand products in films. I was shocked. Commercials shown before a feature film are annoying. Ads sneaked into the films themselves are downright unethical, though. People go to the movies expecting to enjoy a commercial-free film. They see an actor eating Brand X pizza or wearing Brand Y jeans. At the time, they don't realize that they are watching a paid advertisement. Filmmakers have a responsibility to make their audiences aware of these ads. They shouldn't have to interrupt a film to identify an ad. They should be required to list the advertisers in the credits.

_____

_____

_____

_____

_____

_____

_____

_____

_____

_____

_____

_____

_____

_____

_____

_____

Name _____ Date _____ Class _____

WORKSHEET 11

Revising to Reduce Wordiness

Skilled writers make every word count. Avoid using unnecessary words in your writing. To avoid wordiness, keep the following three points in mind: (1) Use only as many words as you need to make your point; (2) choose simple, clear words and expressions over complicated ones; and (3) don't repeat words or ideas unless absolutely necessary.

When editing, you might take out unnecessary words, simplify your language, change a clause to a phrase, or reduce a phrase or a clause to a word or two.

Exercise: Revising Each of the sentences below contains unnecessary words and repeats ideas. Revise each sentence on the lines provided.

1. Most people have heard of the playwright William Shakespeare, the man many people call the greatest writer of all time in the English language.

   _____

   _____

2. Even though William Shakespeare is famous throughout the world everywhere, we can't be certain about his physical appearance—that is, what he looked like.

   _____

   _____

3. From the portraits of Shakespeare that have survived and withstood the passage of time, he appears to have been a slim man of slight build and average height.

   _____

   _____

4. Artists rendered Shakespeare in portraits with well-proportioned features and expressive eyes.

   _____

   _____

5. Although we may never learn more about Shakespeare the man himself, we can continue to learn and gain information about Shakespeare the writer by studying his magnificent works.

   _____

   _____

SENTENCES

Chapter 9: Sentence Style

WORKSHEET 12 *Review*

Exercise A On the lines provided, connect the ideas or show the relationship between them by writing a coordinating or subordinating conjunction or a relative pronoun.

1. Herman Melville's *Moby-Dick* attracted little attention _____ it was published.

2. The sentence "Call me Ishmael," _____ begins *Moby-Dick*, is one of the most famous of all openings for a novel.

3. The main characters are Ishmael and Captain Ahab, _____ sail on the *Pequod*.

4. Ahab is determined to destroy the whale Moby-Dick, _____ he does not understand the nature of his enemy.

5. The book is a classic of American literature; _____ , some people complain that it becomes tiresome during its long, detailed discussions of whales and whaling.

Exercise B: Revising Weak coordination and faulty parallelism make the following paragraphs confusing. On the lines provided, revise each faulty sentence to make it clear and smooth. You may need to add, delete, or rearrange some words in the sentences. Remember to check the placement of correlative conjunctions.

Simon J. Ortiz is an Acoma Pueblo, and he writes eloquently about the experiences of Native Americans. His poems and short stories are infused with Native American history, mythology, and philosophical. Ortiz uses simple, direct language, and his language reflects the oral storytelling tradition of his heritage. Ortiz often employs a sorrowful tone, but he tempers his writings with humor and being optimistic.

Going for the Rain was Ortiz's first full-length collection of poems, and it was published in 1976. *Going for the Rain* depicts a journey that begins in the traditional Native American world, goes through present-day America, and returning to its origin. In these poems Ortiz expresses concern not only for his own people but also American society as a whole.

The collection *A Good Journey* is similar to *Going for the Rain* both in structure and theme. The poems in *A Good Journey* describe Native American history and expressing concern about the environment. The conclusion of this volume is as hopeful as his other works.

_____

_____

_____

_____

_____

_____

_____

_____

_____

_____

_____

_____

_____

_____

_____

_____

_____

_____

_____

_____

Exercise C: Revising   On the lines provided, revise the following word groups to eliminate fragments, run-ons, and unnecessary shifts. If the item is correct, write C.

1. Dorothy West began writing stories when she was seven, and several *Boston Post* prizes were won by her while she was a teenager. _____

   _____

2. *Opportunity* published West's story "The Typewriter." Which later appeared in *The Best Short Stories of 1926.* _____

   _____

3. West was born in Boston but eventually settled in New York City, there she met many writers of the Harlem Renaissance. Including Zora Neale Hurston and Langston Hughes.

   _____

   _____

4. In the early 1930s, she edited *Challenge*, a magazine that published the works of young writers. _____

   _____

5. After West's magazine ventures failed. She took a job as a welfare investigator in Harlem, she later joined the Federal Writers' Project. _____

   _____

SENTENCES

Exercise D: Revising   On the lines provided, revise the following paragraph to vary the sentence beginnings and sentence structure.

Toni Morrison, a gifted African American writer, has earned international acclaim for her works. She won the National Book Critics Circle Award for her third novel, *Song of Solomon*. She received the Pulitzer Prize for her fifth novel, *Beloved*. *Beloved* demonstrates Morrison's talent for portraying complex human emotions and relationships. It tells the story of a former slave haunted by tragic memories. *Beloved* is rich with vivid characterizations, like her other novels. She won the Nobel Prize in literature in 1993.

_____

_____

_____

_____

_____

_____

_____

_____

_____

Exercise E: Revising   On the lines provided, revise the following sentences to eliminate wordiness.

1. Few athletes earn lasting reputations that endure outside the realm of sports.

   _____

   _____

2. However, athlete and baseball player Roberto Clemente is remembered not only as a skilled athlete but also as a compassionate human being. _____

   _____

3. A lifelong opponent of injustice and unfairness, Clemente, who was from Puerto Rico, fought prejudice in the major leagues and in every part of his life. _____

   _____

4. In 1972 Clemente died in an accident in a plane crash on his way to help deliver supplies to the victims of a terrible, horrible earthquake in Nicaragua. _____

   _____

5. His courage and bravery live on in the memories of his fans, who still think of him.

   _____

   _____

Name _____ Date _____ Class _____

Combining by Inserting Single-Word Modifiers and Prepositional Phrases

Combine related sentences by inserting key words or phrases from one or more sentences into another sentence.

> ORIGINAL: The student stared. He stared at the chalkboard. He seemed puzzled.
>
> COMBINED: **Puzzled,** the student stared at the chalkboard.

Sometimes you can insert a word from one sentence directly into another sentence as a modifier. Other times you will need to change the word into an adjective or an adverb before you can insert it.

> ORIGINAL: Her demands for a refund were quickly met. She demanded angrily.
>
> COMBINED: Her **angry** demands for a refund were quickly met.

Exercise: Revising   On the lines provided, combine each group of short, related sentences by inserting adjectives, adverbs, or prepositional phrases into the first sentence. You may change the forms of some words. Add commas if necessary.

> EXAMPLE: 1. Peregrine falcons soar. They soar gracefully. They soar near their nests. *Peregrine falcons soar gracefully near their nests.*

1. Peregrine falcons became scarce. They became scarce in the United States. They became scarce because of the pesticide DDT. _____

   _____

2. No breeding pairs remained. No pairs remained east of the Mississippi. The breeding pairs were gone by 1970. _____

   _____

3. Scientists have reintroduced peregrine falcons. These scientists are from Cornell University. The falcons are wild. The scientists have reintroduced the falcons to the eastern United States. They have reintroduced the falcons under controlled conditions.

   _____

   _____

4. A ban on DDT has helped the falcons. The ban has been effective. It has been a considerable help. _____

   _____

5. Peregrines are hatching eggs. The peregrines are in the eastern wilderness. It is the first time they have hatched eggs in the wilderness since the 1950s. _____

   _____

SENTENCES

Chapter 10: Sentence Combining

WORKSHEET 2
Combining by Inserting Participial Phrases

A **participial phrase** contains a participle and words related to it. It acts as an adjective.

Working for months, Lorinda saved the money for her first semester's tuition.

Sometimes you can take a participial phrase from one sentence and insert it directly into another sentence. Other times you will need to change a verb into a participle before you can insert the idea into another sentence.

ORIGINAL: The woman was impatient. She was asking for a schedule.

COMBINED: The woman **asking for a schedule** was impatient.

ORIGINAL: We scraped off layers of paint. We worked for several hours.

COMBINED: **Working for several hours,** we scraped off layers of paint.

Be sure to place a participial phrase close to the noun or pronoun you want to modify. Otherwise, your sentence may express a meaning you did not intend.

MISPLACED: Flying high above us, a man frantically called the parrot.

IMPROVED: A man frantically called the parrot **flying high above us**.

Exercise: Revising   On the lines provided, combine each sentence pair below by reducing the second sentence to a participial phrase.

EXAMPLE: 1. Marian Anderson showed her love for music early on. She sang in the church choir. *Singing in the church choir, Marian Anderson showed her love for music early on.*

1. Anderson traveled to Europe to study for a year when she was twenty-two. She was awarded a fellowship to do this. _____

_____

2. Anderson became famous. She was well received by audiences all over Europe.

_____

3. She won the praise of U.S. opera lovers as well. She returned to the United States in 1935.

_____

4. Anderson sang in protest on the steps of the Lincoln Memorial on Easter of 1939. She had been banned from singing at Constitution Hall because she was an African American.

_____

_____

5. Seventy-five thousand people came to hear the Easter morning concert. They expressed their disapproval of the discriminatory treatment. _____

_____

Name _____ Date _____ Class _____

Combining by Inserting Appositive Phrases

An **appositive phrase** consists of an appositive and its modifiers. An appositive phrase identifies or explains the noun or pronoun it is next to. Appositive phrases are set off by commas.

His new song, **a mixture of rap and reggae,** delighted the audience.

Sometimes you can combine two sentences by using an appositive phrase.

TWO SENTENCES: Construction on the new housing project will begin in the fall. The project is a temporary solution to the housing crisis.

ONE SENTENCE: Construction on the new housing project, **a temporary solution to the housing crisis,** will begin in the fall.

Exercise: Revising On the lines provided, combine each pair of sentences by turning one of the sentences into an appositive phrase.

EXAMPLE: 1. Elizabeth Bowen became one of the leading fiction writers in England after World War I. She was a native of Ireland.

Elizabeth Bowen, a native of Ireland, became one of the leading fiction writers in England after World War I.

1. In *The Death of the Heart,* the protagonist is a sensitive teenage girl. *The Death of the Heart* is one of Bowen's best-known novels._____

_____

2. Bowen was a nurse and an air-raid warden during World War II. Bowen wrote about the psychological effects of war on civilians. _____

_____

3. Writer Doris Lessing describes people attempting to find meaning in life. She is a sensitive observer of social and political struggles. _____

_____

4. In *Going Home,* Doris Lessing writes about a return visit to Rhodesia. *Going Home* is an autobiographical narrative._____

_____

5. Born in India, Salman Rushdie was educated in England. He won the Booker Prize for his work entitled *Midnight's Children.* _____

_____

Chapter 10: Sentence Combining

WORKSHEET 4

Combining by Coordinating Ideas

You can combine sentences that contain equally important words, phrases, or clauses by using coordinating conjunctions *(and, but, for, or, nor, so, yet)* or correlative conjunctions (such as *both . . . and, either . . . or, neither . . . nor*).

ORIGINAL: The screaming siren of an ambulance shot through my dreams. It left me panting with fear.

COMBINED: The screaming siren of an ambulance shot through my dreams **and** left me panting with fear.

ORIGINAL: I don't like shoveling snow. My brother doesn't like it either.

COMBINED: **Neither** my brother **nor** I like shoveling snow.

You can also form a compound sentence by linking independent clauses with a semicolon and a conjunctive adverb (such as *however, likewise, subsequently*) or with just a semicolon.

Negotiations continue; however, a statement will be released shortly.

Keep your seat belts buckled; we expect to encounter turbulence.

Exercise: Revising   Combine each of the following pairs of sentences by following the directions given in parentheses.

1. Between 1847 and 1850, Canton Province in China had extended periods of drought. Large numbers of Chinese peasants immigrated to the United States. *(Form a compound sentence.)*

   _____

   _____

2. Most of these early Chinese immigrants found no gold. They found no well-paying work.

   (Form a compound direct object.) _____

   _____

3. Ten thousand laborers built the Union Pacific railroad. Nine thousand of them were

   Chinese. *(Form a compound sentence with a semicolon.)* _____

   _____

4. The railroad builders of America initially favored Chinese immigration. The sentiment

   changed when the railroad system was finished. *(Form a compound sentence with a*

   conjunctive adverb.) _____

   _____

5. Despite their hardships, many Chinese immigrants stayed in the United States. They began

   to call it home. *(Form a compound verb.)* _____

   _____

Name _____ Date _____ Class _____

Combining by Subordinating Ideas

You can combine related sentences by placing one idea in a subordinate clause (an *adjective clause*, an *adverb clause*, or a *noun clause*). An **adjective clause,** which modifies a noun or pronoun, is formed by replacing the subject of a sentence with *who, whom, whose, which,* or *that.*

ORIGINAL: The recycling trucks have been rescheduled. They usually run on Wednesday.

REVISED: The recycling trucks, **which usually run on Wednesday,** have been rescheduled.

An **adverb clause** modifies a verb, an adjective, or another adverb in the main clause. To make a sentence into an adverb clause, add a subordinating conjunction such as *although, after, because, if, when, where,* or *while.*

ORIGINAL: Our carpool left without us. We were late.

REVISED: Our carpool left without us **because** we were late.

A **noun clause** is a subordinate clause used as a noun. You can make a sentence into a noun clause by beginning it with a word such as *that, how, what, whatever, who,* or *whoever.* You may also have to delete or move some words.

ORIGINAL: Please give to the relief effort. Give whatever you can.

REVISED: Please give **whatever you can** to the relief effort.

Exercise: Revising   For each of the following items, turn one sentence into the type of subordinate clause indicated in parentheses. Then insert the subordinate clause into the other sentence.

1. Louise Erdrich writes in lyrical prose about the Native American experience. She is part Chippewa. *(adjective clause)* _____

_____

2. The Turtle Mountain Chippewa Reservation is the setting for her novel *Love Medicine.* Erdrich spent time there as a child. *(adjective clause)* _____

_____

_____

3. Erdrich had close ties to the Chippewa community. As a child, she never thought about her Native American heritage. *(adverb clause)* _____

_____

_____

4. As a young adult Erdrich began to realize something. Her Native American heritage was important to her. *(noun clause)* _____

_____

SENTENCES

Chapter 10: Sentence Combining

WORKSHEET 6 *Combining Sentences*

You can combine the words and ideas in separate sentences in several ways: by inserting single-word modifiers; by inserting prepositional, participial, or appositive phrases; by coordinating ideas; and by subordinating ideas.

Exercise: Revising   Using all the sentence-combining skills you have learned, revise the following paragraph for style. Use your judgment about which sentences to combine and how to combine them. Don't change the meaning of the original paragraph. Use the lines provided, and attach additional sheets if needed.

Mount Saint Helens erupted in May 1980. It is near Vancouver, Washington. The eruption was sudden. The explosion had a force over five hundred times that of an atomic bomb. It tore the top off the mountain. It threw ash high into the air. The explosion and resulting mudslides caused more than fifty deaths. The explosions and mudslides left many people homeless. The mud killed hundreds of deer and elk. The mud turned Spirit Lake into a mudhole. Much of the ash fell to earth within a few days. A cloud of dust remained. This cloud was over much of the Northern Hemisphere. People saw spectacular sunrises and sunsets for years. The sunrises and sunsets were rose-colored. The color was due to solar rays striking microscopic particles of ash.

_____

_____

_____

_____

_____

_____

_____

_____

_____

_____

_____

_____

_____

_____

_____

Chapter 10: Sentence Combining

| WORKSHEET 7 | *Review* |

Exercise A: Revising   Each of the following items consists of two short, choppy sentences. Combine the sentences as directed.

> EXAMPLE: 1.   Helen received a job offer. She accepted immediately.
> (Combine by using a *comma*.) *When Helen received a job*
> *offer, she accepted immediately.*

1. She impressed the job interviewer. She knew something about the organization. (Combine into one sentence, beginning with a *participial phrase*.) _____

   _____

2. You should dress neatly. You should arrive on time for a job interview. (Form a *compound sentence*.) _____

   _____

3. The interviewer raises the question of salary. Try to avoid naming a specific figure. (Combine into one sentence, beginning with *If*.) _____

   _____

4. The interview is over. You should thank the interviewer. (Combine into one sentence beginning with *When*.) _____

   _____

5. It is usually a good idea to write a follow-up letter. In it you should again express your thanks for the interview. (Combine into one sentence, using the words *in which*.)

   _____

   _____

Exercise B: Revising   Combine each of the following items. You may have to add, delete, or change some words in the sentences. Add punctuation where necessary.

> EXAMPLE: 1.   *Amazing Stories* was the first science fiction magazine.
> Hugo Gernsback began publishing it in 1926.
> *Amazing Stories, which Hugo Gernsback began publishing*
> *in 1926, was the first science fiction magazine.*

1. Some science fiction contains outlandish speculation. Science fiction has to seem somewhat believable to be effective. _____

   _____

2. *Frankenstein* is an early example of science fiction. The novel describes the scientific creation of life. _____

_____

3. H. G. Wells's *The Time Machine* offers thought-provoking social criticism. *The Time Machine* describes a devastated future world. _____

_____

4. Some critics did not accept science fiction as serious literature. Major authors in the early twentieth century often included science fiction in their works. _____

_____

5. Today science fiction has many supporters. They hold annual conventions and present awards for the best writing. _____

_____

Exercise C: Revising   Revise the following paragraph for style. Using subordinate clauses, appositives, and any other means you wish, combine the ideas in the passage into smooth sentences. Write your improved version on the lines provided or on a separate sheet of paper.

The surface of the planet Mars can be seen through a telescope. It can be seen from Earth. Mars is reddish in color. It was named after the ancient Romans' red god of war. Mars travels in an elliptical orbit. It travels around the sun. It maintains a distance from the sun of at least 128 million miles.

Part of the planet's surface is covered with craters. These craters were caused by meteors. Mars is covered with canyons. It is also covered with deep gorges. Because of these features, some scientists believe that large quantities of water once flowed on the planet's surface. Mars also has plains. The plains are windblown. They are covered by sand dunes and rocks. The rocks are jagged.

_____

_____

_____

_____

_____

_____

_____

_____

_____

_____

_____

_____

Chapter 11: Capitalization

 **WORKSHEET 1**   *First Words*

Capitalize the first word in every sentence.

> **When** is the space shuttle due to land?

Capitalize the first word of a sentence following a colon.

> The senators' statement in support of the besieged civilians could be summed up as follows: **Our** humanity demands that we act, that we act now, and that we act decisively.

Capitalize the first word of a direct quotation. When quoting from a writer's work, capitalize the first word of the quotation only if the writer has capitalized it.

> Just before he died, Walt Whitman muttered, "**Garrulous** to the very last."

> Who are the "**s**omeones" and "**e**veryones" that E. E. Cummings refers to?

Traditionally, the first word of a line of poetry is capitalized.

> **Lightning** that mocks the night,
> **Brief** even as bright.

Percy Bysshe Shelley, "Mutability"

Capitalize the first word of a statement or a question inserted in a sentence without quotation marks.

> I ask you, **What** could he have been thinking?

Capitalize the first word of a resolution following the word *Resolved*.

> Resolved: **That** students be given no homework during the week of final exams.

Exercise: Proofreading   For the following sentences, strike through each error in capitalization and write the correct form above it.

> EXAMPLE: 1. *A*
> ⱥs students, we each should ask ourselves, *A*
> ⱥm I working hard enough?

1. the secretary read the notes from last week's meeting aloud, "resolved: that this year's dues remain the same as last year's."

2. The game of volleyball can be summed up briefly as follows: using only their hands, two teams of six players hit a ball back and forth over a net.

3. Oh, I almost forgot to tell you this: your friend Paula called and said, "don't forget to meet me at the library at noon tomorrow."

4. I can never seem to remember the name of the poet who wrote the famous poem that begins "do not go gentle into that good night . . . . "

5. This critic calls the movie "delightfully weird"; what does she mean by "Weird"?

MECHANICS

Chapter 11: Capitalization

Conventional Situations, the Pronoun I, and the Interjection O

Capitalize the first word in the salutation and the closing of a letter.

Dear Sales Manager,   **My dear Alison,**   **Yours truly,**   **With love,**

Capitalize the Roman numerals and letters in an outline as well as the first word in each heading and subheading.

    I. Literary forms in Elizabethan England
        A. Poetry
            1. Sonnet
            2. Sestina
        B. Drama

Capitalize the interjection *O* and the pronoun *I*. The interjection *O* is usually used only for invocations and is followed by the name of the person or thing being addressed. Don't confuse it with the common interjection *oh,* which is capitalized only when it appears at the beginning of a sentence and which is always followed by punctuation.

Exercise: Proofreading   The following letter has ten errors in capitalization. Correct each error.

dear Rita,

    Well, Thanksgiving is almost here, and i'm still wrestling with my research paper.

Thanks, o wise one, for reviewing my outline and first draft. Following your suggestion,

I've decided to expand "c. Public Response to 'A Modest Proposal'" under "III. effects of

Swift's Satire." This change will add, Oh, about another two pages to the paper. but I think

the result will be worth it.

    I really appreciate your advice, and I'll be sending you a copy of the paper when I'm

finished. Enjoy!

Your Friend,

Luke

Chapter 11: Capitalization

Proper Nouns and Adjectives: People, Places, Things

Capitalize proper nouns and proper adjectives. A **common noun** is a general name for a person, a place, a thing, or an idea. Common nouns are capitalized only if they begin a sentence, a direct quotation, or in most cases, a line of poetry. Common nouns are also capitalized if they are part of a title. A **proper noun** names a particular person, place, thing, or idea. **Proper adjectives** are formed from proper nouns.

COMMON NOUN:	**city**	country	king
PROPER NOUN:	**Moscow**	England	King Arthur
PROPER ADJECTIVE:	**Muscovite voters**	English tweed	Arthurian legend

In proper nouns made up of two or more words, do not capitalize articles, prepositions of five letters or fewer, the word *to* in an infinitive, or coordinating conjunctions.

the Prince of Wales   the Dalai Lama   Trinidad and Tobago

Capitalize the given names of persons and animals. Some names contain more than one capital letter. Usage varies in the capitalization of *van, von, du, de la,* and other parts of many multiword names. Always verify the spelling of a name.

Helen Keller   Lassie   Ludwig **van** Beethoven   John McEnroe

Abbreviations such as *Ms., Mr., Dr.,* and *Gen.* should always be capitalized. Capitalize the abbreviations *Jr.* and *Sr.* following a name, and set them off with commas. Also capitalize Roman numerals (I, III, etc.) but do *not* set them off with commas. Capitalize descriptive names and nicknames.

Adm. Grace Hopper   Luís Ramos, Jr.
Pope John **XXIII**   Ed "Too Tall" Jones

Exercise   The following words and phrases are capitalized incorrectly. Write the words and phrases correctly on the lines provided.

1. Ivan The Terrible _____

2. dr. Antonia Novello _____

3. dickensian character _____

4. janet evans _____

5. Henry viii _____

6. Ms. gloria Steinem _____

7. Roy Roger's horse, trigger _____

8. Hank Williams, jr. _____

9. asian immigrants _____

10. Lawrence "yogi" Berra _____

Name _____ Date _____ Class _____

Proper Nouns and Adjectives: Geographical Names

Capitalize geographical names. However, words such as *north*, *western*, and *southeast* are not capitalized when they indicate direction.

    North America   north of here

    living in the Southwest   southwest Travis County

The abbreviations of names of states are always capitalized. In addresses, abbreviations such as *St.*, *Ave.*, *Dr.*, and *Blvd.* are capitalized. Words such as *city*, *street*, and *park* are capitalized only when they are part of a name. In general, words such as *city*, *state*, and *county* are not capitalized. The second word in a hyphenated number begins with a small letter.

    Twenty-first St., Sioux City, Iowa

    the street east of the city park

Exercise For each item below, strike through capital letters that should be lowercase, and circle lowercase letters that should be capitalized. If the item is correct, make no revision.

        EXAMPLE: 1. just N̶orth of Twenty-F̶ifth (s)treet

1. East of the river

2. Bering strait

3. Fifty-second Street

4. austin, Texas

5. New Jersey turnpike

6. the Iberian peninsula

7. people of the far east

8. Interstate highway 35

9. Plum county

10. the grand Canyon

11. the eastern Seaboard

12. the Nile river

13. an american citizen

14. ranching in the south

15. an african village

16. olympic national park

17. a City like New Orleans

18. that popular spanish singer

19. the eruption of mount pinatubo

20. Bay of Bengal

Name _____ Date _____ Class _____

Proper Nouns and Adjectives: Organizations, Buildings, etc.

Capitalize the names of organizations, teams, business firms, institutions, buildings and other architectural structures, and government bodies.

    National Forensic League   Seattle Seahawks   John's Shoe Store

Do not capitalize words such as *democratic, republican,* and *socialist* when they refer to principles or forms of government. Capitalize such words only when they refer to a specific political party. The word *party* in the name of a political party may or may not be capitalized. Do not capitalize words such as *building, hospital, theater, high school, university,* and *post office* unless they are part of a proper noun.

    Socialist party   Schubert Theater   Howard University
    democratic reforms   a theater downtown   a major university

Capitalize the names of historical events and periods, special events, holidays and other calendar items, and time zones. Do not capitalize the name of a season unless the season is being personified or unless it is part of a proper noun.

    Renaissance   the Spring Carnival   Super Bowl   Thanksgiving

Exercise For each item below, strike through capital letters that should be lowercase, and circle lowercase letters that should be capitalized. If the item is correct, make no revision.

           EXAMPLE: 1. Ernie's (a)ppliance (b)arn

1. in honor of secretaries day
2. the Revolutionary War
3. the world Trade Center
4. itawamba junior college
5. a hotel across town
6. the newport athletic club
7. bureau of the census
8. the university of Texas
9. a winter blizzard
10. the united nations

11. labor day picnic
12. republican supporters
13. a spring shower
14. the world series
15. friday, january 21
16. the Boston celtics
17. the crusades
18. the Barclay Hotel
19. central high school
20. his Socialist ideas

MECHANICS

Name _____ Date _____ Class _____

Proper Nouns and Adjectives: Nationalities, etc.

Capitalize the names of nationalities, races, and peoples.

Moroccan   Caucasian   Cherokee   Greek

Capitalize the brand names of business products. A noun that follows a brand name is not capitalized. Capitalize the names of ships, trains, aircraft, spacecraft, monuments, awards, planets, and any other particular places, things, or events. Do not capitalize the words *sun* and *moon*. Do not capitalize the word *earth* unless it is used along with the names of other heavenly bodies that are capitalized.

Nintendo video game   *Merrimac*   Lincoln Memorial

Mercury   Academy Award   *Air Force One*

Do not capitalize the names of school subjects, except for languages and course names followed by a number. Do not capitalize class names such as *senior*, *junior*, and *sophomore* unless they are part of a proper noun. As a rule, nouns identified by a number or letter are capitalized.

chemistry   during our freshman year   P.O. Box 574

Algebra I   Senior Spring Festival   Suite H

Exercise   For each item below, strike through capital letters that should be lowercase, and circle lowercase letters that should be capitalized. If the item is correct, make no revision.

EXAMPLE: 1. a new Ford Ⱦruck

1. studying Art, English literature, and French

2. this turkish coffee grinder

3. a new sophomore

4. flying the *spirit of St. Louis*

5. a polaroid camera

6. the constellation Cassiopeia

7. chapter 7, page 114

8. a visit to the Washington Monument

9. a swiss pocket knife

10. from Earth to Saturn

11. a cruise on the *cunard princess*

12. winning a pulitzer prize

13. the mexican hat dance

14. a cheyenne tradition

15. the Junior Prom

16. Earth's orbit

17. the state fair of Arkansas

18. art history II

19. tastee peanut butter

20. physics class

Chapter 11: Capitalization

Titles of People

Capitalize a title belonging to a particular person when it comes before the person's name. In general, do not capitalize a title used alone or following a name. Some titles, however, are by tradition capitalized. If you are unsure of whether or not to capitalize a title, check in a dictionary.

| Governor Ann Richards | General Colin Powell | Mother Teresa |
| the governor of Texas | an American general | his mother |

A title is usually capitalized when it is used alone in direct address. Capitalize words showing family relationships when used with a person's name but *not* when preceded by a possessive. A word showing a family relationship is also capitalized when used in place of a person's name, unless it is preceded by a possessive.

Aunt Jean, I'd like to introduce Hal's mom, Mrs. Anderson.

Did my uncle Jack really go to high school with you, Professor?

Exercise: Proofreading   For each of the following sentences, strike through every error in capitalization and write the correct form above it.

EXAMPLE: 1. Is there a problem, ~~O~~fficer?

1. Anne Boleyn was the second wife of king Henry VIII.

2. My Cousin Tamara completed a whitewater canoe course last spring.

3. John Williams was the Conductor of the Boston Pops for several years.

4. English prime minister John Major met with the press.

5. Would your Mom be willing to drive us to the train station?

6. Both Janelle and her Brother made blocks for this quilt.

7. A presentation on preventing crime was given by sgt. Janet Lewis.

8. Who is the President of General Motors?

9. Here is the beautiful flute that aunt Liu carved.

10. We asked dr. Hernández to give the commencement address.

MECHANICS

Chapter 11: Capitalization

WORKSHEET 8 — *Titles of Works*

Capitalize the first and last words and all important words in titles of works, including those shown in the list below.

books	musical compositions	TV and radio programs
cartoons	periodicals	speeches
essays	plays	stories
historical documents	poems	works of art

Unimportant words include articles (*a, an, the*), prepositions with fewer than five letters (*of, in, to, for, from, with*), and coordinating conjunctions (*and, but, for, nor, or, so, yet*). The first word of a subtitle is always capitalized. The article *the* is often written before a title but is not capitalized unless it is the first word of the title.

San Diego Tribune	*Middlemarch*
"The Sky Is Crying"	the painting *Güernica*
Star Trek: Deep Space Nine	**Magna Carta**

Always capitalize the first element in a hyphenated compound used as a title. Capitalize other elements only if they are nouns or proper adjectives or if they have equal force with the first element. Do not capitalize the second element if it is a participle that modifies the first element or if the two elements make up a single word.

"Hide-and-Seek Diplomacy"   German-American Federation   Spanish-speaking

Capitalize the names of religions and their followers, holy days and celebrations, holy writings, and specific deities and venerated beings. The words *god* and *goddess* are not capitalized when they refer to the deities of ancient mythology. Pronouns that refer to a deity may or may not be capitalized.

Exercise   On the line provided, correct any error in capitalization in each of the following items.

1. *Kristin Lavransdatter I: the Bridal Wreath*

_____

2. throughout the English-Speaking world

_____

3. *the victory garden* on PBS

_____

4. worshiped the goddess athena

_____

5. a muslim scholar

_____

Name _____ Date _____ Class _____

 **WORKSHEET 9** *Review*

MECHANICS

Exercise A   For each item below, strike through capital letters that should be lowercase, and circle lowercase letters that should be capitalized. If the item is correct, make no revision.

EXAMPLE: 1. a M̸ovie starring Lena Horne

1. a nation in the middle east

2. the Space Shuttle Columbia

3. at Sixth avenue and Market street

4. taking English, art II, and Chemistry

5. a trip to Yosemite National Park

6. Toni Morrison's *the Bluest Eye*

7. She said, "tell me, too."

8. Hoover dam

9. four miles South on route 10

10. a letter from William Johnston, jr.

11. a beautiful gray arabian stallion

12. the african american novelist James Baldwin

13. Forty-Ninth Street

14. an apple computer

15. "The World Is Too Much With Us"

16. the rings of saturn

17. the medal of freedom

18. the *Los Angeles times*

19. Mildred "babe" Zaharias

20. your Uncle Zeke

Exercise B: Proofreading   Read each of the following sentences to see if it contains any errors in capitalization. If the sentence does contain errors, correctly write the word or words that are in error on the line provided. Supply capital letters where they are needed.

1. According to professor De La Rey, the first of Tennyson's *idylls of the king* was published in 1859, the same year as the publication of Darwin's *the origin of species*, and FitzGerald's translation of omar Khayyám's *rubáiyát*.

_____

2. In ancient egypt the people worshiped many Gods equally until the sun God Ra became the principal deity.

_____

3. The first American woman in space, Sally Ride, was a member of the crew aboard the space shuttle *challenger* launched from cape Canaveral, Florida, on June 18, 1983.

_____

4. The Mountain Ranges in the Western states offer a variety of hiking experiences for those who love the outdoors.

_____

Chapter 11, Worksheet 9, continued

5. From the St. Croix island national monument in Maine to the Huleia wildlife refuge in Hawaii, public lands managed by the federal government, including the military, equal a third of the nation's total acreage.

Exercise C: Proofreading   In the following paragraphs, strike through each error in capitalization, and change lowercase letters to capitals or capital letters to lowercase as necessary.

EXAMPLE: [1] Chattanooga, Tennessee, is the seat of Hamilton ~~C~~ounty.

[1] Chattanooga, on the Georgia border in Southeast Tennessee, is building its future by inviting visitors to explore its past. [2] The city has been welcoming tourists since at least 1866, when an ad in the *Chattanooga Times* invited people from the north to visit with the assurance that the Ku Klux Klan had no power in Chattanooga. [3] Today a multimillion-dollar plaza on the banks of the Tennessee river marks the city's original site, a landing established about 1815 by a trader named john Ross. [4] exhibits throughout the plaza depict the city's history, including the forced removal of the Cherokee to Indian Territory (now Oklahoma) in 1838. [5] Ross, who was himself part Cherokee and who vehemently protested the removal, led that tragic journey, which became known as the trail of Tears. [6] The city of Chattanooga plans to build a trolley system to connect the plaza at Ross' landing to the restored Chattanooga Choo-Choo Terminal and Station on Market Street, where visitors can see a car and an engine from the first train that provided passenger service between the north and the South.

[7] Chattanooga's status as a rail center made the City strategically important to both sides during the Civil War. [8] As the junction point for railroads to Atlanta, Georgia, and Memphis, Nashville, and Knoxville in Tennessee, Chattanooga provided a vital link for the movement of confederate troops and equipment. [9] In fact, the struggle for control of the railroads in the Fall of 1863 led to a series of battles in and around the city that may have determined the outcome of the war. [10] It was the Union general William Tecumseh Sherman's victory in the last of those confrontations, the Battle of Mission Ridge on November 24–25, that cleared the way for his devastating march through Georgia to the Sea.

Name _____ Date _____ Class _____

Using End Marks in Sentences

A **statement** (or **declarative sentence**) is followed by a period.

Pierre and Marie Curie discovered radium in 1898**.**

A **question** (or **interrogative sentence**) is followed by a question mark. However, do not use a question mark after a declarative sentence containing an indirect question.

Have you ever seen the José Greco Spanish Dance Company**?** [question]

Dad wants to know if we're ready to go yet**.** [declarative sentence]

A polite request is often put in question form even when it isn't actually a question. In that case, the sentence may be followed by either a period or a question mark.

Would you please call me**.**   *or*   Would you please call me**?**

An **imperative sentence** is followed by either a period or an exclamation point.

MILD COMMAND: Be quiet, class**.**   STRONG COMMAND: Stop talking**!**

An **exclamation** is followed by an exclamation point. An interjection at the beginning of a sentence is usually followed by a comma but may be followed by an exclamation point. Because an exclamation point is an end mark, the word that follows it should be capitalized.

Wow**,** what a great concert that was**!**   Wow**!** What a great concert that was**!**

A question mark or an exclamation point should be placed inside closing quotation marks when the quotation itself is a question or an exclamation. Otherwise, these punctuation marks belong *outside* the quotation marks.

Elaine shrieked, "There goes a mouse**!"**   Did Coach say, "Fake right**"?**

Exercise: Proofreading   Punctuate the following sentences, providing appropriate end marks. Add closing quotation marks where necessary.

EXAMPLE: 1. The shop owner yelled, "Stop, thief*!*"

1. Mr. Stanton, will you please give me a reference

2. Why does she always say, "Carry on, troops

3. The paramedic shouted, "Stand back

4. Look at the size of the fish I caught

5. The butler said quietly, "Would you please walk this way

6. I can't believe Elliot said, "The term paper's no problem

7. I wonder whether the repair will hold

8. Have you read Poe's short story "The Cask of Amontillado

9. Principal Jackson ordered, "Attend today's assembly

10. Trish is running for president of the senior class

MECHANICS

Chapter 12: Punctuation

 **WORKSHEET 2** *Other Uses of the Period*

An abbreviation is usually followed by a period.

    Dr. Rachel M. Stein   Green Ave.   2:00 P.M. (*or* p.m.)   A.D. 750

When an abbreviation that ends with a period is the last word in a statement, do not add another period as an end mark. *Do* add a question mark or an exclamation point if one is needed.

    Confucius was born in 551 B.C.   Were the first Olympic Games held in 776 B.C.?

Some common abbreviations, such as two-letter state codes, are written without periods.

    TX   WA   CIA   mm   kph   VCR

Note that two-letter state codes are used only when the ZIP Code is included.

    Pittsburgh, PA 15239   *but*   Seattle, Washington

Each letter or number in an outline or a list is followed by a period.

    Embroidery   Large Animals Discovered by Scientists
     I. Supplies   in the Twentieth Century
       A. Thread   1. Okapi
       B. Fabric   2. Long-nosed peccary
     II. Stitches   3. Komodo dragon

Exercise: Proofreading   For each of the following sentences, delete or insert periods as needed.

           EXAMPLE: 1. On Jan⊙1, 2000, my niece will celebrate her tenth birthday⊙

1. Please address all complaints to Dr Joseph S Redwing, Jr, Department of Consumer Affairs, 4749 Prospect St, Tulsa, O.K. 74101

2. In AD 1238, the Thai people created the first Thai nation, named *Sukothai*.

3. Are there any classes offered after 3:00 PM?

4. He's working for Boyd and Co..

5. The doctor increased my allergy shots to 0.5 cc. each week.

6. The last two items on our scavenger hunt list are

    9 an Orioles ball cap

    10 a monkey wrench

7. Did you know that WEB Du Bois was an early civil rights leader?

8. Sandra's new address is PO Box 787, Mt Vernon, NY 10551.

9. The Reardons said that they'd be here by 11:30 AM.

10. Are Mr and Mrs DeJong moving to Orlando, FL.?

Name _____ Date _____ Class _____

WORKSHEET 3   *Commas to Separate Items*

Use commas to separate items in a series.

    Would you prefer an apple**,** an orange**,** or some grapes?

When *and, or,* or *nor* joins the last two items in a series, you may omit the comma before the conjunction if the comma isn't needed to make the meaning clear. Sometimes the presence or absence of a comma changes the meaning of a sentence.

          CLEAR: The day was warm**,** muggy and still.

          CLEAR: Alan**,** Jan and I are leaving. [Alan is being addressed.]

          CLEAR: Alan**,** Jan**,** and I are leaving. [Alan is leaving, too.]

If all the items in a series are linked by *and, or,* or *nor,* do not use commas to separate them.

Do not place a comma before the first item in a series.

        INCORRECT: Loni has read poems by**,** Frost, Hughes, and Moore.

        CORRECT: Loni has read poems by Frost, Hughes, and Moore.

Short independent clauses may be separated by commas.

    Lightning flashed**,** thunder roared**,** and the earth shook.

Use a comma to separate two or more adjectives preceding a noun. When the last adjective before the noun is thought of as part of the noun, as in the compound noun *live oak,* the comma before the adjective is omitted. If one word in a series modifies the word following it, do not separate them with a comma.

    Bob prefers **narrow, colorful ties**.

    They're selling an **antique Western saddle**. [*Western* is part of a compound noun.]

    Have you seen Sue's **bright green convertible**? [*Bright* modifies *green*.]

Exercise: Proofreading   For each of the following sentences, add or delete commas as necessary. If a sentence is correct, write *C* on the line provided.

_____ 1. The firefighters arrived extinguished the blaze and returned to the station.

_____ 2. Jeff or Rafael or Bart will start as quarterback after the half.

_____ 3. In early spring, flowers bloom birds build nests and people's spirits rise.

_____ 4. The company put an intriguing classified ad in Sunday's paper.

_____ 5. My mom always asks me, where I'm going who'll be there and when I'll be home.

_____ 6. Al made a green salad ham and cheese sandwiches and unsweetened iced tea.

_____ 7. Should we go to the mall, or to the park, or to Yoko's house?

_____ 8. Armando sang danced and juggled in the talent show.

_____ 9. I like Renee because she is such a dependable sensitive person.

_____10. Vermont has green rolling valleys and lofty pine-crested mountains.

Chapter 12: Punctuation

 WORKSHEET 4 | *Commas to Join Clauses*

Use a comma before *and, but, or, nor, for, so,* and *yet* when they join independent clauses.

In Greek mythology Hercules battled the Hydra**,** and Perseus slew Medusa.

St. George is said to have slain a dragon**,** but scholars believe that tale evolved from the Perseus myth.

Don't confuse a compound sentence with a simple sentence that has a compound verb. Compound verbs, compound subjects, and compound objects are not separated by commas.

COMPOUND SENTENCE: In early Christian times the dragon was a symbol of sin**,** and many people heard the story of St. George and the dragon.

COMPOUND VERB: The largest living lizard **inhabits** an Indonesian island and **is called** the Komodo dragon.

COMPOUND SUBJECT: The **dragon** or **serpent** has long served as a symbol of humankind's ability to grapple with unknown forces.

COMPOUND OBJECT: The Komodo dragon has a long **tail** and rough **skin**.

Exercise: Proofreading   Add commas as needed to the following sentences. If a sentence is punctuated correctly, write *C* on the line provided.

_____ 1. Dragons never really existed but most ancient peoples believed in them.

_____ 2. Dragons were usually pictured as fire-breathing monsters that could swallow ships and humans in a single gulp.

_____ 3. Dragons were believed to inhabit unknown regions of the ancient world and they were said to destroy all intruders.

_____ 4. They were famous in early myths for people believed that dragons had existed long before human beings appeared on the earth.

_____ 5. In Anglo-Saxon literature Beowulf slew the monster Grendel but many years later the hero himself was killed by a dragon.

_____ 6. The hero died but the dragon was destroyed by Wiglaf, who lived on to rule in Beowulf's place.

_____ 7. The dragon in Chinese lore is very different for Asian cultures honor it as a kingly god.

_____ 8. The dragon disappeared from English literature for a long time but J.R.R. Tolkien introduced the dragon Smaug in *The Hobbit*.

_____ 9. Smaug lives in a mountain lair and there he guards his ill-gained treasure.

_____10. The hobbit Bilbo Baggins and a band of dwarfs defeat Smaug and recapture the treasure.

Name _____ Date _____ Class _____

WORKSHEET 5

Commas with Nonessential Elements

Use commas to set off nonessential clauses and nonessential participial phrases. A **nonessential** (or **nonrestrictive**) clause or participial phrase is one containing information that isn't needed to understand the main idea of the sentence.

NONESSENTIAL CLAUSE: Peggy Moore, **who grows her own vegetables,** finds gardening relaxing.

NONESSENTIAL PHRASE: The Declaration of Independence, **adopted in 1776,** was drafted by Thomas Jefferson.

If a nonessential element is removed from a sentence, the main idea remains clear.

Peggy Moore finds gardening relaxing.

The Declaration of Independence was drafted by Thomas Jefferson.

In contrast, an **essential** (or **restrictive**) clause or phrase is one that can't be left out without changing the meaning of the sentence. Essential clauses and phrases are *not* set off by commas.

ESSENTIAL CLAUSE: I think people **who litter** are thoughtless.

ESSENTIAL PHRASE: The theater **located on Forty-second Street** will be torn down.

The meaning of each of these sentences changes if the essential element is removed.

I think people are thoughtless.   The theater will be torn down.

Exercise   On the line before each sentence, write *N* if the italicized clause or phrase is nonessential. Write *E* if it is essential. Then add commas as needed.

EXAMPLE: ___E___ 1. The old Buick *that I drive* is like Ms. Reno's.

_____ 1. Employees *who always have a ready smile* make the job seem easier.

_____ 2. She is wearing the shirt *that she received for her birthday.*

_____ 3. A chile relleno *consisting of a stuffed, breaded green chile* is an appetizer.

_____ 4. People *who are overly nervous* may not make good drivers.

_____ 5. The watch *that I lost* was my grandfather's.

_____ 6. Cities *that seem alike* bear a closer look.

_____ 7. Lake Chad *covering an area of about six thousand square miles* is West Africa's largest body of water.

_____ 8. The Federal Reserve System *serving as the central bank of the United States* monitors money and credit growth.

_____ 9. That law *which met real needs a century ago* should be updated.

_____10. The Suez Canal *extending more than a hundred miles* links the Mediterranean Sea and the Red Sea.

Chapter 12: Punctuation

WORKSHEET 6

Commas with Introductory Elements

Use commas after one-word adverbs such as *first, yes,* and *no* or after any mild exclamation such as *well* or *why* at the beginning of a sentence.

Well, let's go to a movie.   **Okay,** I'll get my coat.

Hey, do you have the car keys?

Use a comma after an introductory **participial phrase** or a series of introductory **prepositional phrases**. A single prepositional phrase does not usually require a comma.

PARTICIPIAL PHRASE: **Hoping for a lead role,** she auditioned for the director.

PREPOSITIONAL PHRASES: **From the back of the theater,** he listened attentively.

SINGLE PREPOSITIONAL PHRASE: **After her number** the director applauded wildly.

Use a comma after an **adverb clause** at the beginning of a sentence or before any independent clause in the sentence.

When she came home, Letitia told us she got the part.

This is her first leading role; **although she's nervous,** I know she'll do well.

Exercise A: Proofreading   Add commas where they are necessary in each of the following sentences. If a sentence is punctuated correctly, write *C* on the line provided.

_____ 1. Walking as fast as possible we reached the store just before closing.

_____ 2. In the scene at the end of the movie *Casablanca* Rick says goodbye to Ilsa.

_____ 3. Planting onions or garlic next to your roses will benefit the roses greatly.

_____ 4. In a minute the train from Phoenix should arrive on Track 3.

_____ 5. Often confused with Mel Gibson my uncle Pierre is really handsome.

_____ 6. Whenever I see an old Fred Astaire film I regain my interest in dancing.

_____ 7. Why let's take dancing lessons together.

_____ 8. No I really have neither the time nor the talent.

_____ 9. At the corner of Fourteenth Street and Broad Street you'll see a Calder mobile.

_____10. When Johnny Carson retired from *The Tonight Show* Jay Leno became host.

Exercise B   On the line following each of these introductory elements, add words and punctuation marks to form complete sentences.

1. Well _____

2. Because I enjoy adventure movies _____

3. At the top of the hill behind the school _____

4. While sitting in the restaurant _____

5. In June _____

Chapter 12: Punctuation

WORKSHEET 7

Commas with Elements That Interrupt

Use commas to set off elements that interrupt a sentence. For instance, appositives and appositive phrases are usually set off by commas. An **appositive** is a noun or pronoun placed beside another noun or pronoun to identify or explain it. An **appositive phrase** consists of an appositive and its modifiers.

> Will Ann Richards, **the governor of Texas,** run for president?

Sometimes an appositive is so closely related to the word or words near it that it should not be set off by commas. Such an appositive is called a **restrictive appositive**.

> My cousin **Lurleen** grew up in Eureka Springs, Arkansas.

Words used in direct address are set off by commas.

> **Paul,** would you do this math problem?   Okay, **Mrs. Yamaguchi**.

Compound comparisons are set off by commas.

> Daphne's grades this year are as good as, **if not better than,** they were last year.

Parenthetical expressions are set off by commas. **Parenthetical expressions** are remarks that add incidental information or that relate ideas to each other.

> **After all,** we did win the championship.

> Generals who later became president include, **for example,** Ulysses S. Grant and Dwight D. Eisenhower.

> Audrey Hepburn, **not Katharine Hepburn,** stars in this old movie.

Exercise: Proofreading   Add commas as necessary to the following sentences. If a sentence is punctuated correctly, write C on the line provided.

_____ 1. Michael Jordan will be remembered I am sure as a great basketball player.

_____ 2. Right now I don't have time to play catch Joseph.

_____ 3. The poet Carl Sandburg lived in Chicago.

_____ 4. Becky goes to Wittenberg University a liberal arts college in central Ohio.

_____ 5. Tennessee Williams wrote the play _A Streetcar Named Desire_.

_____ 6. The character's name was Indiana Jones not Oklahoma Jones!

_____ 7. Chuck is already as tall as if not taller than his father.

_____ 8. Have you Nikki got any ideas that you'd like to share with us?

_____ 9. Alfred Nobel the man who established the Nobel Prize was a scientist.

_____10. He by the way was the person who invented dynamite.

Chapter 12: Punctuation

 *Commas Used for Clarity*

Use a comma between words or phrases that might otherwise confuse a reader. For instance, use a comma after an introductory adverb that might be confused with a preposition.

> Above, the jet plane roared through the clear blue sky. [comma needed to prevent reading *above the jet*]

Use a comma between a verbal and a noun that follows it if there is any possibility of misreading.

> After weeding, Jules put down a thick layer of mulch and watered the garden. [comma needed to prevent reading *after weeding Jules*]

Use a comma in an **elliptical construction** that replaces an independent clause. (Reminder: An elliptical construction is a word group from which one or more words have been left out.)

> Dinner was delicious; the company, lively. [The construction *the company, lively* takes the place of the independent clause *the company was lively*. The comma takes the place of *was*.]

Use a comma to separate most words that are repeated. However, do not use a comma between repeated words that are part of a verb phrase.

> COMMA: Soon, everyone we knew, knew that our house had been burglarized.

> NO COMMA: By the time we made our statements to the police, Mom and I had had a good talk.

Exercise: Proofreading   Add commas where they are needed in the following sentences. Some sentences may not require any additions.

> EXAMPLE: 1. All the news there was, was hopeful.

1. After we'll go to the skating rink.

2. James Bond is handsome; his manner suave.

3. Until we put the ad in the newspaper, we had had only a few calls about our car.

4. Before passing Janet made sure to signal her lane change with the turn indicator.

5. After warming up the engine runs just fine.

6. The map he has has ketchup on it.

7. Here take this to your mother.

8. The Hendersons having returned my little sister is delighted to have her playmate Sissy Henderson back.

9. After calling Ernesto went looking for the children.

10. Shana's backhand is very good; her forehand even better.

Chapter 12: Punctuation

Conventional Uses of Commas

Use commas to separate items in dates and addresses.

Please come to a party on Friday, July 8, 1994, at my house.

R.S.V.P. to Jackie at 1402 Seventh St., Quincy, MA 02169.

In dates, if the day is given before the month or only the month and year are given, no comma is used.

Where will we be on 1 January 2000?   I visited Hawaii in December 1992.

Use a comma after the salutation of a friendly letter and after the closing of any letter.

Dear Mom,   My dear Sara,   Yours truly,   Sincerely,

Use a comma after a personal name followed by an abbreviation such as *Jr., Sr., R.N.,* or *M.D.* and after a business name followed by an abbreviation such as *Ltd.* or *Inc.* Used within a sentence, such abbreviations are followed by a comma as well.

Jolene Wyatt, M.D., will give our commencement address.

Use a comma in numbers of more than three digits. Place the comma between groups of three digits, counting from the left of the decimal. However, do not use commas in ZIP Codes *(60623),* telephone numbers, house numbers, and four-digit years *(1971).*

$75,104.50   1,572 feet   50,000,000 miles

Exercise A: Proofreading   Add commas as necessary to the following sentences. If a sentence is punctuated correctly, write *C* on the line provided.

_____ 1. Rafael's address is 13 Henry Avenue Akron OH 45507.

_____ 2. On August 9 1934 my grandfather was born in San Juan Puerto Rico.

_____ 3. Marissa Valdez Ph.D. will be our guest on the fifth of October.

_____ 4. Harold P. Levinson Jr. opened a law office at 5 Dale Street Ames Iowa.

_____ 5. The town of Boxford celebrated its bicentennial on 6 June 1966.

Exercise B: Proofreading   In the following personal letter, six commas are missing, and four commas that do appear should be removed. Correct each error.

June 17 1994

Dear Brad

I will be leaving to attend Ohio State on 28 August, 1994. My last day of work at Bob's Diner is August, 26. I look forward to working with you again during my winter vacation, which begins on the fifteenth, of December. Meanwhile, please send my final paycheck to Box 1415, Ohio State University Columbus OH, 45508.

Sincerely

Eugene Roosevelt Jr.

Name _____ Date _____ Class _____

 Chapter 12: Punctuation

WORKSHEET 10 *Semicolons*

Use a **semicolon** between independent clauses that are closely related in thought and are not joined by *and, but, for, nor, or, so,* or *yet*.

Linda trains very hard; she hopes to run in the Boston Marathon next year.

Do not join independent clauses unless there is a close relationship between the main ideas.

NONSTANDARD: Luís is a good cook; I like Cajun food.

STANDARD: Luís is a good cook. I like Cajun food.

Use a semicolon between independent clauses joined by a transitional expression or a conjunctive adverb. Use a comma after the transitional expression or conjunctive adverb.

TRANSITIONAL EXPRESSION: Darnell is on the debate team and the student council; **in addition,** he plays varsity sports.

CONJUNCTIVE ADVERB: The sea is calm; **however,** a storm may be brewing.

Use a semicolon (rather than a comma) before a coordinating conjunction to join independent clauses that contain commas.

Scot, catching the ball, bumped the table; and the lamp fell on the floor.

Use a semicolon between items in a series if the items contain commas.

I would like to visit Madrid, Spain; Florence, Italy; and Fez, Morocco.

Exercise A: Proofreading   In the following sentences, replace commas with semicolons where necessary.

1. Winners included Mary, first place, Julia, second place, and Franco, third place.

2. The workers were dissatisfied, therefore, they considered a strike.

3. We are eager to go on vacation, the past few weeks have been strenuous.

4. Tony has accomplished quite a lot, on the other hand, Janis hasn't.

Exercise B: Revising   On the line provided, combine the related sentences, when appropriate. If the sentence pair is correct, write *C* on the line.

1. We were late for the game. As a result, we missed the kickoff.

_____

2. Jules is the yearbook editor. His father works for a newspaper.

_____

3. The producers are meeting. Please do not disturb them.

_____

4. Many events have been scheduled. For example, there are two concerts coming up.

_____

Chapter 12: Punctuation

Colons

Use a **colon** to mean "note what follows." For example, use a colon before a list of items, especially after expressions such as *as follows* and *the following*.

Please bring the following items**:** canned food, bottled water, and blankets.

Do not use a colon before a list that directly follows a verb or a preposition.

VERB: Some of my favorite poets **are** John Donne, Elizabeth Bishop, and Emma Lazarus.

PREPOSITION: Mrs. Torelli makes pesto **with** basil, garlic, and olive oil.

Use a colon before a quotation that lacks a speaker tag such as *he said* or *she remarked*. Additionally, use a colon before a long, formal statement or quotation.

Mother had had enough**:** "Everyone out of the kitchen right now!"

Use a colon between independent clauses when the second clause explains or restates the first clause. Capitalize the first word of the independent clause following the colon.

The signs are everywhere**:** This ecosystem is in trouble.

Use a colon between the hour and minute *(2:45)*, between chapter and verse when referring to passages from the Bible *(Exodus 1:2)*, between a title and subtitle *(Charles Drew: Surgeon and Teacher)*, and after the salutation of a business letter *(Dear Editor:)*.

Exercise A: Proofreading   Insert colons where necessary in the following sentences.

1. Hikers need the following equipment sturdy boots, light clothing, and a waterproof jacket.

2. The text of the pastor's sermon was Genesis 3 1–21.

3. The actor gave me advice "Learn your lines, be on time, and don't get emotional."

4. My paper was entitled "The Rain Forest Harvest of Shame."

5. You should take the 3 32 train to Columbus, where you'll catch the 5 07 to Dayton.

Exercise B: Proofreading   The following business letter contains five errors in punctuation. Correct each error.

Dear Mr. Lipinski

   Job openings at our store include: stockroom assistant, salesclerk in the linens

department, and secretary to the appliances manager. If you are interested in applying for

any of these positions, please come to my office tomorrow at 9 30 for an application. I feel

that you have the qualities: we at Allbright Stores look for in our employees.

                          Your truly:

                          Julia D. Vasco

MECHANICS

Chapter 12: Punctuation

 *Review*

Exercise A: Proofreading Add commas and end marks to the following sentences. Some sentences will require the addition of closing quotation marks as well as end marks.

EXAMPLE: 1. Well͵I think it's a good idea⊙

1. We went to the mall to the movies and to our favorite restaurant this afternoon

2. Students who do well in academic subjects should in my opinion be commended by their school administrators

3. No Sandy will not leave until the fifth of August

4. Hoping to meet Arsenio Hall we got tickets to a taping of his show

5. On the last day of school the juniors will prepare juice toast and ham and eggs for the seniors

6. Did Principal Reyes really say, "No detention today

7. Anyone who wants a ride should meet by the Fifth St bridge at 6:30 pm

8. My grandmother a housekeeper all her life saved her money invested wisely and put both of her children through college

9. Anne concluded her report on the field trip, saying, "What a wonderful time we all had

10. My best friend has moved to 9782 Revere Avenue New York NY 10465

11. When you go to Jim's house don't forget to return his book

12. Marilyn exclaimed, "It's a great day for a picnic, isn't it

13. We have already decided to hold our first class reunion on July 4 2003 at the Bollingbroke Hotel in San Francisco California

14. Using hyperbole the store claimed in a colorful full-page newspaper ad that it would be having the "World's Most Spectacular Labor Day Sale

15. When they went to the prom did Martha wear a lavender lace gown with blue satin ribbons and did George wear a light blue tuxedo

16. Unfolding the solar panels placing satellites into orbit and conducting medical experiments had kept the space shuttle crew busy

17. Because we had to rekindle the fire twice our cookout was delayed

18. Well if you apply to all eight colleges Paul you will pay a sizable sum in application fees

19. "It is my pleasure to introduce Vernon K Foster Jr. who has recently returned from a visit to Nairobi Kenya," said Adele Peters president of our school's Student Foreign Exchange League

Chapter 12, Worksheet 12, continued

20. The diplomats both educated at American University in Washington DC were assigned posts in Athens Greece and Nicosia Cyprus.

21. "The house is on fire" shouted my father. "Everyone get out right now

22. On the far wall to the right of the main entrance you will see a striking oil painting done in matte black ash white and neutral gray

23. Studying *Beowulf* for the first time the class particularly enjoyed Grendel the grim gruesome monster

24. The treasurer's report did I believe make it clear that the senior class has been very successful in its fund-raising activities this year

25. Interrupting his friends Philip asked, "Are you ready to leave

Exercise B: Proofreading   The following sentences are punctuated incorrectly. For each sentence, cross out the incorrect mark of punctuation and, if needed, fill in the correct mark above it. Add punctuation where necessary.

EXAMPLE: 1. When Jamie had finished, the chicken and salad were all gone; and the beans, carrots, and potatoes had been left untouched.

1. Traffic was stopped for the city's Martin Luther King Day parade consequently a massive traffic jam developed.

2. Don't forget to take your history book home this weekend, the test is Monday!

3. The recipes in *Spirit of the Harvest; North American Indian Cooking* are adapted for modern cooks yet the ingredients are all traditional.

4. One of my favorite biblical passages is the story of Jesus and the Samaritan woman in John 4, 5–42.

5. How good it was to see Aunt Marissa; Uncle Bill; and all of our cousins back in Tennessee.

6. The island of Tierra del Fuego named the Land of Fire by Ferdinand Magellan because of the many bonfires he saw there lies off the southern tip of South America in a cold windy climate!

7. When the doctor informed me that on the one hand only a very small percentage of people suffer a bad reaction to the vaccine and that on the other hand the disease that it prevents is nearly always fatal what could I do but agree to have the shot.

8. Ancient Mayan ruins tropical rain forests and beautiful mountains: are just a few of the sights I saw in Guatemala, where my cousins live.

9. Alex Haley the author of *Roots* attributed his interest in writing to stories his grandmother and great-aunts told.

10. Before you start putting that jigsaw puzzle together Rosa make sure that all of it will fit on the table.

Exercise C: Proofreading   Add semicolons and colons where they are needed in the following paragraphs.

[1] Arthur Mitchell blazed new trails in the world of ballet he became the American Ballet Theater's first African American male principal dancer, and he founded the Dance Theater of Harlem. [2] As a young man, Mitchell studied tap dance, modern dance, and ballet at a special high school for the performing arts, the challenges of ballet especially appealed to him. [3] After graduation from high school in 1952, Mitchell enrolled in the School of American Ballet, part of the New York City Ballet however, he continued modern dancing in other companies.

[4] Mitchell's fine technique and commanding style were impressive consequently, he was invited to join the New York City Ballet in 1955. [5] Director George Balanchine admired Mitchell as a result, Balanchine choreographed dances for Mitchell and cast him in many leading roles. [6] Among the New York City Ballet productions featuring Mitchell were these *Agon, Arcade, The Nutcracker,* and *Creation of the World.* [7] The company was often criticized for showcasing an African American dancer nevertheless, Balanchine remained adamant in his support for Mitchell.

[8] During his years with the New York City Ballet, Mitchell broke racial barriers, received much praise on foreign tours, and helped organize ballet companies in many countries but in 1968 Mitchell decided to form his own ballet company and school, which became the Dance Theater of Harlem. [9] The all-black ballet company quickly established a name for itself in fact, it is acclaimed throughout the world. [10] Critics and audiences have responded enthusiastically to such productions as the following *Creole Giselle, Fancy Free,* and *Firebird.*

Chapter 13: Punctuation

 **WORKSHEET 1** *Italics*

Italics are printed characters that slant to the right. To indicate italics in handwritten or typewritten work, use underlining. If you use a personal computer, you may be able to code words to print out in italics.

PRINTED: This summer I read *The Great Gatsby*.

HANDWRITTEN: *This summer I read* <u>*The Great Gatsby*</u>.

Use italics (underlining) for the following kinds of titles.

books	plays	long poems
periodicals	newspapers	works of art
films	television series	long musical compositions
recordings	comic strips	computer software

Did you see the review of *The Fugitive* in the *Orlando Sentinel*?

Also use italics for the names of court cases, trains, ships, aircraft, and spacecraft.

Someday I'd like to sail on the *Queen Elizabeth II* or ride on the *Orient Express*.

Use italics (underlining) for words, letters, and symbols referred to as such and for foreign words. However, many foreign words are now part of English vocabulary and are not italicized.

The word *eminent* begins with an *e*; *immanent* begins with an *i*.

The masculine symbol ♂ is also the symbol for the planet Mars.

Did you make *arroz con pollo*?   *but*   The house is made of adobe.

Exercise   Underline all items that should appear in italics in the following sentences.

1. Rodgers and Hammerstein wrote the musicals Oklahoma! and Carousel.

2. The presidential candidates made a television appearance last night on 60 Minutes.

3. The French phrase jeu d'esprit means "a witty remark."

4. I often have difficulty keeping the words affect and effect straight in my mind.

5. Die dulci fruere means "Have a nice day" in Latin according to the book Latin for All Occasions by Henry Beard.

6. Frank Capra, a Sicilian immigrant, made such film classics as It's a Wonderful Life and Mr. Smith Goes to Washington.

7. Remember not to use &'s in a formal paper.

8. The Titanic was supposedly "unsinkable," yet the ship sank in 1912.

9. In German, v is pronounced like the English f, and w sounds like the English v.

10. Grant Wood's painting American Gothic hangs in the Art Institute of Chicago.

Chapter 13: Punctuation

 **WORKSHEET 2** *Quotation Marks A*

Use quotation marks to enclose a **direct quotation**—a person's exact words. Do not use quotation marks to enclose an indirect quotation—a restatement of the person's words that is not exact. Notice that a direct quotation is preceded by a comma and begins with a capital letter. However, if the quotation is only a word or a phrase, do not introduce it with a comma or capitalize the first word.

> DIRECT QUOTATION: Grandma exclaimed, **"I'm so glad you've arrived!"**
>
> INDIRECT QUOTATION: Grandma said that she was glad we'd arrived.
>
> DIRECT QUOTATION: Grandma said she was **"so glad"** we'd arrived.

When the expression identifying the speaker divides a quoted sentence, the second part begins with a lowercase letter. However, when the second part of a divided quotation is a complete sentence, it begins with a capital letter.

> "Have you," asked Derek, "**s**een the Statue of Liberty?"
>
> "No, I haven't," I replied. "**M**aybe you can show it to me."

When a direct quotation of two or more sentences is *not* divided, only one set of quotation marks is used.

> "Please put away everything except a #2 pencil. Do not open your test booklets until I tell you to," instructed Mr. Garza.

A direct quotation is set off from the rest of the sentence by a comma, a question mark, or an exclamation point, but not by a period.

> "I don't have anything to do**,"** said Juana.
>
> "Why don't we go to the art museum**?"** Rick asked.
>
> "What a good idea**!"** she exclaimed. "There's always something interesting there!"

Exercise: Proofreading For each of the following sentences, insert or delete quotation marks and other marks of punctuation as needed. Identify each capitalization error by striking through the incorrect letter. Some sentences will also require the insertion of end marks.

1. "We should have started our homework earlier." "We have answered only three

   questions so far," said Beth.

2. Someone once asked Bernard Shaw how old he was, and he answered I'm as old as

   my tongue and a few years older than my teeth.

3. Can you tell me asked Mrs. Ross How many syllables are in a haiku?

4. My uncle Bob always says, If it ain't broke, don't fix it.

5. He ran down the street yelling Wait for me

Name _____ Date _____ Class _____

WORKSHEET 3 | *Quotation Marks B*

When used with quotation marks, other marks of punctuation are placed as follows:

Commas and periods are always placed inside the closing quotation marks.

"Wait a minute," Suzanne said. "I've almost got the answer."

Semicolons and colons are always placed outside the closing quotation marks.

The director said that Larry's English accent is "perfect"; his appearance, "just right": I'm sure he'll get the part.

Question marks and exclamation points are placed inside the closing quotation marks if the quotation itself is a question or an exclamation. Otherwise, they are placed outside.

INSIDE: Marlene wondered, "Which job offer should I accept?"

OUTSIDE: Why did he say, "It's none of your business"?

Use single quotation marks to enclose a quotation within a quotation.

Hillary confessed, "I'm not sure what he means by 'That's just the caterpillar's boots.'" [The period is placed inside the single quotation marks.]

"Would the general say, 'Might makes right'?" asked the reporter. [The question mark is placed inside the double quotation marks because the reporter's words, not the general's, form the question.]

When writing **dialogue**, begin a new paragraph every time the speaker changes.

The Greek philosopher Diogenes the Cynic lived in a huge barrel. One day, Alexander the Great peered in to see the great philosopher. "Is there anything that I can do for you?" Alexander asked.

"Yes," answered Diogenes. "I'd like you to stop blocking my light."

Exercise: Proofreading For each of the following sentences, insert quotation marks and other marks of punctuation as needed. Insert ¶ before a word that should begin a new paragraph.

EXAMPLE: 1. "Who said, 'Beauty seen is never lost'?" asked Robert.

1. Then, the witness continued, we heard someone yell Who's in there?

2. We winced as the umpire called Strike three!; the game was over.

3. How irritating it was to hear him say, All the tickets have been sold!

4. Who said Beauty is in the eye of the beholder?

5. Whistler painted a portrait of a man. Afterward, artist and subject looked at the picture together. "Well, said the subject, you can't call that a great work of art. Perhaps not, replied Whistler. But then you can hardly call yourself a great work of Nature.

Chapter 13: Punctuation

 **Quotation Marks C**

Use quotation marks to enclose titles of short works, such as short stories, poems, essays, articles, songs, TV episodes, chapter titles, and the titles of other parts of books.

> Did the chorus sing "America, the Beautiful"?

> Chapter 4 of *The Life of John Muir* is entitled "To the Sierras."

Neither italics nor quotation marks are used for the titles of major religious texts (the Bible, the Koran) or of legal or historical documents (the Declaration of Independence).

Use quotation marks to enclose the title of a short work that appears within an italicized title. Use single quotation marks for the title of a short work that appears within a title enclosed in quotation marks.

> *"Babylon Revisited" and Other Stories*   "The Elegy Form: 'Lycidas'"

Use italics for the title of a long work contained within a title enclosed in quotation marks.

> "Nature in *The Rime of the Ancient Mariner*"

Use quotation marks to enclose slang words, invented words, technical terms, and dictionary definitions of words.

> In Philadelphia, a submarine sandwich is called a "hoagie."

> The word *commodious* means "spacious; having plenty of room."

Exercise: Proofreading   Add single and double quotation marks to these sentences as needed. Some sentences may also require the addition of end marks.

1. Wilfred Owen's poetry of World War I was adapted by composer Benjamin Britten in the latter's *A War Requiem*, which contains the haunting piece The Next Year.

2. Katherine Mansfield's short story A Cup of Tea is an analysis of the heroine's inability to risk her own domestic security.

3. Gerard Manley Hopkins coined new words such as wanwood in his poetry.

4. Could you find the article *Gulliver's Travels* Revisited in our library?

5. Sheila asked, Is Chapter 3 of *Winter Tales* called Up the Creek?

6. The Sanskrit word *ahimsa* means reverence for life.

7. The Brontë children entertained themselves by telling each other stories about an imaginary country, which they called Gondol.

8. James said my new haircut was rad.

9. Robert Louis Stevenson settled in Samoa, where the native people called him Tusitala, which means teller of tales.

10. The chapter Coketown from Dickens's novel *Hard Times* describes the negative aspects of industrialization.

Name _____ Date _____ Class _____

 **WORKSHEET 5** | *Ellipsis Points*

An **ellipsis** is the omission of a word or words from a sentence or complete thought. Use **ellipsis points** (. . .) to mark omissions from quoted material and pauses in a written passage. If the material that comes before the ellipsis points is not a complete sentence, use three ellipsis points with a space before the first point and after the third point. (You should omit any commas that follow the phrase before inserting the points.)

"A friend is a person with whom **. . .** I may think aloud."

Ralph Waldo Emerson

If the material that comes before or after the ellipsis is a complete sentence, use an end mark before the ellipsis points.

I remember those days on the farm**. . . .**

To show that a full line or more of poetry has been omitted, use one entire line of spaced periods, as long as the line above.

To indicate a speaker's pause or hesitation, use three ellipsis points with a space before the first point and after the third point.

"Um **. . .** well, maybe I was mistaken," muttered Joey.

Exercise Replace the italicized parts of the following passages with ellipsis points.

1. True joy, *that elusive and fleeting spark of light,* makes life's dark sorrows bearable.

   _____

2. "I appreciate your confidence in me, *and I'll do my best to live up to it,*" said the candidate.

   _____

3. The bell rang. *The doors opened.* The playground erupted into a mass of squealing children.

   _____

4. Learn from today; and *when today is over,* store its lesson in your memory.

   _____

5. There was a young fellow of Perth,
   Who was born on the day of his birth;
   He was married, they say,
   On his wife's wedding day,
   And he died when he quitted the earth.

   _____

   _____

   _____

   _____

Name _____ Date _____ Class _____

 **WORKSHEET 6** *Apostrophes A*

The **possessive case** of a noun or pronoun shows ownership or relationship. To form the possessive of a singular noun or an indefinite pronoun, add an apostrophe and an *s*.

a **child's** toy   a **winter's** night   **Joan's** poem   **someone's** coat

To form the possessive of a singular noun ending in an *s* sound, add only an apostrophe if the noun has two or more syllables and if the addition of *'s* will make the noun awkward to pronounce. Otherwise, add *'s*.

for **goodness'** sake   **Ulysses'** travels   the **duchess's** gown

To form the possessive of a plural noun ending in *s*, add only the apostrophe.

the **Reeveses'** dog   the **carpets'** designs   my **aunts'** hats

Plural nouns that do not end in an *s* form the possessive by adding an apostrophe and an *s*.

the **men's** department   **geese's** tempers   **feet's** ticklishness

Form the possessive of only the last word in a compound word, in the name of an organization or business firm, or in a word group showing joint possession. However, form the possessive of each noun in a word group showing individual possession of similar items.

sister-in-law's job   Wilson & **Dulay's** offer   **Ted's** and **my** proposals

When used in the possessive form, words indicating time—such as *minute, hour, day, week, month,* and *year*—and words indicating amounts in cents or dollars require apostrophes.

two **weeks'** vacation   in a **month's** time   five **dollars'** worth

Possessive personal pronouns include *my, mine, your, yours, his, her, hers, its, our, ours, their,* and *theirs*. Do not use an apostrophe with these pronouns or with the possessive *whose*.

Exercise   Most of the following items contain incorrect possessive forms. On the lines provided, give the correct form of each word. If an item is correct, write *C*.

EXAMPLE: 1. Their's is better. *Theirs*

1. Al and her projects   _____

2. the wolves' den   _____

3. Is it your's?   _____

4. anyones' guess   _____

5. my two cent's worth   _____

6. childrens' literature   _____

7. Jenny's and Ramon's skit   _____

8. that girls' car   _____

9. plier's grip   _____

10. Chicago's jazz clubs   _____

Name _____ Date _____ Class _____

WORKSHEET 7   *Apostrophes B*

MECHANICS

A **contraction** is a shortened form of a word, word group, or figure in which an apostrophe takes the place of all the letters, words, or numbers that are omitted.

> hasn't [has not]   o'clock [of the clock]   we've [we have]   '92 [1992]

Do not confuse contractions with possessive pronouns.

> **Who's** coming to the party? [contraction]   **Whose** sweater is it? [possessive]

Use an apostrophe and an *s* to form the plural of all lowercase letters, some uppercase letters, and some words referred to as words. However, you may add only an *s* to form the plurals of such items—except lowercase letters—if the plural forms will not cause a misreading.

> Don't put little hearts over your *i*'s.   Those **TVs** are on sale.
>
> She doesn't want any *if*'s, *and*'s, or *but*'s.   *R*s mean "Referred clients."

NOTE: To form the plural of an abbreviation that ends with a period, add 's.

> B.A.'s   M.D.'s   Ph.D.'s

Use apostrophes consistently.

> I got three *A*'s and three *B*'s on my report card. [Without the apostrophe, the plural of *A* would spell *As*. The apostrophe in the plural of the letter *B* is unnecessary but is included for consistency.]

Exercise: Proofreading   On the lines provided, rewrite the words that are punctuated incorrectly, adding or deleting apostrophes and correcting spelling as needed.

> EXAMPLE: 1. Whose on Vickys bicycle? *Who's; Vicky's*

1. "The box sitting over there is your's, isnt it?" asked Tamara. _____

2. Darnell knew the day would be less than perfect when he heard himself saying, "Don't forget to dot your *t*s and cross your *i*s." _____

3. If your calling the repairman, wait; the TVs working fine now. _____

4. The flood of 32 mentioned in that history book occurred in 1832. _____

5. Leon's sister and my cousin are getting they're M.A.s this spring. _____

6. The *S*s and *I*s stand for "satisfactory" and "incomplete." _____

7. Our apartment is downtown; there's is uptown. _____

8. My brother joined the ranks of R.N.s in 93. _____

9. Their going to exchange VCRs at the flea market. _____

10. You're paper has too many *really*s and *very*s. _____

Chapter 13: Punctuation

WORKSHEET 8 | *Hyphens*

Use a **hyphen** to divide a word at the end of a line. Divide a word only between syllables.

Is your cousin the one who designs **inter-active** video games?　　My mother is learning how to **pro-gram** computers.

Do not divide a one-syllable word.

INCORRECT: His games are lov-ed by millions.　　CORRECT: His games are **loved** by millions.

Divide a word that is already hyphenated only at the hyphen.

INCORRECT: Yes, he's a self-em-ployed designer.　　CORRECT: Yes, he's a **self-employed** designer.

Use a hyphen with the prefixes *ex–*, *self–*, and *all–*, with the suffix *–elect*, and with all prefixes before proper nouns or proper adjectives.

ex-chairman　　**self-**conscious　　**all-**pro　　mayor**-elect**　　**pro-**American

Use hyphens with compound numbers from *twenty-one* to *ninety-nine* and with fractions used as modifiers.

one thousand **forty-eight**　　**three-fourths** majority　　**two-thirds** full

In general, hyphenate a compound adjective only when it precedes the noun it modifies. However, do not use a hyphen if one of the modifiers is an adverb ending in *–ly*.

a well**-**written poem　　a beautifully written poem　　a poem that is well written

Exercise A　On the lines provided, use hyphens to show how each of the following words should be broken at the end of a line. If a word should not be divided, write *no hyphen*.

EXAMPLE: 1. funny *fun-ny*

1. eighty-nine _____
2. mid-October _____
3. handbag _____
4. around _____
5. strength _____

Exercise B　For each phrase below, place a caret (∧) to indicate where a hyphen should be inserted. Some phrases may not require the insertion of hyphens.

EXAMPLE: 1. a well∧traveled route

1. a wooded island in the mid Pacific
2. a four fifths majority
3. a self fulfilling prophesy
4. a fully lined jacket
5. twenty senators elect

Chapter 13: Punctuation

Dashes

Use a dash to indicate an abrupt break in thought. If the sentence continues, use a second dash after the interruption.

"That music—please turn it down—is certainly interesting," said Grandpa.

Use a dash to mean *namely, in other words, that is,* and similar expressions that come before an explanation.

Five dollars—the exact price of a ticket—is missing from my purse.

Use dashes to set off an appositive or a parenthetical expression that contains commas.

The American Transcendentalists—Thoreau, Emerson, Margaret Fuller, and the Alcotts, to name a few—were a band of New England intellectual rebels.

Use a dash to set off an introductory list or group of examples.

Lemonade, cranberry juice, and ginger ale—these are the base of Annie's delicious fruit punch.

Exercise For each of the following sentences, insert dashes where they are needed.

EXAMPLE: 1. W. C. Fields $_\wedge$ I just love his movies $_\wedge$ was born in Philadelphia.

1. This book perhaps you've already read it is excellent.

2. Dr. Percy Lavon Julian, who was born in Montgomery, Alabama, is noted for developing helpful drugs from this surprised me, too soybeans.

3. Some offspring of famous performers Michael Douglas, Liza Minelli, Jeff and Beau Bridges, and Jane Fonda, for example have established award-winning careers for themselves.

4. Zoë is very competitive; she wants only one thing to win.

5. A flashlight, a tire pressure gauge, and a first-aid kit all of these are good things to keep in your car.

6. Eating cruciferous vegetables cabbage, broccoli, cauliflower, and Brussels sprouts is thought to prevent certain kinds of cancer.

7. Please hand me ouch a potholder; this pan is hot!

8. Is that large dog the one with the white, shaggy hair a Hungarian komondor?

9. What great I mean, terrible news: School's closed on account of snow.

10. Michael has one dream to win an Olympic medal that keeps him skating four hours a day.

Chapter 13: Punctuation

Parentheses

Use parentheses to enclose informative or explanatory material of minor importance. Be sure that the material enclosed in parentheses can be omitted without losing important information or changing the basic meaning and construction of the sentence.

Lana (she married my brother) has offered me a summer job.

Lou Gehrig (1903–1941) was a courageous man.

A parenthetical sentence that falls within another sentence should not begin with a capital letter unless it begins with a word that should always be capitalized. A parenthetical sentence that falls within another sentence should not end with a period, but may end with a question mark or an exclamation point.

San Marino (see map on page 126) is a small country, only 23 square miles.

My uncle (do you remember him?) has joined the Peace Corps.

A parenthetical sentence that stands by itself following a sentence should begin with a capital letter and should end with a period, a question mark, or an exclamation point before the closing parenthesis.

The state bird of Texas is the mockingbird. (See figure on page 456.)

When parenthetical material falls within a sentence, punctuation should never come before the opening parenthesis but may follow the closing parenthesis.

In Chief Joseph's speech of surrender (1877), we have a powerful example of Native American oratory.

In a formal research paper, use parentheses to identify the source of quoted or paraphrased material.

The real-life exploits of Jean Rhys gave her invaluable material for her writing (Larson, 322).

Exercise: Proofreading   Parentheses are missing in each of the following items. Insert parentheses, capital letters, and end marks where appropriate.

EXAMPLE: 1. Kirk Douglas (born Issur Danielovitch) has been a popular movie star for years.

1. Diana Ross wasn't she a member of the Supremes starred in a film version of Billie Holiday's life.

2. Thomas Paine 1737–1809 wrote the pamphlet *Common Sense.*

3. The home of Andrew Wyeth is Chadds Ford. That's in southeastern Pennsylvania.

4. When the movie critic mentioned Marlene Dietrich's classic film *The Blue Angel* 1930, only Rachel had heard of it.

5. Goldfish are relatively long-lived animals and even in captivity may live twenty years or more Tanaka, 47.

Name _____ Date _____ Class _____

Brackets and Slashes

Use brackets to enclose an explanation within quoted or parenthetical material.

The actor exclaimed, "This [award] means a lot to me!"

Harry Lillis Crosby (commonly called "Bing" [1903–1977]) was a popular crooner of my grandmother's generation.

Use brackets and the Latin word *sic* to indicate that an error existed in the original of a quoted passage.

"Bing Cosby [*sic*] No Relation to Bill Cosby!" screamed the tabloid's headline.

Use a slash between words to indicate that both terms apply. There is no space before or after the slash.

I've always liked singer/songwriter Kris Kristofferson's gravelly voice.

Each examinee should bring his/her own sharpened #2 pencils and an eraser. [Avoid using terms like *he/she* and *and/or* as much as possible because they can make your writing choppy.]

Within a paragraph, use a slash to mark the end of a line quoted from poetry or from a verse play. In such verse excerpts, the slash has a space on either side of it.

After noting that all superficial attractions pass, Elizabeth Barrett Browning admonishes her lover: "But love me for love's sake, that evermore / Thou may'st love on, through love's eternity."

NOTE: The slash is also commonly used in writing fractions and ratios.

FRACTIONS:	1/3 c	4 3/4 in
RATIOS:	157 ft/sec	65 mi/hr

Exercise Proofread the following sentences, and correct any errors in the use of punctuation. If a sentence is correct, write *C*.

EXAMPLE: _____ 1. The newspaper quoted Mr. Busch as saying, "People who take it [Auto Mechanics I] usually are glad they did."

_____ 1. The Kaufmann house (better known as "Fallingwater" (built in 1936)) is, in my opinion, one of Frank Lloyd Wright's finest structures.

_____ 2. His best tennis serves, clocked at more than 90 mi hr, are quite impressive.

_____ 3. "We ain't '*sic*' leaving until we see the mayor," one citizen said.

_____ 4. Christine was quoted as saying in her valedictory speech: "We are not at an end but a beginning, and it—graduation—marks an exciting time of change in our lives."

_____ 5. What do you suppose the poet means when she says, "The garden of my mind / Is burgeoning with fruit"?

MECHANICS

Chapter 13: Punctuation

WORKSHEET 12 *Review*

Exercise A: Proofreading   On the lines provided, correct the following sentences by adding italics (underlining), quotation marks, other marks of punctuation, and capitalization.

EXAMPLE: 1. Bill said, I've finished reading The Scarlet Letter.
   Bill said, "I've finished reading The Scarlet Letter."

1. Ralph Ellison's essay Hidden Name and Complex Fate is included in his book Shadow and Act. _____

_____

2. Is it true, she asked that only the anthem O Canada would be sung in a World Series between Toronto and Montreal? _____

_____

3. Celeste asked whether the word scissors is considered singular or plural.

_____

_____

4. Our scuba diving instructor tried to encourage us beginners with the words of Franklin D. Roosevelt: The only thing we have to fear is fear itself. _____

_____

5. The French expression sans blague means no kidding. _____

_____

6. Did he mean No, turn right or Yes, turn left. _____

_____

7. For tomorrow's assignment, class, you are to read Chapter One in the book Exploring Physics, said Mr. Abernathy. _____

_____

8. Who wrote the poem Elegy Written in a Country Churchyard? _____

_____

9. If I'd known that you were going to the party, Norris said, I'd have offered you a ride.

_____

_____

10. Salvador announced proudly, I've learned to play The Star-Spangled Banner on the piano.

_____

_____

Exercise B   The following expressions involve the use of dashes, parentheses, hyphens, and apostrophes. Each item consists of three expressions. Two of the expressions are correct; one is wrong. Find the wrong expression, and then write the expression correctly on the line provided.

1. [a] a four-fifths majority [b] one half of the students [c] a magnificently-drawn picture

   _____

2. [a] during it's early years [b] the attorney general's ruling [c] Lewis Cass's speech

   _____

3. [a] They're all in the car. [b] He does'nt think we know. [c] The +'s and −'s are not clear.

   _____

4. [a] I thought—and still think—she knew the answer. [b] Representative Ferraro (New York) had opposed the measure. [c] His remarks were pro Italian.

   _____

5. [a] Sallys and my opinions [b] twenty minutes' work [c] a notebook that is yours

   _____

Exercise C   On the lines provided, rewrite the following items, omitting the parts that appear in italics. Use ellipsis points to indicate where the material has been omitted.

1. Julio is a *hard-working, talented* machinist.

   _____

2. Wherever I go, *whatever I do,* I'll always remember you.

   _____

3. Simone loves rice pudding. *She's coming over.* Let's make some for her.

   _____

4. And did young Stephen sicken, _____

   And did young Stephen die?   _____

   And did the sad hearts thicken,   _____

   And did the mourners cry?   _____

   — Mark Twain, from *Huckleberry Finn*

Exercise D Revise the following groups of words by inserting apostrophes and hyphens where needed.

1. Its a pagoda, isnt it?

2. Shes wearing a sari, Im sure.

3. almost two thirds full

4. Whats its title?

5. mices nest

6. antiimperialism

7. Frank and Carlos party

8. four dollars worth

9. the judges opinions

10. my sister-in-laws job

11. a highly motivat ed employee

12. His grades in French are all As.

13. Lets see whats going on.

14. those firefighters hats

15. that Doberman pinschers owner

16. Maria and Cams trip

17. preColumbian artifact

18. Her cousins choices were the same as hers.

19. speech of the mayor elect

20. a well spoken individual

Exercise E On the lines provided, rewrite each of the following words, using a hyphen to show how they should be broken at the end of a line. If a word should not be divided, write *no hyphen*.

1. self-assured   _____

2. environmentalism   _____

3. friend   _____

4. about   _____

5. daylight   _____

Exercise F: Proofreading Proofread and correct each item by deleting incorrect punctuation and inserting slashes or brackets as needed. If an item is correct, write C on the line provided.

EXAMPLE: _____ 1. Lauren Hutton is an actor⁄model.

_____ 1. Canned and, or boxed food donations will be accepted.

_____ 2. Mark Twain (pseudonym for Samuel Clemens (1835–1910)) wrote powerful satire.

_____ 3. "All's *(sic)* I want is to fight corruption in government," declared the candidate.

_____ 4. "It—the surprise party—was more than I could have hoped for!" Mona told the press.

_____ 5. 34 ft/sec

Chapter 14: Spelling and Vocabulary

Improving Your Spelling

Using the following techniques will improve your spelling.

Pronounce words carefully. Most people spell "by ear"—that is, by how a word sounds. If you are not sure about the correct pronunciation of a word, look it up in a current dictionary.

> ath•let•ic [*not* a•the•let•ic]   soph•o•more [*not* soph•more]

Spell by syllables. A **syllable** is any of the units into which a word can be divided. A syllable is a unit of pronunciation.

> prob•a•bly [three syllables]   co•in•ci•den•tal [five syllables]

Use a dictionary. By using a dictionary, you will become familiar with the correct pronunciations and divisions of words. When you check the spelling of a word, make sure that its use isn't limited by a label such as *British* or *chiefly British*. Also check for labels such as *obsolete* or *archaic*.

Proofread for careless spelling errors. Always reread what you have written in order to eliminate careless spelling errors. For example, avoid errors such as transpositions (*thier* for *their*), missing letters (*libary* for *library*), and the misuse of similar-sounding words (*peace* for *piece*).

Keep a spelling notebook. Divide each page into four columns.
> Column 1: Write correctly any word you find troublesome.
> Column 2: Write the word again, dividing it into syllables and marking the stressed syllable(s). (Use a dictionary to check your work.)
> Column 3: Write the word again, circling any part that causes you trouble.
> Column 4: Jot down any comments that will help you remember the correct spelling.

Exercise On the line provided, write the syllables of each of the following words, placing hyphens between the syllables. Do *not* look the words up in a dictionary. Be sure that the division of each word includes all of the letters of the word. Use your dictionary to check your work when you are finished.

> EXAMPLE: 1. emperor *em-per-or*

1. anonymous _____
2. biscuit _____
3. circumstantial _____
4. espionage _____
5. hygiene _____

6. inevitable _____
7. mediocre _____
8. naive _____
9. propaganda _____
10. vinegar _____

Chapter 14: Spelling and Vocabulary

 **WORKSHEET 2** *Roots and Prefixes*

The **root** of a word is the part that carries the word's core meaning. Many roots come from ancient Latin and Greek words. For example, the root –*aqu*– comes from the Latin word *aqua*, meaning "water." The English words with this root—*aquatic, aquarium,* and *aquamarine,* for example—all have something to do with water. A list of Greek and Latin roots that appear in many English words is given below.

Latin Root	Meaning	Greek Root	Meaning
–aud–, –audit–	hear	–anthro–	human
–bene–	well, good	–bibli–	book
–cogn–	know	–bio–	life
–magn–	large	–chron–	time
–omni–	all	–dem–	people
–par–	equal	–graph–	write, writing, study
–prim–	first, early	–log, –logue	study, word
–uni–	one	–phil–	like, love
–vid–, –vis–	see	–tele–	far, distant

A **prefix** is a word part or syllable added to the beginning of a word to create a new word with a different meaning. The following chart lists some of the Greek, Latin and Latin-French, and Old English prefixes that appear in English words. Their meanings are shown in parentheses.

Old English	Latin and Latin-French	Greek
be– (around, about)	de– (away, from, off)	anti– (against)
for– (away, off, from)	dis– (away, not)	dia– (through, across)
mis– (badly, not, wrongly)	in–, im– (not)	hyper– (excessive, over)
over– (above, excessive)	pre– (before)	para– (beside, beyond)
un– (not, reverse of)	semi– (half)	sym–, syn– (together, with)

When adding a prefix to a word, do not change the spelling of the original word.

Exercise The following words contain prefixes and roots from the previous charts. On the line provided, write the prefix and root of each word. Then write a definition of each word based on the meanings of the prefixes and roots. Check your definitions in a dictionary.

1. biography _____

2. diachronic _____

3. television _____

4. disparity _____

5. bibliophile _____

Name _____ Date _____ Class _____

WORKSHEET 3 *Suffixes*

MECHANICS

A **suffix** is a word part or syllable added to the end of a word to create a new word with a different meaning.

Source	Suffix	Meaning	Example
Old English	–ness	state, quality	loneliness

NOUN SUFFIXES

Greek,	–cy	state, condition	redundancy
Latin, and	–ism	act, manner	criticism
French	–tude	quality, state	fortitude
	–ty, –y	quality, state	subtlety

ADJECTIVE SUFFIXES

Greek,	–able, –ible	able, likely	invisible
Latin, and	–ic	person or thing showing	scientific
French	–ous	marked by	anxious
Old English	–ful	full of	joyful
	–some	apt to, like	nettlesome

VERB SUFFIXES

Greek,	–ate	become, cause	liberate
Latin, and	–fy	make, cause	amplify
French	–ize	make, cause	prioritize

Exercise Underline the suffix or suffixes in each word. Then guess the meaning of each word. Check your guesses in a dictionary.

1. troublesome _____

2. multitude _____

3. outrageous _____

4. magnify _____

5. skepticism _____

6. goodness _____

7. unity _____

8. synchronize _____

9. inaudible _____

10. demographic _____

Name _____ Date _____ Class _____

Spelling Rules A

Write *ie* when the sound is long *e*, except after *c*.

    EXAMPLES: **believe**   **ceiling**   **field**   **deceive**

    EXCEPTIONS: **either**   **leisure**   **weird**   **seize**

Write *ei* when the sound is not long *e*. [Note: These rules apply only when the *i* and the *e* are in the same syllable.]

    EXAMPLES: **forfeit**   **height**   **freight**   **neighbor**

    EXCEPTIONS: **ancient**   **conscience**   **friend**   **mischief**

The only English word ending in *–sede* is *supersede*. The only English words ending in *–ceed* are *exceed*, *proceed*, and *succeed*. All other English words with this sound end in *–cede*.

    EXAMPLES: **accede**   **concede**   **intercede**   **precede**   **recede**   **secede**

Exercise A   On the line provided, correctly spell each word below by adding *ie* or *ei*.

1. th. . .f   _____

2. v. . .n   _____

3. handkerch. . .f   _____

4. for. . .gn   _____

5. f. . .rce   _____

6. interv. . .w   _____

7. sl. . .gh   _____

8. rec. . .ve   _____

9. conc. . .ve   _____

10. . . .ghteen   _____

Exercise B: Proofreading   Correct any errors in spelling in each of the following sentences by writing the correction above the sentence.

           EXAMPLE: 1. The writings of Henry David Thoreau have inspired

                   succeeding   *readers*   *death*

               each ~~succeding~~ generation of ~~reeders~~ since his ~~deth~~.

1. Thoreau's nieghbors conceeded that he was eccentric.

2. Mrs. Byrne proseded to discuss *Civil Disobedeince*.

3. Thoreau, an abolitionist, treid to interceed for John Brown after the arrests at Harpers Ferry.

4. Thoreau's principles often superceeded more practical concerns, and he resigned a teaching job rather then use corpral punishment on his students.

5. The influence of Thoreau's ideas has not receeded; in fact, his writings have inspired such grate twentieth-century thinkers as Mahatma Gandhi and Martin Luther King, Jr.

Name _____ Date _____ Class _____

Spelling Rules B

When adding a prefix, do not change the spelling of the original word.

    re + print = **re**print   over + run = **over**run   un + necessary = **un**necessary

When adding the suffix *–ness* or *–ly*, do not change the spelling of the original word. One-syllable adjectives ending in *y* also generally follow this rule.

    open + ness = open**ness**   soft + ly = soft**ly**   shy + ly = shy**ly**

However, for most other words ending in *y*, change the *y* to *i* before adding *–ness* or *–ly*.

    heavy + ness = heav**iness**   busy + ly = bus**ily**

Drop the final silent *e* before a suffix beginning with a vowel.

    care + ing = car**ing**   active + ity = activ**ity**   use + able = us**able**

Keep the final silent *e* in words ending in *ce* or *ge* before a suffix beginning with *a* or *o*.

    notice + able = notic**eable**   courage + ous = courag**eous**

Additionally, keep the silent *e* when adding *–ing* to the words *dye* and *singe* (*dyeing, singeing*) or when adding *–age* to the word *mile* (*mileage*).

When adding *–ing* to words that end in *ie*, drop the *e* and change the *i* to *y*.

          EXAMPLES: die + ing = d**ying**   lie + ing = l**ying**

Keep the final silent *e* before a suffix beginning with a consonant.

          EXAMPLES: care + ful = car**eful**   amuse + ment = amus**ement**
        EXCEPTIONS: true + ly = tru**ly**   argue + ment = argu**ment**
                     awe + ful = aw**ful**   whole + ly = whol**ly**

For words ending in *y* preceded by a consonant, change the *y* to *i* before any suffix that does not begin with *i*.

          EXAMPLES: funny + er = funn**ier**   reply + ed = repl**ied**

For words ending in *y* preceded by a vowel, keep the *y* when adding a suffix.

          EXAMPLES: gray + est = gray**est**   convey + ing = convey**ing**
        EXCEPTIONS: day + ly = **daily**   say + ed = **said** [the *–ed* drops its *e*]

Exercise On the line provided, spell each of the following words using the given suffix.

  1. silly + ness   _____   6. hope + ing   _____

  2. desire + ed   _____   7. heavy + est   _____

  3. due + ly   _____   8. spicy + er   _____

  4. habitual + ly   _____   9. approve + al   _____

  5. use + less   _____   10. pay + ed   _____

MECHANICS

Chapter 14: Spelling and Vocabulary

Spelling Rules C

Double the final consonant before a suffix that begins with a vowel if the word (1) has only one syllable or is accented on the last syllable *and* (2) ends in a single consonant preceded by a single vowel.

> EXAMPLES: excel + ed = excel**led**   forget + able = forget**table**

For words ending in *w* or *x*, do not double the final consonant.

> EXAMPLES: mow + ing = mow**ing**   relax + ed = relax**ed**

For words ending in *c*, add *k* before the suffix instead of doubling the *c*.

> EXAMPLES: picnic + ing = picnic**king**   frolic + ed = frolic**ked**

Do not double the final consonant unless the word satisfies the conditions (1 and 2) given above.

> EXAMPLES: creep + ing = creep**ing** [has one syllable but does not end in a single consonant preceded by a single vowel]
>
> benefit + ed = benefit**ed** [ends in a single consonant preceded by a single vowel but doesn't have accent on last syllable]

When a word satisfies both conditions but the addition of the suffix causes the accent to shift, do not double the final consonant.

> EXAMPLES: confer + ence = confer**ence** [*but:* confer**red**]
>
> refer + ence = refer**ence** [*but:* refer**ral**]
>
> EXCEPTIONS: excel—excel**lent**, excel**lence**, excel**lency**

The final consonant of some words may or may not be doubled. Either spelling is acceptable.

> EXAMPLE: cancel + ed = cancel**ed** *or* cancel**led**

Exercise   On the line provided, spell each of the following words using the given suffix.

1. commit + ing   _____
2. defer + ence   _____
3. mimic + ing   _____
4. green + er   _____
5. prefer + able   _____
6. defer + ed   _____
7. panic + y   _____
8. repel + ant   _____
9. profit + able   _____
10. billow + ing   _____

11. saw + ing   _____
12. wax + ed   _____
13. red + est   _____
14. patrol + ing   _____
15. run + er   _____
16. omit + ed   _____
17. fool + ish   _____
18. begin + ing   _____
19. infer + ence   _____
20. paradox + ical   _____

Chapter 14: Spelling and Vocabulary

Forming Plurals A

Remembering the following rules will help you spell the plural forms of nouns.

For most nouns, including proper nouns, add –*s*.

artist → artists   journey → journeys   Brady → Bradys

For nouns ending in *s, x, z, ch,* or *sh,* add –*es*.

dress → dress**es**   birch → birch**es**   waltz → waltz**es**

For nouns ending in *y* preceded by a vowel, add –*s*.

monkey → monkey**s**   essay → essay**s**   Friday → Friday**s**

For nouns ending in *y* preceded by a consonant, change the *y* to *i* and add –*es*. For proper nouns ending in *y,* add –*s*.

enemy → enem**ies**   ally → all**ies**   trophy → troph**ies**   Mallory → Mallory**s**

For some nouns ending in *f* or *fe,* add –*s*. For others, change the *f* or *fe* to *v* and add –*es*. For proper nouns, add –*s*.

chief → chiefs   carafe → carafes   wharf → whar**ves**   loaf → loa**ves**
Woolf → Woolf**s**

For nouns ending in *o* preceded by a vowel, add –*s*.

studio → studios   cameo → cameos   igloo → igloos   Matsuo → Matsuos

For nouns ending in *o* preceded by a consonant, add –*es*.

veto → vet**oes**   tomato → tomat**oes**   torpedo → torped**oes**

For some common nouns ending in *o* preceded by a consonant, especially those referring to music, and for proper nouns, add only an –*s*.

soprano → sopranos   photo → photos   alto → altos   Navajo → Navajos

NOTE: For some nouns ending in *o* preceded by a consonant, you may add either –*s* or –*es* (motto → mottos *or* mottoes; zero → zeros *or* zeroes). When in doubt about how to form a plural, consult a current dictionary.

Exercise   On the line provided, spell the plural form of each of the following nouns.

1. dish _____
2. potato _____
3. stereo _____
4. puppy _____
5. roof _____

6. piano _____
7. donkey _____
8. Kennedy _____
9. knife _____
10. patio _____

MECHANICS

Name _____ Date _____ Class _____

 **WORKSHEET 8** *Forming Plurals B*

Remembering the following rules will help you spell the plural forms of nouns.

The plurals of a few nouns are formed in irregular ways.

    mouse → mice   woman → women   tooth → teeth   foot → feet

For a few nouns, the singular and plural forms are the same.

    deer   pliers   Sioux   trout

For most compound nouns, form the plural of only the last word of the compound.

    seatbelt → seatbelts   two-year-old → two-year-olds

    senior citizen → senior citizens

For compound nouns in which one of the words is modified by the other word or words, form the plural of the noun modified.

    runner-up → runners-up   court of law → courts of law

For some nouns borrowed from other languages, the plurals are formed as in the original languages.

    alumnus → alumni   phenomenon → phenomena   datum → data

To form the plurals of figures, most uppercase letters, signs, and words used as words, add an –s or both an apostrophe and an –s.

SINGULAR:	*3*	1800	*Z*	*+*	*if*
PLURAL:	*3*s	1800s	*Z*s	*+*s	*if*s
	or	*or*	*or*	*or*	*or*
	3's	1800's	*Z*'s	*+*'s	*if*'s

To prevent confusion, add both an apostrophe and an *s* to form the plurals of all lowercase letters, certain uppercase letters, and some words used as words.

    These *U*'s stand for "unsatisfactory." [Without an apostrophe, the plural of *U* could be confused with *Us.*]

Exercise On the line provided, spell the plural form of each of the following nouns. (Note: Italics indicate words used as words or letters used as letters.)

1. justice of the peace _____

2. *m* _____

3. scissors _____

4. sheep _____

5. 1400 _____

6. child _____

7. *&* _____

8. baby sitter _____

9. analysis _____

10. *E* _____

Name _____ Date _____ Class _____

Using Context Clues A

WORKSHEET 9

Often, you can figure out the meanings of unfamiliar words by using **context clues.** The **context** of a word is made up of the phrases and sentences that surround it. Here are three types of context clues:

Definitions or restatements: Look for words or phrases that define or restate the meaning of the word.

> He finally overcame his overriding **phobia,** or fear, of heights. [The context indicates that *phobia* means "great fear."]

Examples: A word may be accompanied by examples that illustrate its meaning.

> Typical *Märchen* include "Rapunzel," "Beauty and the Beast," and "Cinderella." [The examples given suggest that *Märchen* are folk tales or fairy tales.]

Synonyms: Look for clues that indicate that an unfamiliar word is similar in meaning to a familiar word.

> Fire department rules demand that theaters mark all routes of **egress** from the building with exit signs. [The context indicates that *egress* means "exit" or "way out."]

Exercise   For the italicized word in each of the following sentences, write a short definition based on the clues you find in the context. Check your definitions in a dictionary.

1. I knew I'd made a bad mistake, but I wasn't prepared for Elton's judgment that it was a

    "totally *egregious*" error. _____

2. *Fabrications* can run the range from "little white lies" to outrageous "whoppers."

    _____

3. Landscapers, nursery owners, and farmers share an interest in *horticulture*.

    _____

4. I didn't want to get into an argument, but Ted insisted on being *contentious*.

    _____

5. If you feel that the *remuneration* is low, you should ask for a raise. _____

    _____

Chapter 14: Spelling and Vocabulary

 **WORKSHEET 10** *Using Context Clues B*

Often, you can figure out the meanings of unfamiliar words by using **context clues.** The **context** of a word is made up of the phrases and sentences that surround it. Here are three types of context clues:

Comparisons: Sometimes an unknown word may be compared with a more familiar word.

> Of all the large rooms in the castle, the ballroom was by far the most **capacious.**
> [The context indicates that *capacious* means "large."]

Contrast: An unfamiliar word may be contrasted with a more familiar word.

> Some of the paintings were serious, but most of them seemed rather *frivolous.*
> [Clues suggest that *frivolous* means "light, not serious."]

Cause and effect: Look for clues that indicate that an unfamiliar word is related to the cause, or is the result, of an action, feeling, or idea.

> If you **remit** the money you owe, you will pay off the entire balance due. [Clues indicate that *remit* means "to send payment."]

When context clues are subtle, you must apply your own general knowledge. You can also draw connections between the unfamiliar word and the other information in the material.

> Len learned that years ago one of his **progenitors** was a hero of the Spanish Civil War. [The general context suggests that *progenitors* means "ancestors."]

Exercise   Use context clues in the following sentences to determine which definition from the list below matches each italicized word. On the line before each sentence, write the letter of the correct definition.

_____ 1. The frightened child answered in a small, *tremulous* voice.

_____ 2. The wealthy do not pay enough taxes to take care of the *indigent.*

_____ 3. The mayor seems very stern and totally *devoid* of humor.

_____ 4. The crowd was silent for a long time and then broke into *profuse* applause.

_____ 5. I washed the *dregs* from my cup of cocoa down the drain.

_____ 6. Unlike the cheery atmosphere at the winner's party, the room where the loser's supporters met seemed overshadowed by a *dolorous* cloud.

_____ 7. I'm not sure that my plan is *feasible,* but I'd like to try it.

_____ 8. A *favonian* wind created small ripples on the surface of the water.

_____ 9. This store carries the *gamut* of footwear from sneakers to formal shoes.

_____10. The colt *gamboled* while the old horse plodded along.

a. shaky	b. plentiful	c. leftovers	d. full range	e. frolicked
f. mild	g. poor	h. without	i. sorrowful	j. possible

Name _____ Date _____ Class _____

 **WORKSHEET 11** *Forming New Words*

New words in the English language are formed in the following ways:

(1) by **combining** two base words (words that can stand alone and that are complete in themselves) to make a compound, or by combining a word with an **affix** (a prefix or a suffix) or a word root

> BASE WORDS COMBINED: base + ball = baseball   self + made = self-made
>
> AFFIX ADDED: un– ("not") + happy = unhappy

(2) by **omitting** part of an original word, either to shorten it or to use it as another part of speech

> airplane → plane   cabriolet → cab   nuclear → nuke

(3) by **shortening** and **combining** two words

> breakfast + lunch = brunch   squirt + swish = squish

(4) by **expanding** the use of a word by using it as different parts of speech

> dump (v.) → dump (n.)

Exercise A   Each of the following words has come into the English language by one of the methods described above. Study the construction of the word. Then, on the line provided, write the letter of the correct definition of each word.

_____ 1. telethon   a. an overnight lodging (blend of *motor* and *hotel*)

_____ 2. hairdo   b. to steal (blend of *sweep* and *wipe*)

_____ 3. el   c. a way of arranging, or "doing," one's hair

_____ 4. swipe   d. a long program (blend of *television* and *marathon*)

_____ 5. motel   e. an elevated train

Exercise B   Each of the following sentences contains an italicized word that has come into the English language by one of the methods described above. On the line provided, write the original word(s) or word parts from which you would guess each new word was formed.

1. Aziz had too many fouls and was *benched* for the rest of the game.   _____

2. Our veterinarian showed us a preserved *tapeworm* in a jar.   _____

3. Rhonda works late every night, but she insists she's not a *workaholic*.   _____

4. Meet me at the *diner* for lunch.   _____

5. Do you know how to *twirl* a baton?   _____

Chapter 14: Spelling and Vocabulary

Choosing the Appropriate Word

Synonyms are words that share the same or nearly the same meaning. However, synonyms often have subtle shades of differences in meaning. Use a dictionary or a thesaurus to make sure you understand the exact differences in meaning between synonyms.

Many words have two kinds of meaning. The **denotative** meaning of a word is the meaning given by a dictionary. The **connotative** meaning of a word is the feeling or tone associated with it.

That **plant** with the purple flowers has spread all over the back yard. [The word *plant* denotes green, growing vegetation. The connotation of *plant* is neutral—neither good nor bad.]

That **weed** with the purple flowers has spread all over the back yard. [Although the word *weed* also denotes green, growing vegetation, the word carries the negative connotation of an unwanted pest.]

Exercise A   For each pair of words in parentheses, underline the word with the more appropriate connotation.

EXAMPLE: 1.   Cook the spaghetti in a pot of (boiling, feverish) water.

1. The (clever, cunning) student will note that there is a flaw in this algebraic formula.

2. Dishes and other artifacts from early civilizations are (infrequent, rare).

3. I (believe, perceive) that Alex Haley's *Roots* is the best book that I've ever read.

4. Howard (fashioned, forged) a quilt from the scraps of cloth.

5. Michael Bolton is a (notorious, popular) songwriter and performer.

Exercise B: Revising   Each of the following sentences is flat and uninteresting because it contains the overused word *nice*. On the line after each sentence, write a more interesting and specific synonym for *nice* that fits the context of the sentence. Change the article *a* to *an* if necessary.

1. The guest speaker gave a *nice* lecture about conservation.   _____

2. We enjoyed the *nice* scenery during our hike up the mountain.   _____

3. The philanthropist gave a *nice* donation to the science museum.   _____

4. The audience gave the chorus a *nice* round of applause.   _____

5. It is not considered *nice* to talk with your mouth full of food.   _____

Chapter 14: Spelling and Vocabulary

 **WORKSHEET 13** *Review*

Exercise A Underline the root and, where possible, the prefix or suffix in each of the following words. Then use the meaning of the word parts and your own knowledge to match each word with its correct definition. Write the letter of the correct definition on the line next to the word it defines.

_____ 1. magnanimous

_____ 2. audiology

_____ 3. univalve

_____ 4. prima donna

_____ 5. vista

a. a shellfish having a one-piece shell

b. a view or outlook

c. the science of hearing

d. generous, noble

e. the principal, or lead, female performer in an opera

Exercise B On the lines provided, spell each of the following words, adding the prefix or suffix given.

1. mis + state   _____

2. manage + able _____

3. bounty + ful   _____

4. spray + ing   _____

5. hurry + ed   _____

6. prefer + ed   _____

7. mad + er   _____

8. re + entry   _____

9. revolt + ing   _____

10. frolic + ing   _____

Exercise C: Proofreading Proofread the following sentences, and circle any misspelled words. On the lines provided, write any misspelled words correctly. If a sentence does not contain any spelling errors, write C.

1. The acter Boris Karloff was born in England in 1887.   _____

2. In a career that spanned more than fifty years, Karloff became fameous in films that repeatedily cast him as a villian.   _____

3. In his first film, *His Magesty, the American* (1919), Karloff played the evil leader of a gang of spies.   _____

4. In one of his final films, *The Incredible Invasion* (1971), he plays a scientist who's body is taken over by an alien from outer space.   _____

5. Other frightning films in which Karloff appeared include *The Ghoul, The Mummy, The Raven, The Black Cat,* and *The Terror.*   _____

6. Probably the most famous of all of Karloff's screen roles was that of the monster in *Frankenstein.*   _____

7. This film, based on a novell by Mary Shelley, made it's debut in 1931.   _____

8. Many movie versions of *Frankenstein* have been made, but
   Karloff was the first person to bring the role of the monster to the
   screen.   _____

9. The movie was so sucessful that sequels followed, including *The
   Bride of Frankenstein* (1935), *Son of Frankenstein* (1939), and *House
   of Frankenstein* (1944).   _____

10. Karloff also stared in some humerous films that made fun of
    typical monster movies, including *Abbott and Costello Meet the
    Killer: Boris Karloff*.   _____

Exercise D   Write the correct plural form of each of the following words.

1. booth   _____   6. beauty   _____

2. echo   _____   7. tomato   _____

3. wrench   _____   8. teaspoon   _____

4. district attorney _____   9. Swiss   _____

5. country   _____   10. loaf   _____

Exercise E   On the lines provided, write the letter of the definition that best fits the
meaning of the italicized word in each sentence. Use context clues for guidance.

a. disease   b. unruly, noisy   c. exciting   d. necessary   e. independent thinker

_____ 1. I got the job because my employer said that I had the *requisite* skills to do it
           well.

_____ 2. I find downhill skiing *exhilarating*, whereas cross-country skiing seems
           boring.

_____ 3. The leaves of the apple tree were black and limp due to *blight*.

_____ 4. Mauricio always follows the rules and agrees with the crowd, but Nigel is a
           maverick.

_____ 5. The kindergarten teacher stopped the lesson to quiet the *fractious* child.

Exercise F   For each pair of words in parentheses, underline the word with the
appropriate connotation.

1. The forest (smelled, stank) of fresh pine.

2. Dusty air had (dimmed, tarnished) the surface of the silver dish.

3. The hike up the steep mountain was (arduous, burdensome).

4. I felt (low-spirited, grief-stricken) when I was late for school.

5. Lizards have (harsh, rough), dry skin.

Chapter 15: The Writing Process

Freewriting and Brainstorming

When you're **freewriting,** you jot down whatever pops into your head.

1. Write for three to five minutes. Keep writing until your time is up.
2. Start with any topic or word, such as *jazz* or *in-line skates* or *freedom.*
3. Don't worry about using complete sentences or proper punctuation. Your thoughts may be disorganized. You may repeat yourself. That's perfectly OK.
4. From time to time, choose one key word or phrase from your freewriting and use it as a starting point for more writing. This **focused freewriting,** or **looping,** allows you to "loop" from what you've already written to something new.

Another way to generate ideas is through **brainstorming,** or using **free association**. You can brainstorm alone or with others by using the following steps:

1. Write a word, phrase, or topic on your paper or on the board.
2. Without any careful thought, begin listing every related word or idea that enters your mind. One person can write for a group.
3. Don't stop to evaluate the ideas. Anything goes, even jokes and ideas that seem to be off the topic.

Exercise A   You can freewrite anywhere. If you have started a journal, you can freewrite there. Start with this question: What's your favorite film? Write a few lines about the main characters. Then, on a separate sheet of paper, give yourself three minutes to write anything about the movie.

_____

_____

_____

_____

Exercise B   Choose one of the following subjects. Brainstorm about this subject either by yourself, with another student, or with a small group. Keep going until you've exhausted every possible idea. On the lines below, list the writing topics from your brainstorming session.

Subjects:

curfews	politics	computers
year-round schools	the "American Dream"	T-shirts

Subject chosen for brainstorming: _____

Possible topics gathered from brainstorming: _____

_____

_____

Chapter 15: The Writing Process

WORKSHEET 2

Clustering and Asking Questions

Clustering is another free-association technique. It is used to break up a large subject into its smaller parts or to gather information, but unlike brainstorming, it also shows connections. Clustering is sometimes called *webbing* or *making connections*.

1. Write a subject in the center of a sheet of paper. Draw a circle around the subject.

2. In the space around the circle, write all the words or ideas that come to mind. Circle each addition, and then connect it to the original subject with a line.

3. Create offshoots by adding and connecting related ideas. Then circle each related idea and connect it to the appropriate circle.

One good way to gather information is to use the reporter's **5W-How? questions:** *Who? What? Where? When? Why?* and *How?* Although not every question applies to every situation, the *5W-How?* questions are a good basic approach. You can also use the same *5W-How?* questions more than once about various aspects of your topic.

Exercise A   Choose one of the following subjects or use one of your own. Write your subject in the circle below. Then create a cluster diagram by thinking of ideas related to the subject and by following the steps listed above.

Subjects:

pollution	nuclear power	favorite vacation spots
television comedians	the Spanish language	women athletes

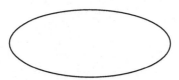

Exercise B   Where will you be at this time next year? Finding the right school or job may depend on asking the right questions. Identify a particular goal—a university, a college, a training program, an apprenticeship, or a job. Then ask at least five *5W-How?* questions about attaining this goal.

_____

_____

_____

_____

_____

_____

Name _____ Date _____ Class _____

Chapter 15: The Writing Process

WORKSHEET 3

Reading and Listening with a Focus

When you read to gather information, you have to be clearly focused. Once you've found a possible source of information, use these hints for finding and collecting information on a specific topic.

1. Give the source of information a "once-over." Look for key words in the index, the table of contents, and chapter headings and subheadings.

2. Skim passages until you find something about your topic; then slow down and take notes in your own words. Be sure to record publishing information for later use.

To listen with a focus, use the following hints.

1. Think ahead. Prepare questions you need to ask.

2. In an interview, concentrate on the question the person is answering.

3. Take notes even if you are recording. Don't try to write every word—use abbreviations and listen for main ideas and important details.

Exercise A "The yo-yo is enjoying a comeback," claims a 1991 newspaper article. When was it popular before? Do a little reading about amusement fads and see if you can find answers to the following questions.

1. What was an amusement fad from the 1950s? from the 1920s? _____

   _____

   _____

2. What are two dance fads from the past, and when were they popular? _____

   _____

   _____

3. What's something that began as a fad but became part of the mainstream culture?

   _____

Exercise B For the next few days, listen to radio (perhaps call-in shows and National Public Radio), television (sitcoms, commercials, "entertainment news," and MTV), and the conversations of students at your school. Then answer the following questions.

1. What fads are people following today? _____

   _____

   _____

2. What might they be doing in the future? _____

   _____

   _____

COMPOSITION

Chapter 15: The Writing Process

WORKSHEET 4 *Observing and Imagining*

One way to gather material for your writing is to look closely at the world around you. Remember, observation is purposeful and deliberate. It's important to use all five of your senses—sight, sound, smell, taste, and touch. It's also important to use your imagination. Try activating your imagination by asking *"What if?"* Here are some sample "What if?" questions:

- What if I could change my circumstances? (What if I had lived during the nineteenth century? What if I lived in the Middle East?)

- What if a familiar thing in our world no longer existed? (What if women could not vote? What if men could not vote?)

- What if major social changes were made overnight? (What if everyone voted on national legislation directly by computer hook-up?)

Exercise   A good story can be about almost anything. Think about the four places listed below. Then choose one and observe it carefully. Write down some descriptive details about each event or place as you might experience it through your five senses. Finally, go one step further by writing a few "What if?" questions that might lead to good story plots.

a park or field   a grocery store   your home at supper time   a hospital

EXAMPLE: Sensory perceptions: *On a boat*

gray sky; storm approaching; loud roar of the engine; smell of rain in the air; rocking of the boat on rough waters; taste of salt water spray

"What if?" *On a boat*

What if the engine failed? What if I spotted a nearby boat sinking?

Sensory perceptions: _____

_____

_____

_____

_____

"What if?" _____

_____

_____

_____

_____

Chapter 15: The Writing Process

WORKSHEET 5 *Purpose, Audience, and Tone*

Your **purpose** is your reason for writing. You can write to express yourself; to create literary works; to explain, explore, or inform; or to persuade.

Your **audience** is the people who will read or listen to your writing. The audience you choose will affect what you say and how you say it. When writing for a particular audience, you need to consider what the audience already knows about your subject, what will interest that audience, and what level of language will be appropriate.

Your **tone** is your attitude toward the subject and toward your readers. The tone of a piece of writing can often be described in a single word: *bubbly, sarcastic, amused,* or *intense,* for example. To create a particular tone, you must be careful in your choice of words, details, sentence lengths, and sentence structures.

Exercise   Read each of the following paragraphs. Then record its purpose, suggest a possible audience, and describe its tone.

1. Well, Talasi, I just wanted you to know that I was thinking about you. It must be hard to move when you're seventeen and have just one year of high school left. How I wish you could have stayed in Des Moines! We all miss you.

   Purpose: _____

   Audience: _____

   Tone: _____

2. What's all this fuss about saving endangered animals? Hasn't anyone heard about survival of the fittest? We can't stop progress. If these species can't make it in the world today, then they'll just have to go. And if one of them is humanity, well, that's just the price we'll have to pay.

   Purpose: _____

   Audience: _____

   Tone: _____

3. In the past fifteen years, the school budget in this town has decreased, in real terms, by sixteen percent. That's over one percent per year. It's an outrage, a disgrace. I'm here to warn you, on behalf of the students and teachers in our community, that if this trend is not reversed, we'll be forced to cut essential services.

   Purpose: _____

   Audience: _____

   Tone: _____

COMPOSITION

Name _____ Date _____ Class _____

WORKSHEET 6 *Arranging Ideas*

Arranging your ideas is an important part of planning. The following chart shows four common ways of arranging ideas.

TYPE OF ORDER	DEFINITION	EXAMPLES
Chronological	Narration: presents events as they happen in time	Story; narrative poem; explanation of a process; history; biography; drama
Spatial	Description: describes objects according to location	Describing from near to far, left to right, top to bottom, and so on
Importance	Evaluation: gives details from least to most important or the reverse	Persuasive writing; descriptions; explanations (main idea and supporting details); evaluative writing
Logical	Classification: relates items and groups	Definitions; classifications; comparisons and contrasts

Exercise   Read the topic sentences below and decide which of the four types of order would be most suitable for arranging details about the topic in a paragraph. On the lines provided, write *C* for chronological order, *S* for spatial order, *I* for order of importance, or *L* for logical order. Be prepared to explain your responses.

_____ 1. The view from the window of José's high-rise apartment was a life-sized picture postcard of the Manhattan skyline.

_____ 2. Considering its past and its potential abuses, the electoral college should be abolished.

_____ 3. Speed skating and figure skating are alike in some ways and different in others.

_____ 4. The progress of miniaturization in electronics is a short but spectacular tale.

_____ 5. I was one of those unlucky people who learned about fire the hard way.

_____ 6. There is much difference between the character in Mary Shelley's novel *Frankenstein* and the monster that Boris Karloff portrayed in the movie.

_____ 7. From roof to veranda, the old house was a study in Victorian architecture.

_____ 8. Our school's Multicultural Day was a great success, from the parade in the morning to the final ceremonies in the afternoon.

_____ 9. Jump-starting a car that has a dead battery requires performing the right steps in the right order.

_____10. State history should be a required subject in all high schools.

Name _____ Date _____ Class _____

 **WORKSHEET 7** | *Using Charts*

Charts are a practical, graphic way to arrange your prewriting notes. Charts group related bits of information and allow you to see the overall arrangement clearly.

When you make a chart, you use the skill of classifying: grouping related information. When classifying information, ask yourself these questions:

- Which items are similar in some way? What heading will show what they have in common?
- Do some items include other items? Which ones?
- Do you have any items left over? Should you create another heading? Should you eliminate the leftovers?

Exercise Look at the following ideas for a paper on diamonds, and complete the assignment that follows.

a. Used for rings, earrings, bracelets, pins, and necklaces

b. Hardest material found in the natural world

c. Koh-i-noor diamond once possessed by Indian and Persian rulers; now one of England's crown jewels

d. Doctors use diamond-edged knives during surgery.

e. Found in meteorites from space

f. Minerals formed from carbon within igneous rock

g. Found in subsurface rock formations called "pipes"

h. Jewelers use diamonds to cut other gemstones.

i. Uncut stones used in automobile and airplane manufacturing and electronics

j. Found in river gravel and coastal sand dunes

k. Most form about 100 miles beneath the earth's surface.

l. Diamond-studded rotary bits used to drill oil wells and bore tunnels in solid rock

1. One obvious heading for items in the list is *Uses*. Which items fall under this heading?

_____

2. The heading *Uses* can be broken down into more specific categories. What are they? On a separate sheet of paper, make a chart of the *Uses* list to show visually the subgroupings and their items.

COMPOSITION

Chapter 15: The Writing Process

WORKSHEET 8

Writing a First Draft

There's no magic formula, no *one* right way to write a first draft. Your prewriting notes may be rough, or you may create a detailed outline. You may like to write fast, or you may write slowly, carefully shaping each sentence. Do whatever feels right for your style of writing a draft. Consider these suggestions:

- Use your prewriting notes or outline as a guide.
- Write freely. Concentrate on expressing your ideas.
- Include any new ideas that come to you as you write.
- Don't worry about making errors in grammar, usage, and mechanics. You can fix them later.

Exercise Read the following prewriting notes about methods of transportation the indigenous peoples of North America used to use during the winter. Then write a first draft of a paragraph on this topic. You may use any or all of the notes. You may also add details or comments if you wish.

proverb: "It is not good to travel far when the pony wears his hair long."

travel difficult during winter

sleds of various types used

some for people, others to carry goods

Iroquois toboggans made of bark

later toboggans made from birchwood planks

Ojibwa hunting sleds with ash tree runners

sleds made so that dogs could be hitched in pairs

sometimes pulled by four or five dogs in single file

sleds often gaily decorated, as by the Cree.

Cree also decorated the dogs that pulled the sleds

snowshoes a primary mode of winter transportation

_____

_____

_____

_____

_____

_____

_____

_____

_____

_____

Chapter 15: The Writing Process

 **WORKSHEET 9** *Peer Evaluation*

Every writer needs an editor—a person who can read critically and with a different viewpoint. You can get your own editor through peer evaluation. Members of a peer-evaluation group read and comment on each other's papers. Take the following steps when you evaluate the work of a classmate.

1. Be sure to tell the writer what's right as well as what's wrong.

2. Make suggestions for improvement. If you see a weakness, give the writer some suggestions to correct it.

3. Concentrate on content and organization. Don't worry about mechanical errors such as spelling or punctuation.

4. Be sensitive to the writer's feelings. Make sure that your comments are constructive—offer solutions, not criticism.

Exercise   Read the following paragraph. Then use the questions that follow to write an evaluation of the paragraph.

Phyllis stearner wanted to play in her high school band even though she did not have full use of her right hand. She was born with cerebral palsy. She talked to the band leader. Soon she was playing the trombone. It doesn't need right finger movement. Another time, she learned that state money was available to her for training. But not for college. She talked to officials and changed their minds. Earned a Ph.D. in zoology, her first step toward becoming an internationally known radiation Biologist.

1. What purpose does the paragraph serve? Does it fully accomplish its purpose?

2. What might the writer do to increase the sentence variety and to avoid repetition in sentence structure?

3. What other problems might the writer address during revision?

_____

_____

_____

_____

_____

_____

_____

_____

_____

_____

_____

COMPOSITION

Chapter 15: The Writing Process

WORSHEET 10

Revising by Adding and Cutting

Two revision techniques are adding and cutting.

You can **add** new information and details in new words, phrases, sentences, and paragraphs.

You can **cut** information, details, examples, or words. For example, you might cut repetition, wordiness, and details unrelated to the main idea.

Exercise   Study the revisions made to the following paragraph. Then answer the questions that follow.

Cubans enjoy many forms of recreation and are especially fond of sports and dancing. For example,

Cubans are known for their love of baseball. ~~In Cuba, many holidays celebrate the~~ *(a Spanish word for soccer)* ~~revolution that brought Fidel Castro to power.~~ Other sports they enjoy include boxing, *fútbol,*
(a court game in which a basket is used to hurl a ball)
and jai alai. Dancing is very popular. Both the conga and the rumba are Cuban dances.
also
~~Cubans are just totally crazy about dancing.~~

1. Why did the writer add the sentence, "Cubans enjoy many forms of recreation and are especially fond of sports and dancing"?

   _____

2. Why did the writer cross out the sentence, "In Cuba, many holidays celebrate the revolution that brought Fidel Castro to power"?

   _____

3. Why did the writer add the information after *fútbol* and *jai alai*?

   _____

4. Why did the writer add *also* to the sentence "Dancing is very popular"?

   _____

5. Why did the writer cut the last sentence?

   _____

Chapter 15: The Writing Process

WORSHEET 11

Revising by Replacing and Reordering

Two ways to revise are replacing and reordering.

You can **replace** weak words, clichés, awkward-sounding sentences, and unnecessary information or details.

You can **reorder** words, phrases, sentences, or paragraphs to add variety or to improve clarity.

Exercise   Study the revisions made to the following paragraph, which is from a report on science fiction for an audience of high school students. Then answer the questions below.

in which the action takes place in space and involves battles between good and evil heroes

There are three main kinds of science fiction. First, there is the kind ~~that has space suits and heroes getting the bad guys out in space~~, such as you might see on *Star Trek*. *Second, there is the kind about* strange-looking little creatures who live in our world or worlds of their own ~~are common in the second type of science fiction~~. Third, there's the kind that puts down modern-day life. For example, "Computers Don't Argue" by ~~a guy named~~ *the noted science fiction author* Gordon R. Dickson criticizes modern life. *Star Trek* is a TV series about spaceships and *other* ~~way-out~~ galaxies~~, etc.~~ *The Hobbit* by J.R.R. Tolkien is about strange little creatures, as is the movie *E.T.*

1. Why did the writer reorder the final two sentences of this paragraph?

   _____

2. Why did the writer replace *way-out* and cut *etc.*? _____

3. Why did the writer replace "that has space suits and heroes getting the bad guys out in space" with "in which the action takes place in space and generally involves battles between good and evil heroes"? _____

   _____

4. Why did the writer replace "a guy named" with "the noted science fiction author"?

   _____

COMPOSITION

Chapter 15: The Writing Process

WORKSHEET 12 *Proofreading*

When you proofread, you catch and correct any remaining errors in grammar, usage, and mechanics (spelling, capitalization, punctuation). If you put aside your paper for a while, you'll spot these mistakes more easily. The following guidelines are designed to help you locate and correct a few of the most common errors.

1. Is each sentence a complete sentence?
2. Does every sentence end with the appropriate punctuation mark?
3. Does every sentence begin with a capital letter? Are all proper nouns and proper adjectives capitalized?
4. Does every verb agree in number with its subject?
5. Are verb forms and tenses used correctly?
6. Are subject and object forms of personal pronouns used correctly?
7. Does every pronoun agree with its antecedent in number and gender? Are pronoun references clear?
8. Are frequently confused words (such as *except* and *accept, imply* and *infer*) used correctly?
9. Are all words spelled correctly? Are the plural forms of nouns correct?
10. Is the paper neat and in correct manuscript form?

Exercise: Proofreading   The paragraph below has ten errors in grammar, usage, and mechanics. Use a college dictionary and your handbook if necessary to identify and correct each mistake.

Many high school students find it real hard to choose a college major. This problem

should not have no affect on a student's decision to attend college however. Tanya and her

teacher, Mrs. Jackson, discussed her feelings about Junior college. Tanya said "My parents

and me agree that junior college will be a good way to save on tuition while I consider my

future and in the meantime, I will be completing my first two years of college. Mrs. Jackson

said that Tanya had chose a good option.

Name _____ Date _____ Class _____

 **WORSHEET 1** *Topic Sentences*

A **paragraph** is a group of sentences that develop a main idea. A **composition,** in turn, can be described as a group of paragraphs that develop a main idea.

A **topic sentence** is a specific, limiting statement about the subject of the paragraph. You can find a topic sentence anywhere in a paragraph. Not all paragraphs have or need topic sentences. However, topic sentences provide a focus for the reader, and they help the writer avoid straying from the topic.

Exercise On the lines provided, write the main idea and topic sentence of each paragraph. If the paragraph does not have a topic sentence, write *No Topic Sentence.*

1. When Native Americans of the Plains moved, they did so in an organized way. Different people were assigned the roles of scouting ahead, flanking the file, and remaining at the previous site until everyone was out. Special care was taken to arrange how and by whom the medicine pipe was carried. Expert and rapid packing allowed the people to be on their way shortly after their morning meal.

   Main idea: _____

   Topic sentence: _____

2. One man was chosen to be the custodian of the medicine pipe. Where he put the pipe before the move depended on the move itself. If the man placed the pipe far away from his tepee, the move would be long. If he placed it nearby, the move would be short. Also, the custodian would place the pipe stem so that the mouthpiece pointed in the direction that the tribe would follow.

   Main idea: _____

   Topic sentence: _____

3. Bags containing all the clothing used for ceremonies were sometimes carried by dogs. Still other dogs pulled the tepee poles or carried household goods. A large dog could pull a load of up to sixty pounds. For many years, dogs were the beasts of burden most commonly used on the Great Plains.

   Main idea: _____

   Topic sentence: _____

4. Later, Native Americans of the Plains used the travois, a device for carrying goods. The design of the travois varied. It usually consisted of two poles with a platform resting between them. Because Native Americans of the Plains moved frequently, the travois was constantly in use.

   Main idea: _____

   Topic sentence: _____

COMPOSITION

Chapter 16: Paragraph and Composition Structure

| WORKSHEET 2 | *Using Details* |

Supporting sentences give details to support or develop a paragraph's main idea. Supporting sentences often consist of sensory details, facts, or statistics. A paragraph may be developed with one type of detail or with a combination of types.

Sensory details are details of sight, hearing, taste, smell, and texture that the writer uses to bring the subject to life for readers.

SENSORY DETAILS: glowing coals   crackling fire   fried fish
                  pine smoke   wooly mittens

A fact is something that can be proved true by concrete information. A statistic is a fact based on numbers. To verify the accuracy of facts or statistics, you can check a reliable reference source.

FACT: The Sargasso Sea lies in the North Atlantic.

STATISTIC: The Sargasso Sea covers roughly two million square miles.

Exercise A   Choose one of the following topics or one of your own. On the lines provided, write the topic and five sensory details related to the topic. If possible, write one detail for each of the five senses.

Possible topics: my dream car; the best job for me; a ride on a bus, plane, train, or boat; my childhood secret hiding place; my favorite dinner; my bedroom

Topic: _____

1. _____

2. _____

3. _____

4. _____

5. _____

Exercise B   Choose one of the following topics or one of your own. On the lines provided, write your topic and three facts or statistics that you could use to support your topic.

Possible topics: healthful snacks; the best park; an outstanding writer, politician, or musician; why conservation of our forests is necessary

Topic: _____

1. _____

_____

2. _____

_____

3. _____

_____

Chapter 16: Paragraph and Composition Structure

WORKSHEET 3

Using Examples and Anecdotes

To make the main idea of a paragraph clear, you may have to develop that idea in detail. Two ways to elaborate on a main idea are to use examples and anecdotes.

Examples are specific instances or illustrations of a main idea.

MAIN IDEA: Exercise is good for your health.

EXAMPLE: Regular exercise can reduce your blood pressure as well as help you control your weight.

An **anecdote,** a little story that is usually biographical or autobiographical, can also be used to support or prove a main idea.

MAIN IDEA: Even a champion needs a cheering section. You can bring out the best in people if you believe in them.

ANECDOTE: In 1951, Leo Durocher, manager of the New York Giants, decided he needed Willie Mays to pull the Giants out of a slump. Mays was then playing for the Minneapolis Millers. When Durocher put the offer to him, Mays declined. In fact, he didn't even want to talk to the famous manager. Why? Mays felt he wasn't a good enough player. Yet Durocher, a man known for bringing out the best in players, persuaded Mays to sign. Once Mays was on the team, Durocher encouraged Mays with praise and attention. In short order, Mays was dazzling fans and the Giants were leaving their slump behind as they took the pennant that year.

Exercise A   Choose one of the following topics or one of your own. Develop a main idea and two sentences that present examples related to the topic. Write the main idea and sentences on the lines provided.

Possible topics: flying; dancing; pets; cooking; political activism

Main idea: _____

1. _____

2. _____

Exercise B   Choose one of the following main ideas. Underline your main idea. Then write an anecdote to support it.

Possible main ideas: my friend's sense of humor always gets us into trouble; playing on a team is a good experience; little things mean a lot

Anecdote: _____

_____

_____

_____

_____

COMPOSITION

Chapter 16: Paragraph and Composition Structure

WORKSHEET 4 | *The Clincher Sentence*

A **clincher sentence** is a final sentence that emphasizes or summarizes the main idea or draws a conclusion.

> Native American place names are very common in the United States. About half the names of the fifty states come from Native American words. Examples include *Mississippi,* which means "father of waters"; *Kansas,* which means "people of the south wind"; *Tennessee,* which was the name of a Cherokee village; and *Oklahoma,* which means "the red people." In addition, Native American names have been given to countless cities, towns, and bodies of water. **In fact, most Americans live in or near a place that bears a Native American name.**

Exercise   For each of the following paragraphs, write an appropriate clincher sentence.

1. Some of our fifty states bear the names of kings and queens. These states are all in the East, and they include Maryland, Virginia, and Georgia, named after Queen Mary, Queen Elizabeth, and King George, respectively. The Carolinas also are named after royalty. Their name comes from *Carolus,* the Latin version of the name of King Charles of England. Louisiana was named after the French king Louis XIV.

   Clincher sentence: _____

   _____

2. Place names have come to us not only from Native Americans and Europeans but also from Spanish settlers. Perhaps the best-known Spanish name is *California.* This state was named after an imaginary land mentioned in a Spanish romance written in 1510. Another state bearing a Spanish name is Colorado. The name *Colorado* described the red earth or red rivers seen by the first Spanish settlers.

   Clincher sentence: _____

   _____

3. The number of bats in several species is declining. Bats live in caves, abandoned mine shafts, and buildings. Cave explorers frighten bats, causing them to abandon their homes. The closing of inactive mine shafts to prevent human accidents causes the death of thousands of bats, who can no longer get in. Also, bats are frequently run out of buildings and are sometimes purposely killed by humans.

   Clincher sentence: _____

   _____

Chapter 16: Paragraph and Composition Structure

 **WORKSHEET 5** *Achieving Unity*

A paragraph with **unity** is one that "hangs together." In other words, all the supporting sentences work together to develop the main idea. Unity can exist whether the main idea is clearly stated in a topic sentence or is implied (suggested). In a paragraph that relates a series of actions or events, the main idea is often implied rather than stated.

In a paragraph with unity, all sentences relate to the stated main idea, to an implied main idea, or to a sequence of events.

Exercise Each of the following paragraphs contains one sentence that destroys its unity. Find that unrelated sentence in each paragraph, and draw a line through it.

1. A person who explores the inner chambers of caves is called a spelunker. The United States has a large variety of caves for enthusiastic spelunkers to explore. Another popular sport that often takes place near caves is rock climbing. Although most spelunkers spend their time in limestone caves, other forms of caves, such as glacier, steam, sea, and volcanic caves, also exist in this country.

2. During the 1950s and 1960s, the movement to achieve civil rights for African Americans became a focus of national attention. One of the most dramatic events of this movement was the August 1963 march on Washington, D.C. On that day, some two hundred thousand Americans congregated in front of the Lincoln Memorial to hear Dr. Martin Luther King, Jr., deliver his "I Have a Dream" address. His speech inspired many Americans to work toward equal rights for citizens of minority descent. Persecution of minorities has occurred throughout history.

3. Book clubs offer two main advantages. Many people collect comic books as a hobby and have huge collections. First, books come right to your door. Second, book clubs offer discounts that enable members to buy books that they could not otherwise afford.

4. The entire senior class volunteered to assist at the local Special Olympics competition. They made housing arrangements, designed name tags, and assigned assistants to individual competitors. Finally, the day arrived, and everything went as planned. A letter of appreciation, which was addressed to all the members of the class, arrived a week later. John did not think the class should have to organize first-aid and comfort facilities.

5. Texas has a most distinctive history. Before being admitted to the United States, it was a separate country, the Republic of Texas. Prior to gaining that status, Texas had been ruled by three other nations. Texas is the second-largest state. Because of its unusual history, Texas has had six flags flying over it: those of Spain, France, Mexico, the Republic of Texas, and the United States, plus, of course, the "Lone Star" state flag.

Chapter 16: Paragraph and Composition Structure

WORKSHEET 6 *Achieving Coherence A*

In a **coherent** paragraph, the relationship between ideas is clear—the paragraph flows smoothly. You can make paragraphs coherent by paying attention to the order in which you arrange your ideas. The chart below lists four basic ways of arranging ideas.

CHRONOLOGICAL ORDER: Arrange events in the order they happen.

SPATIAL ORDER: Arrange details in the order of their location.

ORDER OF IMPORTANCE: Arrange ideas or details according to how important they are.

LOGICAL ORDER: Arrange ideas or details in related groups.

Exercise A The ideas in the following paragraph are not in an order that makes sense. On the line provided, list each sentence by number in order of importance—from the most important supporting sentence to the least important.

[1] When it comes to mystery stories, one woman author is unsurpassed; the greatest plotter of them all is Dame Agatha Christie. [2] Yet even Christie could run out of fresh ideas; the plot of *The Murder of Roger Ackroyd* created a furor among mystery critics and readers, who thought she had "cheated." [3] However, mystery readers have for the most part been satisfied with the technical mastery of her best stories, a reaction that has insured their worldwide success. [4] Perhaps the best indicator of Christie's success is sales of books in the hundreds of millions. [5] Many of Dame Agatha's novels, such as *Murder on the Orient Express, And Then There Were None*, and *The ABC Murders* have thrilled and stumped their readers.

Order of importance (most to least): _____

Exercise B The sentences in the following paragraph are not arranged in an order that makes sense. On the line provided, list each sentence by number in chronological order—from the first event to the last.

[1] Suddenly, the travelers stood transfixed as they heard an extraordinary sound. [2] Quietly creeping closer, the travelers were amazed to see a bird about the size of a crow hanging upside-down from a tree branch, its brilliant, dense, royal-blue feathers spread out in display and accentuated by a shaft of sunlight. [3] It was a throbbing sound like the kind made by synthesizers or electronic organs with all the stops pulled out. [4] Deep in a highland forest of New Guinea, just after sunrise, a group of travelers was exploring. [5] The travelers were quickly told that the sound was created neither by humans nor by machines.

Chronological order (first to last): _____

Name _____ Date _____ Class _____

 **WORKSHEET 7** *Achieving Coherence B*

Direct references and transitional words and expressions can help you achieve coherence. These words and phrases act as connectors between ideas so that a paragraph is clear to readers.

Referring to a noun or pronoun that you've used earlier in the paragraph is a **direct reference**. You can make direct references by using a noun or pronoun that refers to a noun or pronoun used earlier, by repeating a word used earlier, or by using a word or phrase that means the same thing as one used earlier.

A word or phrase that makes a transition from one idea to another is called a **transitional expression**. Such words and phrases include prepositions that indicate chronological or spatial order, as well as conjunctions, which connect and show relationships.

In the following paragraph the direct references to the term *dialogue* are shown in boldface. The transitional words and phrases are italicized.

> *Before* 1980, *when* people with hearing impairments watched TV, they missed out on the real enjoyment of it *because* they could not follow the dialogue. *In* the 1970s, *however*, a technological advance called closed captions opened a way to transmit **speech** in subtitles to a television screen. *Then, in* 1980, the Federal Communications Commission required that *thereafter* part of each television signal be reserved for the broadcast of closed captions. *As a result*, captioning decoding adapters for TVs came on the market *and* made it possible for people with hearing impairments to view **written dialogue** with any closed-captioned broadcast.

Exercise   In the paragraph below, underline as many direct references as you can find, and circle the transitional words and phrases.

Today, Vincent van Gogh is one of the most appreciated artists who ever lived, but during his lifetime virtually no one even liked his art. When he was young, he didn't intend to be an artist, although between the ages of sixteen and twenty-three he worked in art galleries and studied art. Then, for the next four years, he studied for the ministry. At the end of the fourth year, Van Gogh decided to devote his life to art. From that time until his death ten years later, he produced more than fifteen hundred paintings and drawings. Unfortunately, he was able to sell only one during his lifetime. People eventually realized the importance of his art, which has continued to increase in popularity and value.

COMPOSITION

Chapter 16: Paragraph and Composition Structure

WORKSHEET 8 *Description and Narration*

In a **description** you use sensory details (details of sight, hearing, taste, touch, and smell) for support. You'll often use **spatial order** to organize a description, but depending on your subject or purpose, you might also use **order of importance** or **chronological order**.

The strategy of **narration** examines changes over time. You may use narration *to tell a story, to explain a process,* or *to explain causes and effects*. You usually use **chronological order** to present ideas and information in paragraphs of narration.

Exercise A   Choose one of the following subjects. On the lines provided, list five sensory details (details of sight, hearing, taste, smell, and touch) that you could use to describe the specific features of the subject.

  1. a summer night in your back yard
  2. your school the first day after you return from summer vacation
  3. the last second of a tied championship basketball game
  4. yourself—the first time you drove alone
  5. a concert, dance, or jam session you attended

_____

_____

_____

_____

_____

Exercise B   You have probably used the strategy of narration many times, perhaps without even knowing that you were doing so. Now practice the strategy by following the instructions given below.

  1. You are teaching a four-year-old how to ride a bike. List the basic steps and major points of bike riding.

_____

_____

_____

  2. Write down at least three causes that made you decide to go or not to go to college. Then list at least three effects your decision is likely to have.

Causes: **Effects:**

_____   _____

_____   _____

_____   _____

Name _____ Date _____ Class _____

WORKSHEET 9

Classification and Evaluation

The strategy of **classification** is used to examine a subject and its relationship to other subjects. You can classify a subject by dividing it into its parts, by defining it, or by comparing and contrasting it with something else. In paragraphs that classify, writers usually use **logical order:** grouping related ideas together. Classifying by **dividing** means looking at the parts of a subject in order to understand the subject as a whole.

Evaluation means judging the value of something. You often evaluate a subject to inform readers or to persuade them to think or act differently. An evaluation should be supported with reasons showing *why* you made the judgment about the subject. A good way to arrange these reasons is in **order of importance:** You emphasize a point by listing it first or last in the paragraph.

Exercise A Select one of the following subjects or one of your own. Write three or more parts into which the subject could be divided.

  Subjects: high school   a kitchen   a park   the beach

Subject: _____

Parts: _____   _____

  _____   _____

Exercise B Select one of the following subjects or one of your own. Write the name of the larger group or class to which your subject belongs. Then list three details that distinguish the topic from other members of that group or class.

  Subjects: popcorn   pickup trucks   the prom   rap music

Subject: _____

Larger group or class: _____

Details: _____

_____

_____

Exercise C Select one subject from the following list. On a separate sheet of paper, state your overall opinion about it (good, bad, somewhere in between), and list three reasons why you hold this opinion.

   1. the value of a high school diploma
   2. the value of popularity in high school
   3. the quality of public transportation in your city or state
   4. the quality of the last movie you saw

COMPOSITION

Chapter 16: Paragraph and Composition Structure

WORKSHEET 10 *The Thesis Statement*

The **thesis statement** of a composition is like the topic sentence of a paragraph; it expresses the main idea, or thesis, of your paper. Your thesis is not your topic (such as cats) but what you want to say about it (cats are ideal companions).

Exercise A   In the list below, find the four effective thesis statements. They should each have a specific topic and a clear main idea. The remaining thesis statement is weak. It is missing a specific topic or a clear main idea. On the lines provided after sentence 5, rewrite the weak thesis statement as needed to make it more effective.

1. Despite physical disabilities caused by a motor neuron disease, British physicist Stephen Hawking expands our understanding of the universe through his brilliant writing.

2. Bilingual education opens doors to students in two languages; it will be an important part of American education in the future.

3. Rap music, which nobody knew very much about until it became popular a while ago, is a very entertaining form of music.

4. Robots don't perform experiments, but they do carry out many precision tasks in today's laboratories.

5. Would you like to interpret your dreams? Here are keys that will unlock their mysteries.

_____

_____

_____

Exercise B   The limited topic of the following list of details is the effect of houseplants on indoor air pollution. What is a specific main idea you can form from the details? Write a thesis statement for the following topic and list of details. Express both the topic and the main idea clearly and specifically in the statement.

Limited topic: effect of houseplants on indoor air pollution

Ideas and details:

• EPA reports health risks from indoor pollution greater than risks from outdoor pollution

• examples of indoor pollutants: formaldehyde from plywood, carpeting, and some household cleaners; benzene from paints, tobacco smoke, and detergents; trichloroethylene from paints, varnishes, and dry cleaning

• reports that one houseplant per 100 square feet of floor space removes over 85 percent of indoor pollutants

Thesis statement: _____

_____

Name _____ Date _____ Class _____

WORKSHEET 11

Early Plans

The **early plan**—sometimes called a rough, or informal, outline—gives you a general idea of the kinds of information you want to include in your composition. You will need to

- sort related ideas and details into separate groups
- give each group of details a separate label
- make a separate list of details that don't fit into any group. You may use them at some later stage.

Once your grouping is complete, you must choose a strategy for organizing and developing your composition. The four strategies of paragraph development—**narration, description, classification, evaluation**—and the four basic orders—**chronological** (time), **spatial** (space), **logical, order of importance**—are also used for the larger structure of a composition.

Exercise A On the lines provided, group the following details. Above each group of details, write a heading that identifies what the details have in common. Ignore details that don't fit into either group.

magazines	radio	computer files	Congress
broadcast television	cable television	newspapers	videotapes
books	Phil Donahue	audiotapes	movies

Group 1 head: _____   Group 2 head: _____

_____   _____

_____   _____

_____   _____

_____   _____

_____   _____

_____   _____

_____   _____

Exercise B Identify an order for one of the groups of ideas listed above. Then list the ideas in that order.

Group you chose: _____

Order: _____

List: _____

_____

COMPOSITION

Chapter 16: Paragraph and Composition Structure

WORKSHEET 12   *Formal Outlines*

Structured outlines sometimes grow out of early plans. A **formal outline** has numerals and letters to identify headings and subheadings. Indentations show levels of subordination. You may choose a **topic outline** that uses single words and phrases or a **sentence outline** that uses only complete sentences. A formal outline may be used for planning, but it is more often written after the composition is complete, to provide an overview, or summary, for the reader.

Exercise   Study the following outline. Then answer the questions below.

I. Early African American music
   A. Work songs and chants
   B. Spirituals
II. Emergent African American music
   A. Gospel
   B. Blues
III. Later developments of African American music
   A. Jazz (including Dixieland)
   B. Rock
   C. Reggae
   D. Rap

1. Is this a topic outline or a sentence outline? _____

2. In what order do the entries in this outline appear? _____

3. What is the subject of this outline? _____

   _____

4. What would be a good thesis statement for a paper based on this outline?

   _____

   _____

   _____

Chapter 16: Paragraph and Composition Structure

WORKSHEET 13 | *The Introduction*

The **introduction** of an article or composition should

- catch the audience's attention (otherwise the audience may not read on)
- set the tone and show the writer's attitude toward the topic (humorous, serious, critical)
- present the thesis (sometimes at the beginning, but often at the end)

Techniques for writing introductions include beginning with

an interesting or dramatic quotation	an anecdote
an extended example	an unusual or enlightening fact
a question or a challenge	a stand on some issue
an outrageous or comical statement	a simple statement of your thesis

Many introductions use a combination of these techniques.

Exercise For each of the following introductions, identify the thesis statement, the tone, and the technique used for writing the introduction.

1. More than five billion people inhabit this planet, and most of them help to create the chemical wastes that pollute the air we breathe and the water we drink. Because the things we do affect the environment, each of us should know something about our environment and about how our actions affect it. For what we do now may well change the earth for generations to come.

   Thesis statement: _____

   _____

   Tone: _____

   Technique: _____

2. Hey, has hay fever been getting you down even though you never left town? Don't be surprised. Hay isn't always the cause of hay fever. Dust mites, mold, pet dander, and airborne pollen can set off an attack as easily as a haystack. Allergen counts have been on the rise for the last several weeks. Chances are that you've been feeling the effects of these mighty mites. If not, enjoy yourself while you can. The cedars will be releasing their pollen in three more months. You don't have to suffer; there are a number of steps you can take to help reduce the effects of allergens.

   Thesis statement: _____

   _____

   Tone: _____

   Technique: _____

COMPOSITION

Chapter 16: Paragraph and Composition Structure

 **WORKSHEET 14**   *The Body*

The **body** of your composition develops the main idea of your thesis statement. One or more paragraphs support or prove your thesis with details. These paragraphs should connect with one another and should relate directly to your thesis statement. You can achieve these goals if the body has *unity, coherence,* and *emphasis.* **Coherence** is an ordered flow of ideas within and between sentences and paragraphs. You can achieve coherence by using three techniques—*transitional expressions, direct references,* and *a short transitional paragraph.*

Exercise   The following paragraphs form part of a composition. Add transitional words and phrases and direct references. Circle any sentence that is out of order, and draw an arrow to where it belongs. Cross out any sentence that does not belong.

One of the mysteries that surrounds Easter Island is how people reached

_____ . The most likely theory is that the first settlers of Easter Island

were Polynesian voyagers who reached Easter Island sometime _____

the year A.D. 690. A tiny speck of rock with an area of only forty-five square miles, the

island is lost in the vastness of the Pacific Ocean and lies more than a thousand miles

_____ its nearest neighbor, Pitcairn Island. The seventh-century

_____ occurred hundreds of years before the great age of exploration,

long before the time of explorers such as Magellan and Balboa.

A _____ mystery from this tiny island concerns the "talking boards."

The language of these tablets appears to be of Polynesian origin; _____ ,

so few examples remain that it may never be fully translated. Perhaps this language is like

ancient Native American pictographs. These pictographs are inscribed wooden tablets and

chest ornaments.

A _____ mystery—and the major mystery, dwarfing all others—is

how the three hundred or so massive stone figures that dominate the island were carved,

transported, and raised into position. These immense _____ , known as

moia, startled early European sailors and have amazed visitors _____ .

The statues are gigantic and have oddly shaped heads with long ears. Most of

_____ look alike, but _____ sizes vary. The largest

statue is about four stories high and weighs ninety tons. _____ many

theories have been advanced to explain how these stone giants could have been built and

moved, no one knows why _____ were created.

Name _____ Date _____ Class _____

WORKSHEET 15 *The Conclusion*

Compositions need **conclusions** that allow readers to feel that the ideas are tied together and are complete. The following techniques are some options writers have for creating effective conclusions.

1. Refer to the introduction.
2. Offer a solution, or make a recommendation.
3. Restate your thesis.
4. Summarize your major points.
5. Point out consequences or areas for future research.
6. End with an appropriate quotation.

Exercise On the lines provided, identify the techniques used by the writers of the following conclusions.

1. Whatever happened, they would say *kodomo no tame ni*, which means "for the sake of the children." For their children, they put up with rules that kept trained professionals from establishing a practice outside the Japanese community. For their children, they accepted jobs as domestics for white families. For their children, they lived with laws that kept them from owning land or becoming citizens in the very country where they were raising their families.

   Technique: _____

2. In 1942, General DeWitt stood before the House Naval Affairs Subcommittee and said, "I don't care what they do with the [Japanese] so long as they don't send them back here." He wasn't just speaking for himself. He was expressing the view of thousands of Americans at that time.

   Technique: _____

3. We must learn and publish the stories of all those who were sent to relocation camps before it is too late. For only if we record the outrages of the past can we hope to understand and to avoid them in the future.

   Technique: _____

4. So it was that the courage and bravery of the 442nd Regimental Combat Team helped to change prevailing attitudes toward Japanese Americans. The patriotism and sacrifice of the most decorated unit in military history was not in vain.

   Technique: _____

COMPOSITION

Chapter 16: Paragraph and Composition Structure

Transitional Words and Phrases

Whether your piece of writing is made up of a single paragraph or many paragraphs, you will always be connecting ideas. The following chart is a handy guide to words that make the right connections.

TRANSITIONAL WORDS AND PHRASES			
Comparing Ideas/ Classification and Definition	also and	another moreover	similarly too
Contrasting Ideas/ Classification and Definition	although but however	in spite of nevertheless	on the other hand still yet
Showing Cause and Effect/ Narration	as a result because	consequently since	so that therefore
Showing Time/Narration	after at last at once before	eventually finally first meanwhile	next then thereafter
Showing Place/Description	above across around before beyond	down here in inside into	next over there to under
Showing Importance/ Evaluation	first last	mainly more important	then to begin with

Chapter 17: The Research Paper

 **WORKSHEET 1** *Choosing a Suitable Topic*

In exploring subjects for a research paper, begin with your own interests. You will be thinking and reading about your final topic and working hard on it for some time. Also remember that the library is only one of many places to start your exploration.

FAMILY AND FRIENDS: Does someone you know have an interesting job or hobby?

HEROES: Whom do you admire and wish you knew more about?

PLACES NEAR AND FAR: What places have you visited or wanted to visit?

CURRENT EVENTS: Which events and subjects grab your attention?

LIBRARY AND MEDIA: What subjects arouse your curiosity?

Once you have found a subject, you need to narrow your focus to a specific aspect that intrigues you and that can be covered in a composition. To limit a topic, you can analyze it on your own or you can look for subtopics in the card catalog, the *Readers' Guide to Periodical Literature,* and in encyclopedias and specialized dictionaries. Then make sure your limited topic is suitable for a research paper. Use the following criteria.

AVAILABILITY OF SOURCES: Be sure you can find five or six good sources.

OBJECTIVITY AND FACTS: Can you maintain objectivity and stick to the facts?

AUDIENCE INTEREST: If your topic isn't appealing or is widely known, what approach could intrigue your readers?

Exercise Which of the following topics is suitable for a seven- to ten-page research report? Some may be too broad, too narrow, or too personal. For each topic that seems unsuitable, first tell why you think it's unsuitable, and then suggest a more workable topic.

1. urban renewal in Newark, New Jersey
2. the history of slavery in America
3. how Labrador retrievers are trained to detect drugs smuggled as cargo
4. my year as an exchange student in Japan

1. _____

   _____

2. _____

   _____

3. _____

   _____

4. _____

   _____

COMPOSITION

Chapter 17: The Research Paper

 **WORKSHEET 2** *Evaluating Sources*

You can use general reference works like encyclopedias to get an overview of your topic. If you already have a solid background in your topic, go directly to more focused sources, such as the card catalog, on-line catalog, or the *Readers' Guide to Periodical Literature*. Before using a source, you need to evaluate its usefulness to you. One good way to evaluate a source is to use the "4R" test.

RELEVANT: Does the source relate directly to your limited topic? For a book, check the table of contents and index. Skim magazine articles.

RELIABLE: Can you trust it? A respected scholar or a respected magazine such as *Scientific American* can usually be relied on for accuracy.

RECENT: Be sure you aren't using outdated information.

REPRESENTATIVE: If you are working on a controversial topic, you must show different points of view. Your task as a researcher is to study, balance, and interpret the views on all sides.

Exercise   The items below are from the *Readers' Guide to Periodical Literature*.

(A) Did King scholars skew our views of civil rights? D. L. Watson. *The Education Digest* 57:56–8 S '91

(B) Dr. King's widow tells what he would do about today's burning issues. il pors *Jet* 79:24+ Ja 14 '91

(C) Martin and Malcolm [cover story] T. Mikelson. pors *The Christian Century* 108:1031–4 N 6 '91

(D) Martin Luther King's forgotten legacy. S. Perry. il *Utne Reader* p 118–20 My/Je '91

(E) The night Dr. King saved the lives of two white men. R. E. Johnson. il pors *Jet* 79:6–8 Ja 21 '91

(F) The private side of a public man: Martin Luther King, Jr. R. D. Turner. il pors *Ebony* 46:30+ Ja '91

(G) The transformation of Martin Luther King, Jr. D. J. Garrow. il por *The Wilson Quarterly* 15:16 Aut '91

Excerpt from "King, Martin Luther, 1929–1968" from *Readers' Guide to Periodical Literature, 1991*. Copyright © 1991 by the H. W. Wilson Company. Reprinted by permission of *The H. W. Wilson Company*.

You are researching the private life of Martin Luther King, Jr. Answer these questions, on the lines provided, by giving the letter(s) for the entries above.

1. Which entry is probably the most useful for your paper?   _____

2. Which article contains the opinions of Mrs. King?   _____

3. Which articles probably contain biographical information?   _____

4. Which entries are least likely to be useful for your paper?   _____

Chapter 17: The Research Paper

Taking Notes

When you find possible sources, it's important to keep accurate and complete information on them. Your **Works Cited list**—the list of sources at the end of your report—must contain specific information because some of your readers may want to consult your sources.

The best system for collecting accurate information is to put each source on a 3" × 5" card. On each card, record full publishing information, note the call number or location of the source, and assign each source a number.

Read or listen to the source (or a complete section of it) before you begin taking notes. Then go back over the information using 4" × 6" cards to record your notes. Later, when you're organizing your report, cards make it easy to arrange and rearrange information.

Exercise The following excerpt is from a recent article you are reading to gather research for a paper about Mary Shelley. Develop a list of questions using the *5W-How?* questions *(Who? What? Where? When? Why? How?).* Then take notes to answer the questions you have written. Use the space below and additional paper if needed.

In 1797, Mary Shelley was born into an unusual household, one in which both parents were geniuses. Her mother, Mary Wollstonecraft, was the author of *A Vindication of the Rights of Women*, and her father, William Godwin, was an influential philosopher. Mary wrote stories as a young child. At sixteen she met Percy Bysshe Shelley, a young poet, whom she later married. During a visit to Geneva, Switzerland, she wrote a short story, which was later expanded into a novel. Mary Shelley titled the novel *Frankenstein*. It is one of the most famous horror stories of all time; almost everyone is familiar with Shelley's monster.

_____

_____

_____

_____

_____

_____

_____

_____

_____

_____

_____

_____

_____

COMPOSITION

Chapter 17: The Research Paper

WORSHEET 4 | *Writing a Thesis Statement*

The **thesis statement** is a sentence or two stating both your topic and what you will say about it. Your thesis statement may change or be reworded as your writing progresses.

Exercise A   For each topic listed below, write a thesis statement.

> EXAMPLE: 1. **Topic:** fashion in the '90s
> **Thesis statement:** *Fashion in the '90s will emphasize freedom of expression.*

1. **Topic:** changes in the family in the last ten years

   Thesis statement: _____

   _____

2. **Topic:** education in a computerized world

   Thesis statement: _____

   _____

3. **Topic:** violence in our schools

   Thesis statement: _____

   _____

4. **Topic:** individual responsibility and environmental waste

   Thesis statement: _____

   _____

Exercise B   Choose one of the thesis statements you have written in Exercise A (or another of your choice), and write an introductory paragraph for a research report. In the introduction, include your thesis statement, as well as interesting details, ideas, a question, examples, or definitions. Write your introduction on the lines provided, and underline your thesis statement.

_____

_____

_____

_____

_____

_____

_____

_____

_____

_____

Chapter 17: The Research Paper

WORKSHEET 5 *Developing an Outline*

To create your writing plan, start by sorting your note cards into stacks according to their labels. These stacks may immediately suggest the main sections of your report and the ideas you will want to emphasize. Then you can decide how best to order the ideas and which supporting details to use in which sequence.

Your working outline can be rough in form, as long as it is sufficiently detailed to give shape and direction to your drafting. But for your completed paper, your teacher may request a final **formal outline**. A partial example of a formal outline is shown below. Such an outline serves as a table of contents and is prepared *after* you've finished the report.

I. Soil is an outstanding environment for those who live in it.
    A. It is chemically and structurally stable.
    B. There is little change in its climate.
        1. It provides refuge from extremes in temperature, wind, light, and dryness.
        2. It remains full of moisture until soil moisture drops below critical points.

Exercise The following items contain main ideas, subcategories, and details for a second section of the example outline on soil. These headings are in mixed-up order. Decide which sentence should receive the main idea label (II) and how the other ideas should be grouped beneath that (A, B, 1, 2, and so on). Write out the outline in correct order and format in the space provided.

    Heavy rainstorms flood soil and reduce oxygen.

    Most creatures live in pores and cavities not much larger than themselves.

    Soil has its disadvantages as a home, too.

    Movement is made difficult by soil that is too dense.

    Space in the soil must contain the right amount of moisture to be livable.

    Living space is limited beneath the soil.

    Dry soil may crack, exposing creatures to sun and air.

II. _____

_____

_____

_____

_____

_____

_____

_____

_____

_____

COMPOSITION

Chapter 17: The Research Paper

 ## *Documenting Sources*

Deciding which information you must **document,** or give credit for, in a research paper sometimes requires thought. That thought process can start with noticing what is or is not documented when you read reports of research. The following guidelines will also help you avoid pitfalls when documenting your information.

1. In general, don't document information that appears in several sources or facts that appear in standard reference books. For example, a statement like "The Civil War is generally considered one of the bloodiest events in U. S. history" needs no documentation because it clearly relies on several sources. Facts that are widely available in encyclopedias and other standard references also do not need to be credited.

2. Document the source of each direct quotation (unless it's very widely known, such as Shakespeare's "To be or not to be . . .").

3. Document any original theory or opinion other than your own. Since ideas belong to their authors, you must not present the ideas of other people as your own.

4. Document the source of data or other information from surveys, scientific experiments, and research studies.

5. Document unusual, little known, or questionable facts and statistics.

NOTE: Remember that you must give credit when you use another writer's *words or ideas.* Not to do so is **plagiarism,** an extremely serious offense. Even a summary or a paraphrase of someone else's original idea must be credited. When in doubt about plagiarism, give credit.

Exercise   If each of the following items were to appear in a research paper on the Iroquois League, which ones would you need to document? On the lines provided, write *D* for items requiring documentation and *ND* for items that do not require documentation. Be prepared to explain your answers.

_____ 1. In an interview with Bill Moyers, Chief Lyons talked about American democracy and said that "America got it from the Indians."

_____ 2. Originally composed of five nations, the Iroquois Confederacy is believed to date back to 1500.

_____ 3. The Iroquois constitution is known as the Great Law of Peace.

_____ 4. Some historians point out that the writers of the Constitution of the United States studied the Iroquois government.

_____ 5. The nations that were included in the Confederacy were the Mohawks, Oneidas, Onondagas, Cayugas, Senecas, and, later, the Tuscaroras.

Name _____ Date _____ Class _____

WORKSHEET 7 *Parenthetical Citations*

A **parenthetical citation** gives source information in parentheses in the body of a research paper. The citation should provide just enough information to lead the reader to the full source listing on the Works Cited page. Since the Works Cited list is alphabetized by authors' last names, an author's last name and the page numbers are usually enough for a parenthetical citation.

WORKS BY ONE AUTHOR:	(Orwell 58)
SEPARATE PASSAGES IN A SINGLE WORK:	(Orwell 13, 152–155)
MORE THAN ONE WORK BY THE SAME AUTHOR:	(Orwell, *Animal Farm* 4)
MULTIVOLUME WORKS:	(Sandburg 3: 124–125)
WORKS WITH A TITLE ONLY:	(*World Almanac* 523)
CLASSIC LITERARY WORKS PUBLISHED IN MANY EDITIONS:	*Prose:* (Twain, *The Adventures of Huckleberry Finn,* ch. 1, 3)
	Poems and verse plays: (Shakespeare, *Othello* 5.5.17)
	[Note use of Arabic numbers.]
INDIRECT SOURCES:	(qtd. in Campbell 349)
MORE THAN ONE WORK IN THE SAME CITATION:	(Lincoln 46; Ratigan 98)

Place the citation as close as possible to the material it documents, if possible at the end of a sentence or at another point of punctuation. Additionally, place the citation *before* the punctuation mark of the sentence, clause, or phrase you are documenting. For a quotation that ends a sentence, put the citation after the quotation mark but before the end punctuation mark. For an indented quotation, put the citation *two spaces after* the final punctuation mark.

NOTE: A nonprint source such as an interview or audiotape will not have a page number; a print source fewer than two pages will not require a page number. If you name the author in your sentence, you need give only the page number. But if the author has more than one work in the Works Cited list, you will also have to give a short form of the title.

Exercise On the line provided, write a parenthetical citation for each of the following items. Treat the items as if they were all citations in the same research paper. Watch for more than one work by the same author.

1. *Iacocca: An Autobiography* by Lee Iacocca and William Novak, page 69 and pages 179–183, published by Bantam, New York City, 1984.

_____

2. "Ahead: a recovery that goes on and on" by M. W. Karmin in *U.S. News & World Report* magazine, November 12, 1984, pages 31–32.

_____

COMPOSITION

3. "A World View Sampler: The Economy" written by T. Willard. The article appeared in *Futurist* magazine on pages 32–34 of the October 1984 issue.

_____

4. A quotation on page 42 of Leonard Silk's *Economics in the Real World: How Politics Affects the Economy* published in New York City by Simon and Schuster in 1985.

_____

5. "Clinging to the Land" written by Ed Magnuson, page 39 in *Time*, February 18, 1985.

_____

6. Pages 26–28 of an article titled "How the Pentagon Spends Its Billions" by Susan Dentzer, which appeared in *Newsweek*, February 11, 1985.

_____

7. Pages 47–49 of an article entitled "America's Changing Economic Landscape" by James Fallows in *The Atlantic*, March 1985, and "New Look at the Elderly" by John S. DeMott in February 18, 1985 issue of *Time*, page 42.

_____

8. *What They Don't Teach You in Harvard Business School* by Mark H. McCormack, Bantam, New York City, 1985, pages 109–110.

_____

9. Mark H. McCormack's *What They Still Don't Teach You at Harvard Business School*, Bantam, Toronto and New York City, 1989, page 53.

_____

10. *Henry James: Literary Criticism*, edited by Leon Edel and Mark Wilson, volume 2, The Library of America, New York City, 1985, page 72.

_____

Chapter 17: The Research Paper

List of Works Cited

The **Works Cited list** contains all the sources, print and nonprint, that you credit in your report. (The term *Works Cited* is a broader title than *Bibliography,* which refers to print sources only.)

BOOK: House, Homer C., and Susan Emolyn Harman. *Descriptive English Grammar.* 2d ed. New Jersey: Prentice-Hall, 1950. [book by two authors]

ENCYCLOPEDIA: Faron, Louis C. "American Indian." *Encyclopedia Americana.* 1984 ed.

MAGAZINE ARTICLE: Ferris, Timothy, "Einstein's Wonderful Year." *Science 84* Nov. 1984: 61–63. [signed article in a monthly magazine]

NEWSPAPER ARTICLE: "Navahos Upheld on Land Claims." *New York Times* 30 June 1970, late ed.: A20. [anonymous newspaper article]

PERSONAL INTERVIEW: Sanford, Annette. Personal interview. 14 Sep. 1993.

Use the following guidelines for preparing the list of Works Cited.

- Center the words *Works Cited* on a new sheet of paper.
- Begin each entry on a separate line. Position the first line of the entry even with the left margin and indent the second and all other lines five spaces. Double-space all entries.
- Alphabetize the sources by the authors' last names. If there is no author, alphabetize by title, ignoring *A, An,* and *The* and using the first letter of the next word.
- If you use two or more sources by the same author, include the author's name only in the first entry. For all other entries, use three hyphens followed by a period (---.) in place of the author's name. Order the entries alphabetically by title.

Exercise   Use the following items to prepare entries for a Works Cited list. Use correct punctuation and styling; refer to the examples above. In the space before each item, number the items from 1 to 5 to indicate the correct alphabetical order.

_____ 1. A book entitled Troubled Skies, Troubled Waters: The Story of Acid Rain. Author: Jon R. Luoma. Published by Viking in New York in 1984.

_____

_____

_____ 2. A book by Halsey P. Taylor and Victor N. Okada entitled The Craft of the Essay. Published in New York City in 1976 by Harcourt Brace Jovanovich.

_____

_____

COMPOSITION

Chapter 17, Worksheet 8, continued

_____ 3. An article entitled Acid Rain found in the 1987 edition of World Book
Encyclopedia.

_____

_____

_____ 4. An article entitled Cleaning Coal to Cut Acid Rain by I. Peterson in Science
News, the January 18, 1986 issue in volume 129. Reference to pages 37–39.

_____

_____

_____ 5. An unsigned newspaper article with the headline Failure to Address
Problem of Acid Rain, found in the March 15, 1982 issue of the New York
Times, on page 15 of Section I.

_____

_____

Name _____ Date _____ Class _____

 **WORKSHEET 9**   *Proofreading and Publishing*

Checking the mechanics of your parenthetical citations and list of Works Cited is a very important part of proofreading a research paper. Remember that your documentation is there for readers to use: Accuracy is necessary so that they may find your sources.

A research report is a substantial piece of work, a paper to be proud of and to *publish*. If you discover persons or groups especially interested in your subject, consider sending them a copy of your report. Save a copy of your report as an example of your writing and research skills for a college or job application. You might make your report the basis of a videotape documentary, or you could make an audiotape of the report, adding sound effects or music.

Exercise: Proofreading The following paragraphs are part of a research report. Proofread for errors in grammar, spelling, punctuation, and capitalization, and put the Works Cited list in the correct form.

On a fall evening in 1927, the first movie with sound premiered. It's huge earnings, over two million dollars, (Taylor, Peterson, and Hale, 202) launched a revolution. But the new age of the "talkies" was not without its price.

Film directors now had to work under a handicapp. Instead of having extensive freedom of movement, actors and actresses had to hover near a microphone. Consequently, audiences that had been used to seeing action-packed adventures found the new "speakies" boring and artificial. The careers of many writers were over.

Additionlly, some actors and actress was unable to make the transition. There voices simply did not appeal to their audiences. Oscar winner Emil Jannings returned to germany when fans rejected his voice. Yet actors like Laurel and Hardy enjoyed increased popularity because their voices enriched their characterizations. (Maltin, 114.) Still other actors, like the still famous Rin-Tin-Tin were unaffected by the crisis.

By the 30s the crisis was largely over. Although initially studios had been reluctant to spend money acquiring sound equipment and installing speakers in theaters those expenses had become sound investments.

Works Cited

Leonard Maltin, *The Great Movie Comedians: From Charlie Chaplin to Woody Allen*, Crown. New York, 1978.

A Pictorial History of the Movies. Deems Taylor, Marcelene Peterson, and Bryant Hale. Simon and Schuster: New York. 1949

COMPOSITION

Name _____ Date _____ Class _____

Using Notes in a Research Paper

Exercise   You are writing a research paper about computers. The purpose of your paper is to answer the question, "How will computers change newspapers in the future?" Below are two notes that you have taken during your research. Use the notes to write a paragraph for your report on a separate piece of paper. Summarize or paraphrase some of the material, and quote some of the material directly. Be sure to include a topic sentence in your paragraph as well as a list of Works Cited.

Note 1:

"Imagine that your home computer is connected to a large, nationwide network. That network carries news and weather and sports from every conceivable source. (It also carries movies and mail, but that's another story.) Now suppose that you can tell your computer to scan the network during the night. While you are sleeping, your computer calls far and wide on the network, searching for stories on whatever topics you've told it to look for. When the computer finds such a story, it prints it, along with some nifty color photos, on your fifty-dollar, color laser printer. The next morning you simply walk over to your printer and pick up your own Personal Newspaper. Sounds like science fiction, doesn't it? But it's not. Some people are creating their own personal newspapers right now. In a few years, the practice will be commonplace."

—from "The New Network News," an article by Janell Robinson in *MAC's
   Media World* magazine, January 4, 1993.

Note 2:

"Who wants to read a newspaper made for everybody? I, for one, could care less about the race results or local traffic accidents or winning hands in bridge. I want to read a newspaper made for me, one that reports what I want to know about. That's what's so exciting about this Personal Newspaper idea cooked up by the people at MIT's Media Lab. When the Personal Newspaper hits the scene, the age of the mass media will be over. Instead, we'll have individualized media. No one will read *The Daily Metropolis* anymore. They'll read *Dee Dee's Daily* or *Glenette's Gazette* or *Geraldo's Herald*. Now that's what I call a democratized press."

—from an interview with Pegeen O'Donnell, freelance journalist and writer,
   January 6, 1993.

Your paragraph will be judged on the basis of these criteria:

1. The paragraph is developed from both sources.
2. A thesis statement explains what the paragraph is about.
3. The tone of the paragraph is appropriate for a research paper.
4. Facts and ideas are stated mostly in the writer's own words.
5. Both sources are credited.
6. The paragraph is relatively free of errors in spelling, grammar, usage, mechanics, and manuscript form.

Name _____ Date _____ Class _____

 **WORKSHEET 1** | *Finding Books in the Library*

In most libraries, books are assigned **call numbers** to identify each book and to indicate where it's shelved. Call numbers are assigned according to one of two classification systems: the *Dewey decimal system* or the *Library of Congress system*. In the **Dewey decimal system,** nonfiction books and some works of literature are grouped by subject into ten general subject areas, each assigned a range of numbers. Books of fiction are grouped in alphabetical order according to the authors' last names. The **Library of Congress system** uses code letters to identify subject categories. The first letter of a book's call number tells the general category. A librarian can provide you with a complete list of letter codes for Library of Congress categories.

The **card catalog** is a cabinet of drawers filled with alphabetically arranged cards: *title cards, author cards*, and *subject cards*. Catalog cards may give publication facts, list the number of pages, and tell whether the book contains illustrations or diagrams. The **on-line catalog** is a computerized version of the card catalog. The on-line catalog can help you locate information quickly and may tell you if a book you are looking for is checked out or if it is available at another library.

Exercise A   On a separate sheet of paper, draw a diagram of your school library, and label the areas where the following resources are found (computers may or may not be available in your school library).

1. the card catalog (or on-line catalog)
2. the fiction section
3. the reference section
4. current magazines
5. the librarian's desk
6. computers

Exercise B   For each of the following numbered descriptions, use the card catalog or the on-line catalog to find a specific book. On the line provided, write each book's title, author or editor, and call number.

1. a collection of essays about ecology _____

_____

2. a guide to career choices _____

_____

3. a recent book on a specific sport _____

_____

4. a book by each of the following authors: Sandra Cisneros, John Cheever, and James Baldwin

_____

_____

5. a biography of a particular scientist _____

_____

RESOURCES

Resources

WORKSHEET 2   *Using Reference Materials*

Your library may contain many or all of the following sources of information.

- *Readers' Guide to Periodical Literature*   The *Readers' Guide* indexes articles, poems, and stories from more than one hundred magazines.
- **Vertical File**   A vertical file is a cabinet with up-to-date materials organized by subject; it often contains government, business, and educational publications.
- **Microfilm and Microfiche**   Many libraries photographically reduce periodicals and newspapers and store them on microfilm or microfiche.
- **Audiovisual Materials**   Libraries often keep audiocassettes of famous speeches or poetry readings as well as videotapes of documentaries.
- **Reference Section**   Most libraries have a separate reference section. Ask your librarian about its location and what works are available.

Exercise A   In your school or your local library, find answers to the following questions about the *Readers' Guide*.

1. Where are the *Readers' Guide* volumes kept in your library? _____

    _____

2. In the *Readers' Guide*, find a subject heading for popular music. List any *see* or *see also*

    references that you find under this heading. _____

    _____

    _____

3. Check in the *Readers' Guide* under the subject heading of health. Write down the title,

    author, magazine, date, and page numbers for one of the listed articles. _____

    _____

4. Find an entry for a review of a book that interests you. Write down the information given

    in the entry, spelling out any abbreviations. _____

    _____

Exercise B   Name a reference book you could use to find each of the following items of information.

1. the source of the expression "the apple of his eye" _____

2. the current population of Brazil _____

3. biographical information about Sandra Day O'Connor _____

4. colleges offering majors in horticulture _____

Name _____ Date _____ Class _____

Types of Dictionaries

An **unabridged dictionary** is the most comprehensive source for finding information about a word. Unabridged dictionaries offer more word entries and usually give more detailed information, such as fuller word histories or longer lists of synonyms or antonyms, than abridged dictionaries do.

The *Oxford English Dictionary (OED)* is the largest unabridged dictionary. The *OED* gives the approximate date of a word's first appearance in English and shows, in a quotation, how the word was used at that time. The *OED* also traces any changes in the spelling or the meaning of a word.

An **abridged** or **college dictionary** is one of the most commonly used reference books in the United States. Abridged dictionaries do not contain as many entries or as much information about entry words as unabridged dictionaries do. However, abridged dictionaries are revised frequently, so they give the most up-to-date information on meanings and uses of words. Besides word entries, most abridged dictionaries contain other useful information, such as tables of commonly used abbreviations, selected biographical entries, and tables of signs and symbols.

A **specialized dictionary** contains entries that relate to a specific subject or field. For example, there are specialized dictionaries for terms used in art, music, sports, gardening, mythology, and many other subjects.

Exercise   Using an abridged or college dictionary, look up the answers to the following questions.

1. From what language does the word *dungaree* come? _____

2. Which is the correct spelling: *argile, argyle, argiel,* or *orgyle?* _____

3. What is *Bay State* the nickname for? _____

4. How do *canvas* and *canvass* differ in meaning? _____

   _____

5. What is the meaning of the Latin phrase *vide supra*? _____

6. How many different meanings are given in your dictionary for the word *shuffle?*

   _____

7. Give the slang meaning or meanings for the word *lug.* _____

8. Copy the correct pronunciation for *mucilaginous,* including diacritical marks. Be able to

   pronounce it correctly. _____

9. Write the plural of *analysis.* _____

10. What meaning does the word *passive* have in chemistry?_____

Name _____ Date _____ Class _____

 **WORKSHEET 4**   *The Dictionary Entry*

A **dictionary entry** contains a lot of information about a word. The boldfaced **entry word** shows how the word is spelled and how it is divided into syllables. The entry word may also show capitalization and provide alternative spellings. The **pronunciation** is shown by the use of accent marks and either diacritical marks or phonetic respelling.

Part-of-speech labels (usually in abbreviated form) indicate how the entry word should be used. Some words may be used as more than one part of speech. For these words, a part-of-speech label is given before each numbered (or lettered) series of definitions.

The **etymology** is the origin and history of a word. Etymology tells how the word (or its parts) came into English. The etymology for the word *raccoon* looks something like this:

    [< Virginia Algonquian (*aroughcun*)]

The example shows that *raccoon* comes from the Virginia Algonquian word *aroughcun*. Sometimes etymologies contain symbols such as < or *. These symbols are usually explained in the front of the dictionary or at the bottom of each page.

Special usage labels (such as [Archaic] or [Slang]) may show that a definition is limited to certain forms of speech. Other labels may indicate that a definition is used only in a certain field, such as *Law, Math.* (mathematics), or *Bio.* (biology). Here are two usage labels for the word *order:*

    Law command of a court   *Bio.* a group of plants or animals

Dictionaries may also contain the following information.

EXAMPLES:	phrases or sentences that may demonstrate how the defined word is to be used
OTHER FORMS:	full or partial spellings of plural forms of nouns, different tenses of verbs, or the comparison forms of adjectives and adverbs
RELATED WORD FORMS:	usually words created by adding suffixes or prefixes to the entry word
SYNONYMS AND ANTONYMS:	words with the same or opposite meanings

Exercise   Use a dictionary to answer the following questions. Write your answers on the lines below.

1. What is the plural form of *farrago*? _____

2. What does the adjective *lupine* mean? _____

3. How are the letters *ch* pronounced in *choric*? _____

4. Which syllable is accented in the word *syllepsis*? _____

5. How else can *gussy* be written? _____

 **WORKSHEET 5** *Business Letters: Form*

A business letter contains six parts.

- The **heading** usually consists of three lines: your street address (or post office box number); your city, state, and ZIP Code; and the date of the letter.

- The **inside address** shows the name and address of the person or organization you are writing to. If you're writing to a specific person, use a courtesy title (such as *Mr., Ms.,* or *Mrs.*) or a professional title (such as *Dr.*) in front of the person's name. After the person's name, include the person's business or job title (such as *Owner* or *Sales Manager*), followed by the name of the company or organization and the address.

- The **salutation** is your greeting. If you are writing to a specific person, begin with *Dear,* followed by a courtesy title or a professional title and the person's last name. End the salutation with a colon. If you don't have the name of a specific person, you can use a general salutation, such as *Dear Sir or Madam.* You can also use a department or a position title, with or without the word *Dear.*

- The **body** of your letter contains your message. If the body of your letter contains more than one paragraph, leave a space between paragraphs.

- **Closings** often used in business letters include *Sincerely, Yours truly, Respectfully yours,* and *Regards.* Capitalize only the first word of the closing.

- Write your **signature** in ink, directly below the closing. Sign your full name. If you type your letter, type your name neatly below your signature.

There are two styles frequently used for business letters. With the **block form,** every part of the letter begins at the left-hand margin, and paragraphs are not indented. In the **modified block form,** the heading, the closing, and the signature are aligned along an imaginary line just to the right of the center of the page. The other parts of the letter begin at the left-hand margin. All paragraphs are indented.

Exercise   On the back of this sheet, write a business letter in block form. Invent all of the information. Your purpose can be to request information, to express appreciation, or to register a complaint about a product or service.

Name _____ Date _____ Class _____

Name _____ Date _____ Class _____

 **WORKSHEET 6** *Business Letters: Content*

The purpose of a **request letter** is to ask for something. You may want to request a catalog, a brochure, or information about a product or service. An **order letter** is a special kind of request letter that is written to order merchandise by mail. Remember the following guidelines when you write a request or order letter.

1. State your request clearly.
2. If you're asking for information, enclose a self-addressed, stamped envelope.
3. Make sure that your request is reasonable and that you have allowed enough time for the person to respond.
4. Include all important details, such as size, color, style, catalog number, and price. Compute correctly any costs involved, including any necessary sales tax or shipping charges.

The purpose of a **complaint** or **adjustment letter** is to report a problem and to request a satisfactory resolution to the difficulty. Remember the following guidelines when writing a complaint or adjustment letter.

1. Register your complaint as soon as possible.
2. Explain exactly what is wrong, and provide all necessary information.
3. Keep the tone of the letter courteous.

An **appreciation** or **commendation letter** is written to compliment or to express appreciation to a person, a group, or an organization.

Remember that all business letters usually follow a few simple guidelines. *Use a courteous, positive, and professional tone.* Rude or insulting letters are counterproductive. *Use formal standard English.* Avoid slang, dialect, contractions, and abbreviations. *State your purpose clearly and quickly.* Assume that the person reading your letter is busy. *Include all necessary information.*

Exercise   After you graduate this summer, you would like to volunteer to help build houses for the homeless with a charitable group called Operation Shelter. On the back of this sheet, write a letter of request to the manager of Operation Shelter. Invent the address and any other information you include in the letter. Be sure to request an application form and any other available information.

Name _____ Date _____ Class _____

_____

_____

_____

_____

_____

_____

_____

_____

_____

_____

_____

_____

_____

_____

_____

_____

_____

_____

_____

_____

_____

_____

_____

_____

_____

_____

_____

_____

_____

_____

_____

_____

_____

_____

_____

_____

Letters of Application and Résumés

You write a **letter of application** to provide a selection committee or a possible employer with enough information to determine whether you are a good candidate for a position. When you are writing a letter of application, remember the following points.

1. Identify the job or position you are applying for. Tell how you heard about it.
2. Depending on the position you are applying for, you might include
   • your age, grade in school, or grade-point average
   • your experience or your activities, awards, and honors
   • personal qualities or characteristics that make you a good choice
   • the date or times you are available
3. Offer to provide references. Your references should include two or three responsible adults (usually not relatives) who have agreed to recommend you. Be prepared to supply their addresses and telephone numbers.

A **résumé** is a summary of your background and experience. For many job positions, a résumé should be submitted along with a letter of application. There are many different styles of arranging the information on a résumé. Whatever style you select, be sure your résumé looks neat and businesslike.

Exercise A   You have seen an ad for an after-school job that suits your qualifications and needs. Write the body of a letter of application to the person in charge of hiring. Keep the body of your letter brief, but include enough information to show that you are a good candidate for the position.

_____

_____

_____

_____

_____

_____

_____

_____

_____

_____

_____

_____

_____

_____

_____

Resources, Worksheet 7, continued

Exercise B   Choose a job that interests you. On a separate sheet of paper, write a personal résumé that shows you are qualified for such a position. On the lines below, write a short letter explaining how you heard about the job and requesting a personal interview. You may invent some or all of the information.

_____

_____

_____

_____

_____

_____

_____

_____

_____

_____

_____

_____

_____

_____

_____

_____

_____

_____

_____

_____

_____

_____

_____

_____

_____

Name _____ Date _____ Class _____

Printed Forms and Applications

When you fill out forms, keep the following guidelines in mind.

1. Always read the entire form to make sure you understand exactly what information you are being asked to supply.
2. Type neatly or print legibly, using a pen or pencil as directed.
3. Include all information requested. If a question does not apply to you, write *not applicable* or *N.A.* instead of leaving the space blank.
4. Keep the form neat and clean. Avoid smudges or cross-outs.
5. When you have completed the form, proofread it carefully to correct any spelling, usage, punctuation, or factual errors.
6. Submit the form to the correct person, or mail it to the correct address.

Exercise   Complete the following application form for a summer job at an amusement park. Make up any or all of the information. Print neatly.

Name _____
          Last   First   Middle Initial

Address _____
          Number and Street   City   State   ZIP Code

Home phone _____   Work phone _____

Date of birth _____   Sex: _____ Male _____ Female

Social Security No. __ __ __ – __ __ – __ __ __ __

Job(s) in which you are interested (circle all that apply):

accounting   clerical   drink concessions
janitorial service   management—trainee   mechanic
performance—dance   performance—musical   performance theater
receptionist   rides operator   ticket taker

Other _____

Skills, Honors, Awards, Accomplishments: _____

_____

_____

Other Work Experience: _____

_____

Education: _____

_____

Resources

WORKSHEET 9 *Writing Social Letters*

When you want to thank someone formally, to congratulate someone, to send an invitation, or to respond to an invitation extended to you, you should write a social letter.

Social letters are much less formal in style than business letters. For example, social letters don't include an inside address, and most use the modified block form.

Thank-you letters. The purpose of a thank-you letter is to express appreciation for a gift or a favor you have received. Try to say more than just "thank you": Give details about how the person's gift or efforts were appreciated or helpful.

Invitations. An invitation should contain specific information about a planned event, such as the occasion, the time and place, and any other details guests might need to know.

Letters of regret. If you have been invited to a party or another social function and will be unable to attend, it is polite to send a letter of regret. A written reply is especially appropriate if you were sent a written invitation that included the letters *R.S.V.P.* (In French, these letters are an abbreviation for "please reply.")

Exercise On the lines provided, write a social letter for one of the following situations.

1. Write a thank-you letter to your aunt and uncle who took you on a weekend camping trip.
2. Write a letter of regret explaining that you will not be able to attend a friend's birthday party.
3. Write an invitation letter for a graduation party you are planning.

_____

_____

_____

_____

_____

_____

_____

_____

_____

_____

_____

_____

_____

_____

_____

Resources

Manuscript Style A

Abbreviate given names only if the person is most commonly known that way. Leave a space between two such initials, but not between three or more.

   P. D. James   **F.** Scott Fitzgerald   **W.E.B.** Du Bois

Abbreviate social titles whether used with the full name or with the last name alone. The social title of *Miss* is not an abbreviation, so it is not followed by a period.

   Mr.   **Mrs.**   **Ms.**   **Sr.** [*Señor*]   **Sra.** [*Señora*]   **Dr.**   **Miss**

Abbreviate civil and military titles used before full names or before initials and last names. Spell out such titles before last names alone.

   Capt. Sarah Douglas   **Captain** Douglas

Abbreviate titles and academic degrees after proper names. Use such abbreviations only after a person's full name, not after the last name alone. Except for numerals such as *III* or *IV,* abbreviations of titles and degrees used after a name are set off by commas. Do not include the titles *Mr., Mrs., Ms.,* or *Dr.* when you use a title or degree *after* a name. Also, do not leave a space between the letters in academic degrees.

   The research team included **Dr.** Cynthia Kaloma and T. Mark Famako **III, Ph.D.**

Spell out most company names in text. They may be abbreviated in tables, notes, and bibliographies. The abbreviations *Inc.* and *Ltd.* are set off by commas; however, they may be omitted in text. *After* spelling out the first use of the names of agencies, organizations, and other things commonly known by their initials, use abbreviations.

Exercise: Proofreading   The following sentences contain errors in the use of abbreviations. On the line provided, correct each error.

1. Mr Edwards, I'd like you to meet my good friend Lt. Weinberg.

   _____

2. We at Better Baked Breads Inc. refer to the company as B.B.B., Ms Turner.

   _____

3. Will Dr. Ellen Patterson, Ph.D be leading the question-and-answer period?

   _____

4. Dr. Joe C Stamos III, M.D., and Ms. Diaz, M.D. are opening a new office.

   _____

5. My aunt, Lieutenant H. M. I. Piotrowski, has been in the military since she graduated from high school.

   _____

   _____

RESOURCES

Resources

WORKSHEET 11 *Manuscript Style B*

In a written passage (text), spell out the names of states, countries, and other political units whenever they stand alone or follow any other geographical term. Abbreviate them in tables, notes, and bibliographies.

TEXT: California   Alberta   France   TABLES, ETC.: Calif.   Alta.   Fr.

In text, *United States* may be abbreviated to *U.S.* only when it is used as an adjective. However, spelling it out is never incorrect.

How long may **U.S.** citizens live abroad?
or
How long may **United States** citizens live abroad?

In text, spell out every word in an address.

Please contact the main office at 5398 Talbot Avenue.

NOTE: In letter and envelope addresses, the two-letter state code may be used when followed by a ZIP Code. Addresses may be abbreviated in tables, notes, and bibliographies.

In text, spell out references to the points of the compass.

She told us to travel **southwest** [*not* SW] from Albuquerque.

Exercise: Proofreading On the line provided, correct the manuscript style in each of the following sentences. If a sentence is correct, write *C*.

1. The overseas operator will help you place a call outside the United States.

_____

2. I had thought the compass was pointing S, but it was pointing N; we were heading for So. Car.

_____

3. In the U.K., people refer to a cookie as a "biscuit."

_____

4. Address all entries to 32 E. Elm St., Carson City, Nev.

_____

5. The next song is dedicated to our guests from Mex.

_____

Resources

WORKSHEET 12   *Manuscript Style C*

Abbreviate the two most common era designations, *A.D.* and *B.C.* The abbreviation *A.D.* is used with dates in the Christian era. When used with a specific year number, *A.D.* precedes the number. When used with the name of a century, it follows the name. The abbreviation *B.C.* is used for dates before the Christian era. It follows either a specific year number or the name of a century.

> Europe's Dark Ages began around A.D. 476.

> Siddhartha Gautama was an Indian philosopher who lived and taught around 500 B.C.

Spell out the names of months and days whether they appear alone or in dates. Both types of names may be abbreviated in tables, notes, and bibliographies.

> TEXT: Tuesday, October 25, 1994   TABLES, ETC.: Tues., Oct. 25, 1994

Abbreviate the designations for the two halves of the day measured by clock time *A.M. (ante meridiem)* and *P.M. (post meridiem)*. Both abbreviations follow the numerals designating the specific time. Do not use *A.M.* or *P.M.* with numbers spelled out as words or as substitutes for the words *morning, afternoon,* or *evening*. Also, do not use the words *morning, afternoon,* or *evening* with numerals followed by *A.M.* or *P.M.*

> The next session will begin at 6:00 P.M.
>
>   *or*
>
> The next session will begin at six o'clock this evening.

Spell out the English equivalents of common Latin expressions. For example, use *and so forth* rather than *etc.* In tables, notes, and bibliographies, use abbreviations for the Latin expressions. In text, spell out the words *volume, part, unit, chapter,* and *page* as well as the names of school subjects.

Exercise: Proofreading   On the line provided, correct the manuscript style in each of the following sentences.

1. On p. 325, you can see the area of the Roman Empire outlined in red on the map.

   _____

2. Tutankhamen ruled Egypt around B.C. 1355.

   _____

3. The conference is scheduled to begin at 9:00 A.M. in the morning.

   _____

4. Dictionaries, encyclopedias, almanacs, etc. are available in the reference section of the library.

   _____

5. All entries must be processed by Mon., May 3.

   _____

RESOURCES

Resources

 **WORKSHEET 13**   *Manuscript Style D*

In text, spell out the names of units of measurements whether they stand alone or follow a spelled-out number or a numeral. Such a name may be abbreviated in tables and notes when the name follows a numeral.

The rescuers tunneled for twenty-five **feet** to reach the boy.

In text, spell out the words for the symbols % (percent), + (plus), – (minus), = (equals), and ¢ (cents). The dollar sign ($) may be used whenever it precedes numerals. Do not substitute the symbol for the words *money* or *dollars* after numerals.

At least 30 **percent** [*not* %] of the survey's responses were against the proposal.

Project costs are estimated to run over $1,250,000.

In text, spell out a **cardinal number**—a number that states how many—if it can be expressed in one or two words. Otherwise, use numerals. Cardinal numbers in compounds, such as *thirty-three*, are hyphenated.

twelve cents	**three hundred** people	**one fifth** of the farmers
549 steers	**78,536** miles	**2 1/2** (or **2.5**)

In a particular context, be consistent in your use of numerals. If any of the numbers require numerals, use numerals for all of them. However, to distinguish between numbers appearing beside each other, spell out one number and use numerals for the other.

We should need only about a **dozen 10**-penny nails.

Each of the **three** clubs collected over five hundred dollars.

Exercise: Proofreading   On the line provided, correct the manuscript style in each of the following sentences.

1. With these 11 volunteers + the fifteen who have promised to help, we should be able to do the job.

   _____

2. To my chagrin, I discovered that I had left five $ on the counter.

   _____

3. From our small garden, we harvested 52 pounds of tomatoes.

   _____

4. Please send me 5 2-gallon barrels.

   _____

5. The ball lay motionless on the two-yd line.

   _____

Name _____ Date _____ Class _____

 **Manuscript Style E**

Spell out a number that begins a sentence. Also, spell out an **ordinal number**—a number that expresses order.

> **One hundred twenty-five** [*not* 125] interactive compact disks are on order at the library.
>
> Who was the **first** [*not* 1st] emperor of Rome?

Use numerals to express numbers in conventional situations. Spell out a number used with *o'clock*.

February 14, 1962	SS # 135-90-4209	3 pints	12:00 P.M.
or	Interstate 4	30 Fifth Street	*or*
14 February 1962	1 by 10 inches	the 1500s *or* the 1500's	twelve o'clock noon

Nonsexist language is language that applies to people in general, both male and female. When you are referring to a profession or to people in general, use nonsexist expressions rather than gender-specific ones. For example, you might use the nonsexist terms *humanity*, *human beings*, and *people* instead of the gender-specific term *mankind*.

Exercise: Proofreading   On the line provided, correct the manuscript style in each of the following sentences.

1. "33 flavors are too many to choose from," he said.

    _____

2. Even at 4:00 A.M. in the morning, traffic is heavy on Interstate Ten.

    _____

3. During the late eighteen hundreds, the future of humans was changed by the horseless carriage.

    _____

4. Be there at 9:00 o'clock sharp, or we will leave without you.

    _____

5. The 2nd contestant received a free set of 3 mixing bowls.

    _____

Resources

WORSHEET 15 *Review*

Exercise A   Go to a library to look for books with the following descriptions. Write the author, title, and call number of each book.

1. a book written by Toni Morrison _____

    _____

2. a book about astronomy _____

    _____

3. a book of poems _____

    _____

4. a reference work _____

    _____

Exercise B   You are writing a paper about a current, nationally known political figure. Go to the most recent volume of the *Readers' Guide.* Write the names, authors, and descriptions of two articles you find in the *Readers' Guide* under your subject heading. If there is no heading for the person you chose, find a related subject that interests you. Write the names, authors, and descriptions of articles listed under that subject heading.

1. _____

    _____

2. _____

    _____

Exercise C   On the lines provided, write the titles of reference works that you might use to find information on the following topics.

1. the age of Robert Frost when he started writing poetry _____

    _____

2. a word that means the same as *strong* _____

    _____

3. a general description and history of photography _____

    _____

4. the location of the island of Sardinia _____

    _____

5. the birthplace of Noam Chomsky, the well-known linguist _____

Name _____ Date _____ Class _____

Exercise D   On the lines provided, write a business letter to the program director of a local radio station expressing your appreciation for her decision to allow four hours of student programming each weekend. Use block form.

_____

_____

_____

_____

_____

_____

_____

_____

_____

_____

_____

_____

_____

_____

_____

_____

_____

_____

_____

_____

_____

_____

_____

_____

_____

_____

_____

_____

_____

_____

Resources, Worksheet 15, continued

Exercise E: Proofreading   On the line provided, rewrite each of the following sentences to correct errors in manuscript style.

1. 1,500 troops were quickly dispatched to the scene. _____

   _____

2. My mother was the 1st woman in her family to graduate from college. _____

   _____

3. Imagine all this for just thirty nine $ and ninety-nine cents! _____

   _____

4. Won't you please ask Maj. Parks to come for dinner next Sat.? _____

   _____

5. Goods' Furniture, Inc. will close at 5:00 o'clock P.M. _____

   _____